ADVANCE PRAISE FOR

Love Without Martinis

"Regardless of where a couple is on their recovery journey, *Love Without Martinis* is essential reading. Couples impacted by one or both partner's recovery often struggle to find a path forward. *Love Without Martinis* provides a clear and practical approach that couples can implement to work towards peace, trust, and happiness. This book doesn't just talk the talk. It also walks the walk in sharing moving, honest stories of real couples who have worked hard and found their way together. It is the rare book that both teaches and inspires."—**LISA SMITH**, author of *Girl Walks Out of a Bar*

"The author brilliantly balances her personal experience and well-researched information on this topic to create a much needed hand-book appropriate in clinical settings and for the general public. The ASCENT Model provides an organized and practical plan for goals and action towards healing. In the end, readers are left with hope and a sense of connection to stories of the couples who have supported each other in finding meaning along the often confounding road to recovery."—**SARAH ALLEN BENTON**, author of *Understanding the High-Functioning Alcoholic: Breaking the Cycle and Finding Hope*

"*Love without Martinis* is brilliant! This is an important read for couples who are interested in rewriting the story of recovering love together. This work gives life to the idea that addiction is not just personal suffer-ing, but a family issue that must be addressed by all parties involved. This work is a long overdue resource for couples who are valiantly brav-ing the work of recovering love and healing. Too often recovery books are centered on the individual rather than the relational dynamic—which for many is the most central part of their lives. The ASCENT approach offers a skillful map of healing practices to guide couples in a dynamic journey of recovery in a way that is easy to follow and imme-diately accessible."—**KATHLEEN MURPHY**, Executive Clinical Director, Breathe Life Healing Center

"*Love Without Martinis* goes right to the soul of the haunting issues that couples in long-term recovery face and provides useful tools to overcome them. These strategies go above and beyond the actual substance abuse to tackle the underlying feelings of shame, fear, and guilt that so many of us grapple with. Forgiveness and love are always waiting on the other side, and Chantal shows us it's all possible through these powerful stories of hard work and hope."—**DAPHNE WILLIS**, singer/songwriter (Sony/ATV) of hit song "Somebody's Someone"

"Sometimes we think that our relationships, if meant to be, shouldn't need as much attention as our recovery, or our physical health or our work. This book dispels that notion and provides a straight forward and joy-filled set of practices and principles to grow our relationships. Kind of like growing a garden, the tools in this book can function like sunshine, water, nourishment, weeding, and pruning to keep our relationships healthy and strong in recovery."—**DR. CASSANDRA VIETEN**, Executive Director, John W. Brick Mental Health Foundation

"*Love Without Martinis* captivate readers with dynamic case studies in the form of stories that demonstrate a clear systems approach to engaging loved ones in the recovery process. This book is beneficial for all who face and treat substance use disorders!"—**DR. GREGORY HOBELMANN, MD**, Senior Vice President, Chief Medical and Clinical Officer, Ashley Treatment Center

"Finally a book to recommend to couples facing the debilitating effects of alcohol on their personal lives and relationships. We don't always see the full picture ourselves, but we can often identify with stories. This book offers the unique opportunity to witness addiction and the journey of recovery through the lens of each partner's experience in six very different couples."—**DR. MEGAN FLEMING**, leading sex therapist and relationships counselor for national media including shows anchored by Anderson Cooper and Lawrence O'Donnell

"Unflinchingly honest and remarkably candid, *Love Without Martinis* invites us to grapple with the lessons of romantic relationships and recovery and to see that the point is not sobriety, since sobriety is never enough, but true recovery, which calls us to rebuild and re-ignite the passion and love in our relationships."—**ANNIE GRACE**, author of *This Naked Mind: Control Alcohol, Find Freedom, Discover Happiness & Change Your Life*

"Chantal Jauvin astutely explores addiction as a disease of emotional isolation. She captures the power of narrative to reveal the opportunity of committed relationship to deepen the recovery of the participants. The reader is offered a lucid lens into the essential building blocks of emotional intimacy. Couples can immediately apply the material to the construction of workable boundaries, the honoring of desire and to hold the tension of diverse needs and beliefs with compassion and generosity."—**DR. PAUL DUNION**, author of *Shadow Marriage: A Descent into Intimacy*

"*Love Without Martinis* is an important and very readable book. The authors introduce the ASCENT Approach to support couples, helping them navigate some pretty rough waters that occur in intimate relationships when addiction occurs. Their approach is specific, manageable, and written by two authors who have earned their expertise through personal and clinical experience. Knowing that being vulnerable is one of the essential ingredients necessary for successful treatment, both authors are terrific role models." —**DR. DAN GOTTLIEB**, Host of *Voices in the Family* and author of *Letters to Sam* and *The Wisdom We're Born With: Restoring Faith In Ourselves*

"Happy families are all alike; every unhappy family is unhappy in its own way." So begins Tolstoy's *Anna Karenina*. With a novelist's skill and precision, *Love Without Martinis* details the unique ways that six unhappy couples struggle with addiction and how their struggles enrich them with humility, courage, caring, and a wisdom that make them all more whole human beings. These stories are inspiring because they are true. They show us that the work of recovery is soul work. This book will be a wonderful help to those in recovery, those who love them, and those who help them."—**DR. RICH BOROFSKY** and **ANTRA BOROFSKY**, Co-directors, Center for the Study of Relationships

"I highly recommend this book to all therapists with clients in early recovery! The power of stories and the healing insights of these stories will help couples and individuals relationally repair core family systems. *Love Without Martinis* transcends not just substance abuse, but mental health as well."—**MICHAEL BLANCHE**, Co-Founder, Ethos Treatment

"*Love Without Martinis* contributes much to the field of addiction treatment, and particularly to the sensitive dynamics that arises in both the addict and their partner in early recovery. Each couple's narrative highlights an important aspect of the need for transformation, change and a healthy social connection in the recovery process for couples. This book should be required reading in every treatment center!"—**Dr. William Heran, CEO** and Co-Founder, Providence Treatment Center

"*Love Without Martinis* is vivid, detailed, nuanced, and evocative. Jauvin has a novelist's eye and heart, and the language to express them. The stories would be meaningful for anyone in a long-term partnership, even one without addictive problems. For Jauvin to recruit these couples was a small miracle in itself (and their gift to us needs to be acknowledged). Then each account was structured for maximum benefit by Jauvin's story-telling artistry. The ASCENT model, for organizing the change process, also makes a meaningful contribution. For a couple grappling with addictive problems, whether they embrace 12-step fellowships, methods such as SMART Recovery, or any other pathway, there is much to learn here."—**A. Tom Horvath, PhD, ABPP**, Practical Recovery Psychology Group, La Jolla, California; Past president, SMART Recovery; author of *Sex, Drugs, Gambling, & Chocolate: A Workbook for Overcoming Addictions* (Impact, 2003)

"Chantal Jauvin and her collaborator Jeremy Frank have written a superb book in an area that has been neglected. They have developed a solid, useful outline for guiding couples through the process of recovering from addiction. The well-crafted ASCENT framework provides a clear, lucid orientation to navigating the difficult path to restoring a healthy relationship—or in some cases, establishing one anew. Jauvin is an exceptionally facile writer and the writing is never less than compelling, both in the opening formal chapters explaining the approach, and then in the stories of people in recovery which follow. Each couple is treated with even-handed compassion, even when pointing out significant dysfunctional patterns of behavior. This is a very powerful contribution to the literature on couple's recovery; clinicians will find it valuable, but its primary benefit will be to those couples in recovery who may recognize, in this description, many of their own dilemmas, and gain hope, perspective and tools to help them on their journey. Kudos to Jauvin and Frank!"—**Dr. Mark Schenker,** author of *A Clinician's Guide to 12-Step Recovery* (WW Norton 2009)

"*Love Without Martinis* offers a unique and intimate look into a far-reaching but often unspoken about piece of the addiction recovery puzzle: The spousal relationship. As a society, we typically focus on the individual's journey of addiction to recovery. The strain that alcoholism and addiction can put on a romantic relationship is apparent. While addiction recovery for the one is vital, the reconstruction of the couple's relationship cannot be overlooked. With the ASCENT Approach, in conjunction with book's the supplemental storytelling, Jauvin paints a clear picture of the impact addiction and alcoholism can have on both partners in a relationship, while offering practical actions that couples can take in order to support both sustainable recovery and a healthy, successful partnership."—**ZACH SNITZER**, Co-Founder, Maryland Treatment Center and Innovo Detox

"*Love Without Martinis* is believable, at times personal; compelling, as well as psychologically nuanced and coherent. A particularly important contribution this book makes to the literature on recovery for couples is its description of the arc of recovery over years, often involving periods of relapse, disappointment, conflict, and emotional pain, which can also offer opportunities for growth and ultimately healing and real connection. Ms. Jauvin and Dr. Frank are to be commended for this wise and hopeful message to couples dealing with alcoholism and its discontents." —**DR. ROGER CAMBOR, MD**, Bryn Mawr Psychiatry

"*Love Without Martinis* shows couples how to address their miscommunication, rebuild their trust, and deal with the most troubling aspects of their relationships while they navigate their recovery. Based on my life-long study of human nature, psychology, and neuroscience, I believe the ASCENT Approach rightly focuses on self-awareness as a building block to develop a healthy partnership."—**DR. NICOLE LIPKIN, PsyD**, Organizational Psychologist & CEO, Equilibria Leadership Consulting

"As a married couple in long-term recovery, this book is a must-read. We've learned that our stories matter and we have a voice, that people need to take their "mess" and "make a message." *Love Without Martinis* offers practical tools to get couples back on track and inspire people out of their isolation. It encourages couples to look inwards, consider all options for recovery, and build a truly loving relationship. Marriage,

partnerships, and recovery are constant works in progress and well worth the effort. Please don't give up before the miracles happen."
—**TIM RYAN**, A&E's *Dope Man* and Founder of *A Man in Recovery;* and **JENNIFER GIMENEZ RYAN**, model, actress (*Charlie's Angels*: Full Throttle Nun), reality television (*The Bold and The Beautiful*) and recovery advocate

"*Love Without Martinis* clearly demonstrates how important our commitment to recovery and deep work is if we want to be true to ourselves and successful in our partnerships. The couples in this book courageously share their personal stories with honesty and vulnerability no matter how challenging their journeys. Nothing is more powerful for healing than giving voices to our stories of recovery."—**ELIZABETH EDWARDS**, singer, songwriter, and recording artist and recovery advocate

"As a couple, Andrea and I are well aware of the isolating effects a life of sobriety can potentially cause. *Love Without Martinis* reads like a refreshing tonic without the gin and reminds us we are not alone in our pursuit of long lasting love and recovery."—**SÉAN MCCANN**, author of *One Good Reason: A Memoir of Addiction and Recovery, Music and Love* and Founder of Great Big Sea

"I highly recommend *Love Without Martinis*. I know first-hand the pain of relationship failure wrapped around substance use. I often say Trauma and Shame are the Gatekeepers to Happiness. The stories and tools in this book help you open the gates to long-term recovery from addiction."—**BRIAN CUBAN**, author of *The Addicted Lawyer: Tales of the Bar, Booze, Blow and Redemption*

LOVE

WITHOUT MARTINIS

LOVE

WITHOUT MARTINIS

How Couples Build Healthy Relationships
in Recovery, Based on Real Stories

Introducing the Six Practices of
The ASCENT Approach to Recovery from Addiction
with Jeremy Frank, PhD, CADC

CHANTAL JAUVIN

SelectBooks, Inc.
New York

This edition published by SelectBooks, Inc.
For information address SelectBooks, Inc., New York, New York.

First Edition

ISBN 978-1-59079-511-8

Library of Congress Cataloging-in-Publication Data
Names: Jauvin, Chantal C., author.
Title: Love without martinis : how couples build healthy relationships in
    recovery, based on real stories / Chantal C. Jauvin ; introducing the
    six practices of the ASCENT approach to recovery from addiction with
    Jeremy Frank, PhD, CADC.
Description: First Edition. | NEW YORK : SelectBooks, 2021. | Includes
    bibliographical references and index. | Summary: "Author with a partner
    in recovery from addiction to alcohol presents The ASCENT Approach she
    developed with Jeremy Frank, PhD, a Licensed Clinical Psychologist and
    Certified Alcohol and Drug Counsellor. Six practices to help couples
    rebuild their relationship are demonstrated in real-life stories of
    couples navigating the difficult process from early recovery to a
    successful long-term recovery"-- Provided by publisher.
Identifiers: LCCN 2020042033 (print) | LCCN 2020042034 (ebook) | ISBN
    9781590795118 (paperback) | ISBN 9781590795125 (ebook)
Subjects: LCSH: Alcoholism counseling. | Alcoholics--Rehabilitation. |
    Alcoholism--Treatment.
Classification: LCC HV5275 .J38 2021 (print) | LCC HV5275 (ebook) | DDC
    362.292/86--dc23
LC record available at https://lccn.loc.gov/2020042033
LC ebook record available at https://lccn.loc.gov/2020042034

Book design by Janice Benight

Manufactured in the United States of America
10 9 8 7 6 5 4 3 2 1

For my husband, William Thomas,
The love of my life

CONTENTS

✳

Foreword

When Chantal and her husband, Bill, informed me that she was planning to write a book about "stories of couples in recovery" from the point of view of both partners, I was intrigued. Having been in the recovery field for 36 years—and personally in recovery for 11—I know of countless books about addiction and recovery from the perspective of experts, therapists, parents, children, individuals, and friends. However, I could not recall a book specifically about couples in recovery from the perspective of each partner. Since there is a void of literature about this important topic and clearly a need for this, I encouraged her to "go for it!"

Substance Use Disorder is a family disease, meaning it affects everyone in the family unit, especially the partners. As in every chronic disease, recovery from substance use disorder does not stop when a person leaves treatment. It is something they must live every day. This can be taxing on couples as they struggle with the realities of the disease. They need to understand that recovery is not just about their partner being sober or abstinent but also about each of them engaging in recovery from the effects of the disease.

Having been around thousands of couples both in and out of recovery, I offered Chantal and Bill my observations from the past decades. Specifically, I had identified three typical situations of couples struggling with Substance Use Disorder: In the first category only one partner is in recovery and the other is not; in the second category one partner is in recovery while the other person is ambivalent; and in the third category both are in recovery.

One partner in recovery, and one not: This first category can take on all kinds of forms. The patient either willingly or unwillingly seeks treatment and their partner resents them for their disease, either resenting the impact that this now has on their life together or resents how it either changed them or did not change them. I have seen partners resent the fact that their spouse got sober and other cases where they felt resentment toward a spouse who did not become sober. Without some type of therapeutic or recovery engagement of the codependent, these relationships end either legally or emotionally.

In this category, when one of the partners with substance use disorder gets sober and the other resents the sobriety, the now-sober person is confused. The person cannot understand, now that he or she finally "got better," why the relationship did not also get better and, in fact, can still end. The answer unfortunately is simple: the partner did not also become well.

One person enters recovery and the other is ambivalent: A curious but real situation occurs when a person enters recovery, and their partner is disengaged or ambivalent. Unfortunately, I have seen this too often where one person embraces a level of recovery and their partner is neither resentful nor supportive—just ambivalent. The partner's view is something like this: It's your problem. I'm not going to stand in the way of your recovery, but I'm certainly not going to do anything regarding myself. Although these relations often stay in place, I will frequently hear the individual in recovery relate with sadness their desire for their partner to experience the same kind of emotional and spiritual growth that they have.

Both partners embrace recovery: In this third category, the person with the substance use disorder receives treatment and their partner also does his or her own work. Both partners appreciate that the dysfunction of substance use disorder impacted them personally and affected the dynamics of their relationship. When the individual suffering from substance use disorder gets well, it changes the patterns of behavior and interaction of the couple. When the other person joins his or her partner in recovery to "do their own work," this enhances the new dynamics of the couple and strengthens the relationship.

Seeing couples that heal and grow both individually and collectively is exhilarating. These couples have a newfound relationship that exceeds anything they could have expected.

I am fortunate to be in this third category. Before my recovery eleven years ago, my wife and I had been married for twenty-five years. To outsiders—and even to our extended family—our marriage relationship seemed fairly normal and maybe even healthy. We probably thought so ourselves. When I entered recovery for my addiction to alcohol in 2008, and my wife did her own codependency treatment and group work, we began exploring how to improve our relationship by going to several retreats and attending Recovery Couples Anonymous meetings. By working on this together, we realized how much was missing from our relationship before our recovery. We'd gone from being casual about how we spent our time together to now looking forward to and enjoying those special times. Once we were wondering what we would be doing together when I retire, and now we both look forward to that day.

One of my all-time best birthday presents was when I turned 60 and my wife mentioned to me, "Who would have thought that such an awful illness would make our marriage so good!" I certainly would not have imagined this, nor would most people who embark on the journey of recovery. But this new relationship is truly one of the "Promises of Recovery"—and it does, indeed, materialize if you invest yourself in reclaiming and rebuilding a healthy relationship.

Love Without Martinis provides you with an opportunity to observe a variety of couples and how they are doing in recovery. My hope for all the readers of *Love Without Martinis* is that both partners will be inspired to "do the work." This has rewards beyond your wildest expectations. A special thank-you to Chantal and Bill for their vision, courage, and candor in helping other couples on their recovery journey.

DOUG TIEMAN
President and CEO
Caron Treatment Centers

Introduction

CHANTAL: *Why I Wrote This Book*

Call me naïve, but I was completely unaware that addiction had entered my home. It made its presence known very slowly, randomly, and by degrees.

In my childhood, I would explore the little patch of forest next to the house in Cumberland where I grew up by the Ottawa River in Canada. I would peek and poke at the bugs and insects that lived under the rocks. The creatures that slithered in the dark soil captured my attention, but not for long. I was quickly distracted by noises in the trees or by a rhubarb bush begging to be picked. It would take many more trips along the same trail before I had examined the bugs in sufficient detail to look them up in my Larousse Encyclopedia. If I couldn't find them in the big golden volumes, I would pester my mother until she took me to the local library. Books were the definitive answer to all the questions in my universe.

Books have remained a constant in my life. From my early childhood favorite, *Le Petit Prince (The Little Prince)* by Saint-Exupéry, to my French classroom at Ashbury College where I was the only female student in an all-boys' class and had the burden of defending Simone De Beauvoir's *Le Deuxième Sexe (The Second Sex)*—and later in law school followed by my MBA years—my love of reading remained necessary and central. As my professional career reached its apex, books were my solace during the long-haul flights from Newark to Johannesburg and from Vienna to Mexico City. Many friendships and romantic relationships were formed through the exchange of books.

When my husband Bill and I first moved into our home together in Philadelphia, I thought I knew him. However, somewhere between unpacking the first box of books in May 2008, our sudden departure for Canada to be by his mother's side until she passed, and our return home after Labor Day weekend, I realized I didn't know him anymore.

Bill's character seemed to have undergone major changes. I empathized with the combined traumas of his mother's death, his divorce, his cross-country move, and his paused executive career. Those events were enough to explain the shaky start to our life together, I told myself. But there was a much deeper and greater undercurrent that I could not see: the underlying existence of a family disease. I had no personal experience with addiction. I was blind to its presence. What I knew about drinking was mostly based on Hollywood depictions. We were already trapped in a dark forest.

Bill struggled against the pull of addiction that was dragging him into a losing battle with himself. Dominated by his genetic instincts, he drank secretly and with increasing obsession. He became a shadow of his former self as a successful CEO. In some strange irrational dance, my healthy self, deprived of conscious understanding, became entangled in a blur of activity aimed at saving Bill. I forgot myself. My life force transformed into anger. Addiction disrupted and interrupted our lives.

In our story in part three of this book, you will read how I came face-to-face with the reality of Bill's addiction. This discovery broke the powerful trance that commanded our lives. In that moment, when confronted by the unknown, I turned to books. I was convinced that they would hold the answers to all my questions. I did find many answers. In *Alcoholics Anonymous,* known worldwide as the *"AA Big Book,"* I learned a great deal about the disease and the diagnostics of high-functioning alcoholism and the need for treatment.

I soon made the discovery that I too had a disease because alcoholism, also referred to as a "substance use disorder," is a family disease that reaches back to the family of origin and forward into romantic relationships. I found out about Al-Anon and codependency. Before long, the only reading materials I had were self-help books, "crash and burn" memoirs, and recommended readings from Caron Treatment Center.

What I did not find were stories of couples like Bill and me. How had couples talked with one another, healed their scars, forgiven each other, made themselves vulnerable again, and recovered their intimacy? I wanted to read their words, see them interact, and feel their emotions at times when the person they loved walked out of rehab, or had a relapse, and especially when sobriety was not enough.

With the support and help of many people, I've written *Love without Martinis* in the hope that others will find it when they turn to books for knowledge and understanding.

Stories are a powerful medium for self-understanding. They help us find ourselves or remember who we are. They carry lessons and, like an instruction booklet, show us how different models fit together. Stories let us "practice" without getting hurt. They show us patterns and how to resolve similar situations. We develop empathy when we identify with characters, and can even allow ourselves to be convinced to change our minds and challenge our own thinking. Stories of people who have walked before us provide an opportunity to do soul work. Recovery is soul work.

Recovery, not sobriety, gave us back our lives. Recovery was the voice that said, "This is the way forward." Sobriety grounds recovery but does not complete it. My husband was sober for nearly six years before we fully reclaimed our relationship. Recovery requires the ability to live within a healthy relationship. It took us that long to build the necessary skill set to love each other within a wholesome relationship. As you will read in our story, we both had to engage in a long and at times tumultuous journey of the self. We each had to invent new parts of ourselves and heal some old wounds.

Love existed between us, but we needed to create a satisfying degree of intimacy in our relationship so that each of us could thrive. To accomplish that, we needed new tools. The ones we have acquired throughout our lives, and especially through the chaos of addiction and codependency, are inadequate. In recovery, each of us has rebuilt a solid sense of ourselves and constructed a healthy framework to support both our individual growth and commitment to each other.

I am not a therapist or counselor or doctor. I am a storyteller. What follows are my stories of six couples in recovery based on interviews I conducted with each of them. These couples have bravely and generously agreed to share the truth of their lives with you. Each individual has read their story and confirmed that the story represents the essence of their experience of recovery. For storytelling purposes, some details of the dialogue and scenes have been imagined by me. The characters first names, localities, and many details are real. But the accuracy of each detail is not what matters. What matters most is that these couples are living proof that we have the opportunity to reclaim our lives from addiction and create a healthy relationship in recovery.

The stories of the couples in part three are organized by the length of time each couple has been in recovery. You will notice that whether partners have celebrated a few months or a decade of recovery, conflicts continue to surface in their relationship. However, the longer the couple has been engaged with their recovery, the more resilient and better equipped they are to face these challenges in a healthy manner.

You will read about the gut-wrenching fight against addiction. What I hope you will remember is the courage it took each of these persons to stand face-to-face with what they saw in themselves without looking away. These stories are for you to contemplate. They can provide markers along the way as you explore your inner landscape and embrace your own recovery.

Writing a book shares many parallels with recovery. When you enter into recovery, you must be willing to go where it draws you while holding in the deepest folds of your being the conviction that it will lead you to a new place worth discovering. This book started as solely a storytelling book. However, it took my hand and said "This way. Your work is not done."

Indeed, it was not. I hadn't yet met Dr. Jeremy Frank. We shared our personal experiences of recovery from opposite sides: His came from his addiction to drugs and alcohol, and mine came from loving someone who battled addiction. We discussed our individual pathway to recovery and the stories of the couples I had interviewed. Patterns, habits, and wisdom emerged as we followed the threads of our discoveries. Jeremy and I realized we could meld these insights into six practical behaviors to guide partners in their quest to build a healthy relationship. We named this The ASCENT Approach.

As you read the stories in parts two and three that tell the experiences of couples finding their way to the full benefits of recovery in their relationship, my hope is that *Love Without Martinis* will provide solace, impetus, and support as you travel your path to creating a healthy relationship with the person you love.

—Chantal C. Jauvin, LLB, MBA

JEREMY: *Why Embrace the Work of Recovery?*

A breakthrough happened five years into my recovery when I just couldn't understand why I was so afraid of getting married. Was I just terrified of growing up and becoming a man? My father, a psychoanalyst, and my mother, a social worker, had the perfect marriage, and despite the jokes about how shrinks' kids are always messed up, I was doing pretty well. Aside from the small issue of recovering from addiction to alcohol and drugs, I was studying in grad school to be a psychologist, I had hobbies, friends, and many interests. And I felt healthy. Yet I knew I still had more personal work to do to get my act together. In my second year of therapy with my second therapist, we were discussing my fear of intimacy, whether it was too much or not enough. I was describing an anxious pit in my stomach when Dan asked me a perplexing question.

"Jeremy, is it better to be loved by Jen (my girlfriend at the time) or to be known by her?" he asked.

"To be loved by her," I said. I thought it was a trick question. After all, Dan was Dr. Dan Gottlieb, PhD, the well-known Philadelphian and accomplished voice of WHYY's *Voices in the Family* radio talk show. Dan had a way of making you feel off-balance and unsure, and then all of a sudden something would hit you and you would just feel your feelings. Later the insight would come. I've since learned that there are two ways to "get an A in therapy." You either make some changes and then the insight will follow, or you learn some things about yourself and then you will make those changes when you are ready. I wasn't certain about much when it came to the decisions before me in my relationship with my girlfriend. However, I clearly knew I wanted nothing more than to be loved by Jen.

Fear of loss was a strong shadow in my life, a trigger that could easily pull me back over the line from recovery into active addiction. Jen and I had already been together for four years. We loved each other. At the top of my "fear of losing list" was fear of losing attention, especially from Jen. Maybe this came from a familiar fear of losing attention from my busy parents. This combined with a constant battle to fend off critical thoughts about myself and all the people in my life (more family of origin issues) left me paralyzed, stuck in my head, isolated and always knowing that drugs and alcohol could offer temporary solace.

The silence between Dan and me grew, as did my unease. That's how Dan would get me to feel my emotions. I began to doubt my answer. I riffled through the research stored in my head from my hot-off-the-press doctoral dissertation on adult attachment and substance dependence. I scolded myself for not knowing the answer to his question. More feelings, more shame . . .

"Jeremy, being known is more important than being loved. You can't be loved without being known. Jen has to know your real and genuine self. If she doesn't know you, you will never know if she truly loves you. If you don't know yourself, how can she know and love you?" he said.

I was all caught up in my head. I always intellectualized everything as a defense against feelings. Were we right for each other? Maybe marriage could be fun? Would Jen get bored with me? . . . I with her? The feelings rising in my stomach getting stuck in my head.

I have so much gratitude that after 21 years of marriage my wife, Jen, has never known me as an active addict. But she has certainly seen my addictive tendencies. I can easily tend towards obsessive thinking and compulsive behavior around eating, exercising and family relationships. I must have my Kombucha and blackberries. I must not skip my daily workouts. I must dedicate enough time to my parents and children. These preoccupations may appear normal. But for someone like me, meaning a person in recovery, these drives can take on an unwarranted sense of urgency and compulsivity.

Even without the martinis, Jen and I tread water at times, trying to get to understand or accept why the other stacks the dishwasher "the wrong way," drives too slowly, or insists the kids should be picked up when they are totally capable of taking the bus. When we're not resolving these mundane conflicts that almost always have deeper-seated origins, we're still trying to teach each other who we are and what it is like to be ourselves. We try to learn about our desires to find purpose or just how to enjoy some lighthearted fun and closeness. Our relationship works best when we engage in discovering each other on a daily basis and giving each other the freedom to grow and change. It's a process without an end that would be impossible without recovery.

In my nearly 30 years working in this field, I've often been asked: At what point is someone recovered from their dependence on alcohol? How long should someone be in recovery before it is safe to have a relationship with them? When will a partner finally get over the past and trust a boyfriend, wife, or partner that has been sober for years not to relapse? When will the relationship be reclaimed from the chaos of addiction?

There are at least as many definitions of the word "recovery" as there are pathways to recovery. Dictionary.com offers a plain and straightforward definition: "restoration or return to health from sickness."[1] But what does that mean in the context of addiction to alcohol?

Recovery from substance dependence usually requires not only sobriety but learning who we are—our becoming more aware, mindful, and conscious. For a couple to be healthy and happy, each member must negotiate the sharing of their conscious selves with their partner.[2]

Addiction is the antithesis of conscious awareness. It has been described as a defense against awareness. It is a disease that manifests in the denial of feelings, the denial of problems and the blunting and numbing of who we really are. It is the only disease that tells us that we do not have a disease.

When it comes to couples, the disease of addiction is the garrotter of love. If we do not know ourselves because of the hazy fog of alcohol, there is no room for love. We will be "trapped in a dark forest," as Chantal alludes.

---

1 https://www.dictionary.com/browse/recovery?s=t

2 Freud, despite some of his assertions, remains the father of psychoanalysis for his contribution to the understanding of the "unconscious" in psychology. His main idea was that the purpose of psychotherapy was to make that which is unconscious conscious. Freud, S. (1922). A general introduction to psychoanalysis. New York: Boni and Liveright.

Earnie Larsen, a pioneer in the field of recovery from addictive behaviors, believes that once a person breaks the primary addiction (becomes sober) the next stage is "learning to love." Since love only exists in a relationship, "the core of recovery is becoming a person increasingly capable of functioning in a healthy relationship."[3]

Addiction has been described as a disease of social isolation. Recovery is a type of "coming out process" which involves digging down deep to know oneself with some external help to learn how to relate with others. We need connection to be fully realized as human beings. In the words of Harville Hendrix, PhD, the creator of Imago Relationship Therapy, "The most fulfilling love relationship is one in which two people are intimately connected with each other, yet keep a respectful distance apart by acknowledging each other's 'otherness.'"[4] This is the "hard work" that Doug Tieman discusses in his foreword and the "soul work" that Chantal refers to that is indispensable to recovery.

While there is extensive research on addiction, couples, and recovery, there is less agreement on how to integrate this empirical knowledge into a comprehensive understanding of the impact of addiction on couples. There is even less knowledge, and less agreement, about how to determine the best practices for treatment and recovery for couples because individuals struggling with a substance use disorder can be so different from each other, and their needs for treatment and recovery can be specific, vast, and diverse.

Some treatment providers believe that everyone in recovery individually and jointly with their partner must pass through developmental stages to achieve and maintain the full benefits of long-term recovery. But more likely there are underlying factors that can drive

3 Larsen, Earnie. *Stage II Relationships: Love Beyond Addiction*. New York: Harper One, 1987 (page 13).

4 Hendrix, Harville, *Getting the Love You Want: A Guide for Couples*. New York: St. Martin's Press, 2008 (page xix).

or fuel addiction and recovery. If active addiction is the tip of the iceberg, we see only the one-tenth above the water, the behavior fueled by alcohol or drug use, gambling, eating disorders, etc. This leaves over 90 percent of the effects of addiction under the water and unseen. For each individual and couple, it is this underwater part of the iceberg which must be investigated, treated and known for couples to recover.

Based on my thirty years of studying and treating individuals and couples, not to mention facing my own addiction, I strongly believe there is no one path to recovery. There are as many ways to recover as there are people who want to recover. But I have also learned that there are common themes that transcend cultural, socio-economic, gender, and other unique conditions. These commonalities are what we need to understand.

The framework that informs my practice the most draws on the research work of Harvard psychiatrist George Vaillant. In addition, I've been influenced by evidence-based practices and general prevailing understandings of what is effective according to clinicians' anecdotal experiences.[5] Over the years I've come to realize that there are major areas of concern that people must address in order to recover. I refer to these as The Seven 'S's:

1. Steps of care and stages of change

2. Structure of time

3. Supervision of recovery process

4. Spirituality and belief systems

5. Social support

---

5 Vaillant, George E. "Alcoholics Anonymous: Cult or Cure?" *Australian and New Zealand Journal of Psychiatry*; 39: 431–436. *https://doi.org/10.1080/j.1440-1614.2005.01600.x*

6. Substitutes for alcohol or substance addiction

7. Sustenance of recovery

Many of these elements overlap. One need not address all of the factors to develop sustainable recovery. However, one cannot focus on only one or two of them.

When Chantal approached me to participate in *Love Without Martinis*, she asked how my framework specifically applied to couples. Did each partner need to work on these factors individually or together? Could only one partner work on these areas while the other ignored them? What if each partner's views of the importance of these areas were at odds with each other? This began a conversation based on my experience and research in the field and her learnings from interviewing couples and reading books to inform her writing. The result of our conversations and reflection is The ASCENT Approach.

Before you open yourself to the powers of the stories written by Chantal in parts two and three, we will present The ASCENT Approach in part one.

Whether we turn to books for knowledge and understanding or to mutual support groups such as Alcoholics Anonymous, Al-Anon, and SMART or to therapists, medical doctors, and alternative practitioners or places of worship, we need to ask for help and support from others who may have been there before us.

Recovery from addiction involves finding and baring our soul. While that may seem daunting at first, others' stories can show us the way to do this "safely." It is important to remember that we must reserve the right to advance at our own pace. If our relationship is to survive the disease of addiction, it can only happen in the context of engaging with a partner who is also willing and able to do similar hard work. Addiction causes real trauma to the individual, partners, and family. The antidote to active addiction is to become known to ourselves and others.

Trauma-informed clinicians, in particular, have learned the importance of storytelling in recovery from trauma. Each time we share our story, we grapple with different aspects of our experience with its broad and varied feelings. In doing so, we come to know ourselves more fully.

—Jeremy Frank, PhD, CADC
Licensed Clinical Psychologist,
Certified Alcohol and Drug Counselor at
Jeremy Frank Associates in Philadelphia

PART I

✳

The ASCENT Approach to Building Relationships in Recovery

The ASCENT Approach:
Six Practices to Build a Healthy
Relationship in Recovery

When we are in recovery, we often hear the words disease, co-dependency, and treatment attached to other words such as journey, healing, and even spiritual awakening. The underlying message, whether blatantly stated or gently hinted at, suggests that we need to change. In a relationship, it implies each of us must grow for the relationship to have even a chance of succeeding.

Addiction breaks our connection to ourselves, to the world, and to one another. We experience estrangement from ourselves and separateness in all our relationships.

Similarly, the battle of an addicted person's partner to either strong-arm a person they love into sobriety, or ignore them until they become sober, often draws a wedge between the partners and the world within us and around us.

In therapy rooms, in the relationships of the couples interviewed for this book, and in our own relationships, we have felt lonely while being together. Conflicts arise that pit us against each other with a mounting list of unresolved issues we label as insurmountable differences, lack of trust, miscommunication, absence of intimacy, and disagreements about money, sex, and control. Although we can dream that sobriety will chase away these intruders from our otherwise happy world, this is unlikely.

Underlying causes rooted in the shadows of our being will most likely prevail against such a swift and tidy resolution of the tension between us. These wounds and traumas require time to be healed. We need the support of counselors, spiritual advisors, sponsors, doctors, and people in long-term recovery to show us the way. Because we do not live in a perfect world, life does not stand still to give us the opportunity to entirely dedicate ourselves to our recovery. And other new challenges and traumas continue to emerge to remind us of the familiar slogan that we must "Live life on life's terms."

The goal is not to resolve all our problems or eliminate all our pain and discomfort so that we can finally start living the life we want. Life is simply not that linear and tidy. Instead, what we aim for is to develop the ability to navigate the richness and the challenges of life in harmony with our partner.

My favorite definition of recovery remains one written by Earnie Larsen, a pioneer in the field of recovery from addictive behaviors: "The core of recovery is becoming a person increasingly capable of functioning in a healthy relationship." The reason I prefer this definition is twofold. It recognizes that recovery starts where we are in our life with the goal to improve our ability to grow in relation to ourself and another person. Secondly, it recognizes that the relationship must itself grow into a positive connection between two persons.

This definition of recovery by Larsen captures the essence of long-term recovery. There are various ways to describe the progression from early to long-term recovery, most of which focus on the individual and not the couple. Because recovery is considered a lifelong and nonlinear process accompanied by other unattended psychological and or emotional considerations, the distinctions between the different stages of recovery are often considered subjective. For the purposes of this book, when we refer to "early recovery" we mean the period following sobriety when the couple is able to recognize that there is a substance use disorder affecting each of them and their relationship. They begin to shift their focus from "who" is wrong to "what" is wrong.

After an initial understanding that the partners are facing a disease, they begin to reach for support outside their family unit and to listen and speak to one another in their partnership with less reactivity. However, resentment, blame, shame, mistrust, and many other emotions and perhaps coexisting psychological conditions need to be addressed and healed. As the couple moves through mid-recovery, their individual recovery begins to intersect as they learn to talk through past hurts, understand their personal responsibility for the relationship, and formulate a new vision for their union. This period can also be more tumultuous as the pair starts to tackle tougher issues of trust and physical and emotional intimacy along with practical matters of finances and health as the couple deepens their ability to communicate.

With continued soul work, the couple will grow into long-term recovery. This is not nirvana or a place of perfection. Rather it is the point where the couple has created a stable and intimate environment in which they are able to (1) deal with problems without needing immediate resolution to resolve the tension, (2) balance the short-term as well as the long-term issues, and (3) grow both individually and as a couple.

One of the aims of recovery is to strive to build a fresh connection within the couple that can withstand the ebb and flow of temporary disconnects as well as individual growth. While each partner addresses their own growth at their own pace, the couple also requires guidance and attention. The goal is not so much to get the relationship back but to heal the disconnect. As we commit ourselves to recovery, we want to develop an increasingly intimate connection with one another. In long-term recovery, we create a new and healthy foundation upon which to relate to one another both as "me" and as "us," which we can then bring forth into our communities. Recovery calls upon us to relate and connect with each other as well as to broaden our participation in positive relationships.

As I interviewed couples for *Love Without Martinis*, I also read about addiction, recovery, and relationships to train myself to listen more deeply to their stories. When the listening, the reading, and the writing were done, my hope was that I had not only effectively reported the stories of tremendous courage and love but also imparted what these couples had learned about recovery.

Traditional storytelling is a custom of sharing knowledge, interpreting experiences, and passing on collective wisdom to others through the power of stories. I knew that I had told each story to the best of my ability, and this was confirmed as I received each couple's approval to include their story in this book. Still, I felt that to fully engage in storytelling, I needed to go further. I wanted to share their collective wisdom and felt that this required expertise in the field of recovery, which I do not possess.

I approached Dr. Jeremy Frank, a psychologist and certified alcohol and drug counselor, to help me with my book. He, himself, is in recovery. He is also a husband, an avid soccer player, gardener *extraordinaire*, father of two great teenagers, and as I learned, a fabulous collaborator. Together we explored the stories of the couples in *Love Without Martinis* using his knowledge from private practice, our personal experiences, and the recovery literature to understand what they have in common. This chapter tells the result of what we found.

Jeremy and I discovered common threads that could be woven together to support couples in recovery. In the spirit of traditional storytelling, we have interpreted the wisdom that emerged from our exploration and formed the six practices we call The ASCENT Approach to make each practice easier to remember.

Here are the practices of The ASCENT Approach for couples in recovery:

> **A**ssess your readiness to change
>
> **S**tructure your time
>
> **C**reate your community
>
> **E**ngage in your life
>
> **N**urture your spirituality
>
> **T**reasure your partnership

Beware. These practices are not magical formulas. Nor are they substitutes for individual recovery work. They do not replace external guidance whether offered by a therapist, a fellowship, a spiritual guide, or a counseling professional—particularly in early recovery. What we have observed, however, is that the couples who developed certain habits were successful in building healthy relationships in recovery. It became evident to us that we could learn from them how to acquire particular behaviors that are conducive to long-term recovery.

Much like the lessons we discern from hearing our elders tell stories, the narrative of couples who have reclaimed their relationships from addiction and built *healthy* unions can serve as examples. Their accounts show us habits that spurred their growth and others that were self-defeating. We can observe how, in the midst of anguish, they handled their emotions, experienced missteps and changed their behaviors.

The American novelist, Tim O'Brien, summarized well the importance of sharing our experiences with others and learning from people who have journeyed before us. He said, "Storytelling is the essential human activity. The harder the situation, the more essential it is."

I cannot think of any experience in my life that was harder than living through the disintegration of the connection with the man I love as he battled with his addiction and we struggled to find a meaningful connection together in recovery. I often turned to the anecdotes shared by others to give me hope and show me the way.

We hope that as you read the stories that follow, you will see how Tom and Carole, David and Leslie, Luke and Nadia, Tim and Chuck, my husband Bill and I, and Sherri and Larry engage in these behaviors. They were not trying to apply The ASCENT Approach as it had not yet been created. However, each couple exhibited these habits, often enough for us to recognize their value as supportive practices for their recovery as a couple.

We encourage you to engage as a couple with as many of these practices as you can reasonably and safely manage. These practices are not steps and do not need to be tackled in a specific order since they often overlap. It is important, however, that each of you go at your own pace or pause when necessary. These practices are intended to establish a fresh connection between the partners and create new behaviors that will guide you toward long-term recovery.

Assess Your Readiness to Change

You and I, and the people we love, don't grow at the same pace. Most often we travel through life to different beats. When my husband and I hike, we have different strides. I charge up hills, and he paces himself. Some days he walks ahead and must wait for me to catch up. Sometimes I trot down the hills and in turn must wait for him. At other times, we fall into a natural rhythm, walking side-by-side, chatting and figuring out the world around us.

Growth and recovery are similar processes since each of us progresses at our own pace. Although we may rationally understand that each of us must deal with hurts or troubling emotions to heal, our perception of what needs to be addressed, in what order and how fast, often differs. One of the most significant shifts in early recovery is moving from *who* is wrong to *what* is wrong. Often we blame our partner or ourselves for the chaos of addiction because we do not comprehend the nature of addiction. Once we begin to understand that neither of us is to blame, we naturally start to search for what is to blame.

We must come to terms, both individually and as a couple, with the reality that we are dealing with a disease that affects both of us. As we work through a gradual acceptance of the impact on our lives and the recovery that lies ahead, we may differ in our grasp of what needs to be done. Assessing your readiness means determining how willing you both are to accept that there are problems that need to be addressed and to explore and evaluate a range of options to solve them.

In early recovery, it is not uncommon for people to believe that if their partner or they themselves stop drinking, the "problem" will be solved. Their lives and relationships will fall into place. The focus often centers on abstinence. The individuals and the couple shift their struggle from stopping the drinking to ensuring that their non-drinking continues. This battle to maintain sobriety often consumes them and prevents both the individuals and the couple from engaging in recovery.

This practice consists of assessing our readiness to accept that each of us requires some combination of counseling, fellowship, spiritual guidance, and perhaps medication or other medical attention to address our recovery needs. It involves coming face-to-face with the reality that addiction is a disease requiring treatment beyond achieving sobriety. Cravings, feelings, poor communication skills, buried emotional issues, health, finances, and other issues arise and need to be addressed.

The importance of assessing our readiness with respect to co-dependent behavior can be acute. Resistance to accepting the idea that each of us has been affected by this family disease can be high. For example, issues of self-worth, anger, guilt, abandonment, and harmful behaviors need to be addressed. The partners affected by addiction need to do their own soul work to heal and develop new attitudes and behaviors and integrate new ways of thinking. We also need a plan of action to prevent us from reverting to negative habits.

Perhaps the simplest way to evaluate our progress with this practice of assessing our readiness to change is to see it as a continuum of four levels:

I do not see the problem, or I am not currently ready to address it.

I recognize there is a problem, and I am thinking about how to tackle it.

I am now ready to take action to effect change.

I am absorbing this change and learning how to maintain it.

It is important to individually assess where we stand in this continuum when we consider which problem to tackle. We must assess our willingness and ability to absorb any change that personally affects us. For example, we may be ready to rebuild the relationship with a relative, but our partner may not be ready to accept that particular family member back into their life. This practice encourages us to identify differences in the partners readiness to change.

The complexity of this practice becomes evident when we try to assess where we stand, not only individually but as a couple. There is much debate about whether in early recovery the couple "needs to go on hold" while each partner engages in their own therapy, or whether it is advisable for the individual and couple's work to be parallel. We may require external support to help us determine whether we are ready as a couple to engage in joint work.

Three distinct units (me, my partner, and us) need to be simultaneously and regularly assessed. Each unit may not always be at the same place in the continuum of readiness to change. We don't need to be.

The continuum is also not a one-way street. As we move from early recovery to later recovery, we may find ourselves moving back and forth along the continuum. For example, we may be ready to accept that it's time to seek counseling but may not be aware that an issue such as a childhood trauma can be undermining our individual or joint recovery.

This practice encourages us to focus on assessing our readiness and communicating it to each other. We do not need to agree with each other. However, the process of naming for ourselves the areas in which we wish to grow, and communicating with each other about how ready we are to tackle them, enhances our connection to one another. The challenge is to accept each other's level of readiness, to be aware that one of us is tackling a specific issue and to support each other as we move toward action. In this practice, we strive to find the balance between too little or too much, too slow or too fast, so that we maintain a sense of balance in our relationship as we move forward in our recovery.

When you read the story of Carole and Tom, you will see how Carole believes that Tom drinks to relax because he is tired and under a lot of stress at work. As problems progress in their lives, Carole's denial leads her to believe that Tom has a medical condition rather than a struggle with alcohol. In Tom and Carole's story, the growing anxiety between them becomes palpable. Carole eventually breaks through her denial when she comes face-to-face with the amount of money Tom is spending on alcohol. This is the first time she considers the words "alcoholism," "disease," and "addiction." Carole is scared. Even after Tom and Carole first discuss the possibility that Tom cannot control his drinking, their level of readiness to address Tom's need for treatment is mismatched. Carole attends Al-Anon before Tom accepts his addiction. Their commitment to embrace recovery differs. Tom faces stress caused by intense feelings of CEO "Imposter Syndrome." Carole's focus on Tom's condition of feeling like a "fake" overshadows her own need to address some childhood issues that fuel her inability to detach from her husband. Each of them is angry and blames the other for the chaos in their lives. Their conflicts mount until they each become ready to act and seek outside support.

As you read the stories of the other couples, you'll notice that each person's level of readiness to address issues that relate to one another often varies. Leslie tells David that he is no longer retired but has a full-time job called "recovery." She supports David with this job as she did when he was an executive at Procter & Gamble. However, she chooses to concentrate on other aspects of her own recovery, such as her community. In other stories, you'll see that one partner is ready to address certain issues in their relationship while the other does not perceive a need for change. Observe how the different levels of readiness affect the couple's ability to deal with sexual intimacy, finances, and emotional availability.

As a couple engaged in the process of early recovery, the key is to understand whether both of you are ready to make a change to deal with a specific issue. If not, we need to respect this fact about the other person. We can seek ways to support our partner or ourselves, often with external help, to move closer toward being ready. In the meantime, it is best to concentrate on something we are both ready to address. In later recovery, we develop a greater ability to hold the tension between us. We learn how to avoid disconnecting when we are not both ready to change. We have become more comfortable with giving each other support and the time to ready ourselves for change because we understand that growth is part of life and many problems do not need an immediate resolution.

Structure Your Time

Recovery does not happen by accident. Making progress requires careful structure of your time. Idle time too easily lulls us back into habits, behaviors, and thinking patterns that are counterproductive to our growth. The practice of organizing activities, making a schedule, and committing to obligations creates a container that holds us.

In early recovery, having a routine creates predictability and calms the previous chaos wreaked on our relationship by addiction. Adhering to a schedule makes us accountable (being where we say we'll be) and promotes trust between us by following through on our commitments (doing what we say we'll do). We also form new habits that create a strong defense against slipping back into harmful habits such as spending time alone, romanticizing drinking, or focusing too much on our partner's life.

Structuring our time is critical in early recovery. We are often so enmeshed as a couple that we're unable to operate without constantly surveilling each other. This need to know all the details of our partner's affairs stems from the trust that was destroyed throughout active addiction. During the turmoil preceding early recovery, each of us was trapped in a cat-and-mouse game focused on figuring out ways to escape from the other or catch our partner in wrongdoing. Alternatively, we may be so disconnected that our lives rarely intersect. In this situation, we learned throughout active addiction that the only way to survive conflict was to avoid each other at all costs. We became the cliché of two ships passing in the dark giving each other a very wide berth. In either situation Structure guides us towards taking personal responsibility for ourselves and for our welfare.

Regular commitments provide a form of external supervision necessary in early recovery. When you agree to meet with a therapist, sponsor, friend, or colleague, someone outside the couple provides a form of oversight. The person you are meeting expects you to show up, to be on time, and to participate in what you've agreed to do. The commitments don't always have to be one-on-one meetings; they can include other kinds of time obligations such as signing up for a class, volunteering at an animal shelter, or joining a meditation group. In the chaos of addiction, we shied away from such obligations. In recovery, it is important that we are accountable for being present.

Finding your own structure and balancing your needs and wants as a couple helps address the "people, places, and things" of active addiction and codependent behavior. It encourages you to explore new interests and meet new people. This is essential to avoid a return to old habits. In early recovery, having impulsive urges caused by feelings of confusion, dependency and grief, to name a few strong emotions, can create turbulence that pulls you and your partner into old, familiar dysfunctional patterns in an attempt to create certainty rather than dealing with the uncertainty of these new feelings. Structure provides a counterweight. It encourages accountability and predictability, which are fundamental components of trust.

In later stages of recovery, you will need more time as a couple for deeper personal growth and your joint healing. This can be challenging when we are juggling all our daily obligations. Structuring our weeks to set aside time together is important. As we develop greater communication skills, more time is required to talk through past hurts and to create a new vision of our partnership for the future. We begin to experience a greater need to address not only short-term goals but also long-term ones. Predictability allows us to consider the home improvement project that was shelved, the trip that was postponed, or the dog adoption we abandoned. It encourages us to explore what we want for the next stage of our lives together. What do we aspire to individually and as a couple?

With later-stage recovery we learn to navigate our increasing involvement with a larger community, balance the distribution of joint responsibilities, and make time for intimacy as a couple. Structure continues to be the container that holds us accountable to one another in our pursuit of growth and a deepening of our bond.

Structuring our time is the practice that overlaps the most with the other practices. It is the trifecta of: 1) Creating our community, (2) Engaging in our life, and (3) Nourishing our spirituality. Whether it is joining a baseball league, having a regular date night, signing up for guitar lessons, journaling each morning, and spending time with the kids; or gardening, going to church or volunteering in the neighborhood; these commitments are all forms of structuring.

After returning home from treatment, Tom and Carole look at their calendars and plan the next ten months. Tom joins the fellowship of Alcoholics Anonymous and engages in individual therapy. Carole mirrors this by also beginning therapy with an addiction counselor in addition to attending Al-Anon meetings. They both focus on the goal of Tom's return to work after 90 days of sobriety. Later in their recovery, Tom begins to volunteer as a mentor for a boys' after-school program. He takes up a new hobby (fly fishing). Carole becomes comfortable with Tom's absences when he takes the mentored boys on weekend sailing trips. They create a new family tradition of Sunday barbecues with their adult children. Tom and Carole also set some boundaries to protect their time alone and encourage their sexual intimacy.

As you read the stories of the other couples, see how they develop their own structures by establishing a routine for specific mealtimes, exercising to fulfill fitness goals, and meeting deadlines for every-day responsibilities like bill-paying and coordinating their weekly schedules. More ambitious goals are set, such as deciding to launch a small entrepreneurial business, attend fellowships, take a singing class, individually join siblings and parents for annual celebrations, see a therapist, and determine to meet friends regularly and partic-ipate in clubs. We can see that in later recovery, couples increas-ingly organize their lives in ways that free them to engage with a greater circle of people, to help them to grow spiritually and to pursue creative aspirations.

Create Your Community

The benefits of engaging with other people to combat loneliness can be said to be even more important during recovery. Having a com-munity is a cornerstone of sobriety because it breaks the isolation that has crept into our lives. Our ability to survive and thrive as people is largely dependent on our ability to create bonds with oth-ers, whether they are friends, family, neighbors, or coworkers. Only by fulfilling our need for intimacy with others can we enjoy the full benefits of recovery.

We are pack animals, and we need each other to survive. We have evolved over several hundreds of thousands of years through bonding within our tribes. During our battle with addiction, we used alco-hol to ease our social relationships. Alcohol "loosened" us up. We believed that we needed to drink "to cope" with work, loneliness, boredom in our relationships, fear of rejection, failure, success, and the list goes on. Drinking was our attempt to facilitate entry into the social world or to navigate its complexities.

In early recovery, we build new relationships to connect with people who are not burdened by the pain of our addictive or chaotic behavior. We owe them no emotional debts. Forming new bonds is an effective way for us to break down our isolation while we get to know ourselves in recovery. When we engage with others, especially other couples, it provides us an opportunity to put our own relationship into perspective. We discover our strengths and weaknesses as we observe them in others. This validates that relationships are complex and beautiful bonds that need care.

When we join with others who share our views and interests, such as in book clubs, sports teams, and neighborhood classes, we gradually reintegrate into a community that is not an emotionally charged situation for us. As a member of these groups we develop our ability to listen to others and engage in dialogue. This helps us develop healthy ways of behaving since we are required to focus on something other than ourselves. Being surrounded by members of our community also provides us with a safety net, providing us with a group of acquaintances to contact when we feel vulnerable and need connection.

Each relationship offers us a mirror to better understand ourselves. By observing people new to us, we become better able to discern their positive behaviors without feeling guilt or shame for our past actions and are more willing to emulate these healthy interactions. When we introduce ourselves to new people, and when we spend time with old friends or family members who are safe for us, we share stories. Each time we tell a story we grapple with different aspects of ourselves. Every time we listen to other people's stories we nurture our ability to be compassionate towards others. These experiences begin to alter us and the way we behave; we are honing our communication skills and our empathy and are becoming more self-aware. We bring these learnings back into our relationship with the person we love. By bonding with others, we grow and deepen our connection as a couple.

Once we are more grounded in our recovery, we are encouraged to reach out to broader, less homogeneous groups such as school parent committees, professional associations, fundraising drives, and neighborhood organizations. Interacting with people who embrace diverse views, habits, and experiences challenges us to grow in several ways. We need to find commonalities with people who may disagree with our views of the world in order to relate with one another. This provides us an opportunity to speak for ourselves. It forces us to develop flexibility in our thinking and awareness of ourselves. We learn to extend ourselves to others and to understand when we are overextending ourselves.

Relationships require us to develop appropriate boundaries. When addiction wreaked havoc in our lives, our ability to manage our boundaries was compromised. One moment we could be too rigid (everything became black-and-white with no ability to see or operate in grey areas) or too fluid (nothing mattered but surviving the moment). Recovery requires us to develop semi-permeable boundaries. We become gatekeepers for what we may safely allow in or what we must keep out.

As we learn to say no, we can't pick up the team's equipment again or stand up to support new club regulations, as we lobby strangers to sign a petition for climate change or leave a meeting early to take the bus before it's too dark or step in to help because a committee member got sick, we grow individually. In turn, we then bring freshness and new ways of behaving into our intimate relationship with our partner and grow as a couple.

In the story of Tom and Carole, you will observe that early in his recovery, Tom creates new relationships with his sponsor and AA fellowship. He also learns to create boundaries with his brother who is in denial concerning Tom's dependence on alcohol. Carole relies on one long-standing friend for support but learns that Al-Anon is the safest place to wrestle with her codependency. Tom, never one to join social clubs, decides to participate in Sober Bikers United.

Carole builds on her yoga background by volunteering to teach a weekly class. As Carole becomes more self-aware, she grapples with her tendencies to control others and her need for predictability. As an antidote, she joins a book club. Although reading is normally a calming hobby, she realizes that the monthly meetings will force her to visit the home of strangers and eventually host them. She will not be able to control how the club members behave and will have to trust herself to handle the situations that arise.

The first summer into their recovery, Tom and Carole host a Sunday barbecue with their new friends. They experience the freedom of being themselves with people who know them for who they are now without the confusion of the wine and whiskey-soaked evenings. Tom and Carole realize that no one pays attention to whether Tom is drinking; what they prize is the laughter and the fun of getting together.

In the stories of the other couples, you will observe how they turn to their families, their friends, and their fellowships for support. In early recovery, each couple wrestles with how much to reveal to people around them concerning their sobriety and recovery. Each couple finds a way to navigate the social challenges created by the prevalence of social drinking but not at the expense of isolation. Notice how they learn to travel with others, participate in clubs, visit their families, and spend time with friends. The success of our long-term recovery requires moving from "you and I" to "us and our community."

Engage in Your Life

The practice of engaging constructively in your life is perhaps the most general of the practices. It calls upon each of us to affirm ourselves through personal development. Addiction and codependency cause us to have a single-minded fixation on a substance, such as alcohol, or a dysfunctional pattern of relating, including attempts to control our partner. In recovery we must learn to expand our interests and welcome growth into our lifestyle. We must not remain stagnant. We need to educate our minds, care for our bodies, and take charge of our lives.

Ultimately, this is our life, and we are responsible for it. In early recovery it is crucial to develop a healthy relationship to something positive which calls us strongly enough to thwart our desire to drink or revert to behaviors that place our sobriety at risk. Similarly, to avoid slipping back into codependent thinking or behaviors that undermine our personal growth, we must cultivate interests that shift our focus and energy away from our partner toward activities we find rewarding. We know this intuitively to be true. We know we must replace a bad habit with a healthy one. The disease of addiction has trained us to engage in many unhealthy ways.

Early in our recovery, it is very challenging to develop positive habits. We must choose to work out instead of drinking. We must decide to call a friend instead of fretting over our partner. We must nurture our interests even though we often have forgotten what previously fascinated us. We must find a purpose that is meaningful to us individually rather than what our partner, parent, or child tells us is important. We must choose to care for our body instead of ignoring it. These choices promote a positive self-image, a sense of well-being and a greater self-awareness.

While searching for, or rediscovering, the activities and interests that bring us joy and fulfillment, we should consider which of our responsibilities have been neglected. Perhaps it is time to look at our finances, evaluate our careers, take care of health issues, talk to our estranged kids, visit an aging parent, or fix our house. Addiction is all-consuming; it tricks us into disregarding or avoiding our responsibilities. In recovery we need to pace ourselves but also attend to the obligations that are rightfully ours. Our inaction not only impacts our partner. It affects others we have neglected. Ultimately we are preventing ourselves from flourishing.

In later recovery, we use this practice to recalibrate when we lose perspective. Are we focusing too much on going to the gym with our headsets plugged in and not signing up for that yoga class because we are afraid to try? Are we staying late at work every night at the expense of spending time with our children, disregarding our role as a present parent? Are we waiting for the neighbor to fix the fence? Are we spending sufficient quality time with our partner? We need to honestly evaluate ourselves and the choices we are making to ensure that we maintain a healthy and balanced life.

When we fully engage in positive ways in our lives, we are lighter and more joyful. If we feel better in our skin, we laugh more often, respect our boundaries and remain open to change. These are all factors that deepen our connection to one another. We recognize the benefits of being connected to one another and also gain new respect for our "otherness," feeling less threatened than previously by our differences.

In the first story, Carole experiences people laughing at themselves during an Al-Anon meeting. She comes to understand that by assuming responsibility for themselves, they can put their behavior into perspective and even laugh about it. Through his interaction with his AA peers, Tom realizes he wants to return to work to fulfill his professional aspirations.

The couples in these stories take charge of their lives, their relationships, and their interests. This happens tentatively at first, but as their recovery progresses, so does their desire to live fuller lives. Many turn to sports and yoga to heal their bodies and nerves. They decide to be mindful parents who share the joy of their hobbies with their children. They set aside time for date night or cuddling to watch their favorite TV series. They try fishing, dust off their tools, write a book, make plans for the weekend, and start online businesses to provide for their future.

Nurture Your Spirituality

Let's be clear about what this practice entails. It is to encourage us to delve into our human spirit to find a belief outside of ourselves, one that affords us hope, comfort, and serenity. It is about knowing what brings us inner peace. It is not necessarily about religion or belief in a god. In recovery circles there is perhaps no more difficult topic than that of our spirituality. The idea that we must identify a "Higher Power, and that by believing in this "power greater than ourselves" we will "be restored to sanity," creates the most tension and resistance. It provokes reactions ranging from passive skepticism to outright anger. Many people come to spirituality with rigid or hurtful religious constructs or have had confusing childhood experiences with their family's religion or hold dogmatic positions.

Others arrive fighting a war against the idea of surrendering to something greater than themselves. It is far more important that we identify what brings us inner peace than to continue these battles with ourselves about religion and the meaning of a god in order to arrive at a specific definition of a higher power.

As a couple, both people do not need to believe or disbelieve in a higher power or turn to the same external source for guidance. What we do need is to develop a spiritual practice that supports our individual healing. Whether we turn to religion, a universal god, collective wisdom, *Dharma* or Nature, or another belief, we must simply acknowledge that we should discover what spiritual practices give us comfort and guidance. While many of us may struggle with identifying a higher power, some may be atheistic or agnostic. Or others may have a clear belief in a god. It is imperative that we respect our partner in his or her spiritual journey.

What calms our emotions, our "spirits"? Perhaps it is prayer, meditation, journaling, reading reflections, communing with nature, or mindful breathing. This practice is about caring for our souls. The more ways we find to nourish our inner peace, the greater guidance and serenity we will find from within.

It is worth repeating that this is an individual pursuit, a renewal of our personal spirit. By nurturing our spirituality, we learn to turn to our inner beliefs to guide our actions. We connect with our emotions, which leads us to be more present to ourselves and our partner.

Whether in early recovery or later-stage recovery, spirituality provides a useful tool to deal with uncertainty and conflict. This inner knowing of something greater than ourselves provides us with serenity in the face of struggles or peacefulness. We learn to forgive others and ourselves. These are all gifts to our relationship.

In the story of Tom and Carole, they both join a 12-step fellowship that called upon them to look into their hearts. By moving through the steps, they each identify a power that is greater than themselves to turn to for guidance. This journey deepens their self-awareness and leads them to learn to forgive themselves and each other. Breaking the cycle of blame, in turn, cultivates their intimacy.

In the stories of the couples, some people keep journals, others practice yoga or meditation, some go to church, and others embrace Buddhism. They find ways to ground themselves through their love of nature or religious celebrations. As people grow, their spirituality evolves, and the ways in which they find inner peace might change.

Treasure Your Relationship

With this practice, we focus on honoring each other and our relationship. Addiction blinds us and contorts our views of ourself and the person we love. At times, we both despise ourself and our partner. We feel inadequate or justified in negative attitudes. We experience a roller coaster of emotions that we often misdirect at our partner. Loving someone in addition to ourself gives rise to many conflicting emotions that range from righteousness to loathing ourselves for our inability to either save or leave the person we love. Untangling this bundle of emotions takes patience, effort, and strong external support.

In early recovery, our ability to listen to each other and communicate respectfully is very hit-and-miss. With the support of others and the passage of time, we learn to control impulsive reactions to each other's expression of feelings and thoughts. We learn to speak more openly and begin to break down the negative personal defenses we relied upon in the past. This personal work is best undertaken with external support from professionals, sponsors, and spiritual advisors who can guide us through what can be tumultuous periods.

Still, we must lean in and begin very gently to step toward one another. We focus on identifying the qualities we appreciate in our partner. We practice verbally communicating this to them. We recognize who they are to us. Are they patient, caring, funny, sexy, determined, creative, or generous? We verbally express this to them on a regular, even daily, basis, but are careful to avoid excessive praise.

The key is that we keep our comments short and direct. "I love your sense of humor" is better than "When I am exhausted, you figure it out, and then you make me laugh and everything is fine again." We must not have any hidden agendas. "I love your generosity means "I love your generosity." It does not mean "I am pointing this out because I am preparing to ask you to buy or give something to me or someone else." We do not qualify what we say. Saying "I love your patience when you are not so tired" diminishes our appreciation. It is a quality we personally appreciate in our partner, not what others say or believe. "My mother says you are so determined, and I agree with her."

At a different time, we also tell our partner that they did something that we liked. Here we focus on how they behave. It does not have to be something they did for us. Again, we keep it direct and genuine: "I love how you play with our son." "I like it when you bring me coffee in the morning." "I appreciated the call that you were running late." "I enjoy it when you volunteer at the community garden." We are telling each other that we respect and enjoy specific ways in which our partner behaves. It's that simple, and we must strive to keep it so.

On other occasions, we express what we like about our relationship. We want our partner to know what we value in our partnership and what we enjoy doing with them. Always, we keep it authentic. "I enjoy cooking together." "It is so much fun when we garden side-by-side." "I love how we travel so well together." "I enjoy our intimacy." "It's special for me when we sit on the dock alone and watch the sunset." "I love it when we hold hands." "I like how we can be silly and laugh so hard when we play charades."

Human communication is a complex field. Books, podcasts, workshops, and so many other tools abound and present us with theories and how-to skills that offer to help us be more effective. Add to this the trauma of all the miscommunication in addiction, it is enough to want to stay quiet for a very long time or not say anything meaningful that might make us vulnerable. It is tricky to be fully simultaneously conscious of what we are saying and what we are transmitting through our nonverbal communication.

In this practice, we emphasize telling each other what we like about the other and what we like about us. The key is that we are building gratitude for each other and our relationship. This strengthens our connection to one another. When I express my appreciation for who you are and how you behave, I am saying, *I see you*. When you express your appreciation for who I am and how I behave, you are telling me, *I see you*. That exchange is a very intimate experience for us to share. We are creating meaning together.

In the story of Tom and Carole, Carole *sees* Tom when she tells him he is a good role model for the boys he mentors. Tom *sees* Carole when he tells her he appreciates that she respects his decisions.

When you read the stories, notice how this practice often marks the transition from addiction to sobriety. Couples begin by expressing their gratitude for the presence of sobriety in their lives. As they progress in their individual recovery, they start to see one another again without the fog and chaos of addiction. With this renewed appreciation of the person they love, they learn to express themselves with less urge to control and more genuine desire to praise their partner. Whether it is Nadia expressing how Luke is a good father to their son, David, or Tim telling Chuck that he is always there for him, or Bill acknowledging how Chantal is so giving, each person is telling the other "I see you." "I appreciate what we have together." In each of those moments, they heal their relationship a little more. They are shining a light on the healthy part of who they are together.

✳✳✳

When we engage in practices that help us become a person who is able and willing to grow within a healthy relationship, we reap more and more benefits from recovery. If we understand where we and our partner stand in the continuum of change, we can identify issues that both of us are ready to tackle. When we structure our lives so that we can build new relationships and develop existing ones, we are fine-tuning our ability to connect with our partner. When we individually pursue hobbies, take care of our health, and take charge of our responsibilities, we strengthen our relationship. When we focus on our inner peace and attend to our spirituality, we reinforce our relationship. When we express gratitude for each other, we are giving each other the gift of being seen. These practices require an effort but reward us with joy in our relationship. These practices guide us as a couple while we attend to our individual work.

As you read through the stories of Tom and Carole, David and Leslie, Nadia and Luke, Tim and Chuck, Bill and Chantal, and

Sherri and Larry, keep in mind The ASCENT Approach. Dr. Frank and I invite you to look for parallels in your own life and where you might learn from these couples who have created a connection. Sharing stories is a powerful way to experience the journey of others in a safe way. We hope you take hold of your own story, share it with others, and participate in the increasingly large community of people who live meaningful lives in recovery.

PART II

✳

The Story of
Carole and Tom

Storytelling is the essential human activity.
The harder the situation, the more essential it is.

—TIM O'BRIEN
American author and winner of the
National Book Award for Fiction

Carole and Tom represent all of us who have faced substance use disorder in our partnership and are now in recovery. The incidents in the narrative of Carole and Tom are a blend of true events I learned about from my interviews of several couples in various stages of recovery.

The feelings and behaviors of Carole and Tom should be familiar to those of us who have worked hard to save our relationship from the chaos of addiction and to build a healthy relationship in recovery. We hope that reading their story and observing their experiences in the light of the six practices of The ASCENT Approach will be comforting and inspiring.

2006

Tom

His life was a masterpiece of balance.
He believed everything was under his control.

Carole

She could watch without shuddering because
she couldn't see the storm gathering strength.

Tom: In control

Tom loved his bourbon, his black dog, and his barbecue—and he loved them in that order. He told himself, however, that he first loved his wife Carole, and second his daughter, Sarah, and son, Peter, and third his baby brother Michael. In the end, the order did not matter much. Every week, they all came together under the roof of his suburban home.

It was early morning on the 5th of April, 2006, and summer had already made its appearance in Philadelphia. Tom glanced at the headlines of the *Inquirer* without much interest. His coffee was steaming on the kitchen table next to his orange juice, fish oil, CoQ10, glucosamine, and whatever the hell other supplements Carole thought he should take. The pink package of fake sugar, another of his wife's healthy demands and his concessions, was squarely aligned with his spoon on the folded napkin. She had already mixed his Cheerios with chia seeds and placed the bowl in the center of his placemat atop a bread plate he would not use. All that was left to create the perfect breakfast was for him to pour his almond milk and toss in the apportioned blueberries. His wife often reminded him that a healthy breakfast set him up for a perfect day. That was a lot to expect every morning.

Tom's gaze moved from the blur of the front page to his backyard. He loved that the summer had arrived early. Everything was more natural in the summer, freer. The family was no longer cooped up and on top of each other in the kitchen and living room. Why did they always convene together as if they didn't have the luxury of 4,000 square feet to spread out? The air flowed through from the front to the back door. The kids and his wife went in and out of their activities, barely noticing him.

He would soon be able to throw open the garage door and shine up his Harley. And this year, Carole would finally let Peter, who had just turned 21, share a beer with his Dad as they talked shop. Tom and Buddy could resume their toss-and-fetch ball game at the back of the yard, just beyond the pool, out of earshot but within sight of the family. Buddy was always eager to hear Tom's unfiltered view of the world.

Caught up by spring fever, Tom thought maybe tonight he would prep the barbecue grill. Why not even tell Carole to pick up some steaks—well, maybe some salmon—on Friday for the first outdoor feast of the season. Michael would come. His brother could never turn down a few cold Budweiser and a cigar on the deck. Although Michael could let his love of beer get away from him, the brothers had shared some of their best conversations on that deck.

"You seem in a good mood. I'm sure it's not the stock market, so you want to let me in on the secret?" Carole said as she entered the kitchen and reached for her green morning concoction. Everything about her was slim: her nose, her waist, and the yoga pants that hugged her thighs.

"No secret." After 22 years of marriage, he still felt it necessary to reassure her, even if he was not entirely sure of what. "The paper says it might get as high as 90 degrees today. Can you believe it?"

"It's a bit soon for this heat. I guess we can stop taking our vitamin D." She sat cross-legged across the table from him. She placed her green drink on her placemat, next to her journal, her much smaller stockpile of supplements, and her tiny cup of cottage cheese. He was happy she had given up insisting he joined her for morning yoga. He did not see the point of breathing from his core when his hamstrings were screaming for relief and his head was heavy from lack of sleep.

"I was thinking we should have Michael over and have our first family barbecue of the season on Friday night. Sarah will be all too happy to chill in the hammock and flip through her *Vogue* magazines to figure out her summer fashion. We can let Pete have a beer with us this summer instead of pretending he doesn't drink. The kid's now officially 21." He saw her grimace. What did she expect from chugging ground-up grass for breakfast? Coffee was the way to get your engine going in the morning, not kale.

"Tom, leave him alone. He's not like you. He's into Debbie, not beer."

"Hey, I resent that." He teased her. "Since you've been on that health kick, when do you see me with a beer?" he said, breathing in his belly and stretching out his hands in Zen-like fashion.

"Ok, mister, you have a point. But that Wild Turkey isn't exactly calorie-free. Anyway, can't we just have an us-and-the-kids barbecue? I'm sure Michael has hot plans now that he's single."

"Come on, sweetheart. Michael is family. He's my baby brother. Besides, dating in your mid-40s is not as much fun as you think."

"Oh, I don't know. To be alone and not have to worry about anyone but yourself, with the kids grown up, doesn't sound too bad to me." Sometimes there was a tone in her voice that made Tom anxious. Carole would say something that was intended to sound funny, but more than once, it boomeranged with repressed anger. Tom could feel in his gut that precise moment when things changed directions. Far less easy was figuring out whether to laugh or make a quick exit.

"Sweetheart, I have to run. I need to prepare for my meeting with the advertising team. It's our first barbecue of the summer. Let's invite Michael. Give the guy a break, at least until his dating calendar fills up. Let's invite Debbie, too. The more, the merrier." With years of practice, in one leap, Tom grabbed his briefcase, planted a kiss on his wife's forehead, and escaped before she could negotiate with him.

❋❋❋

"Waiter, a bottle of champagne, please. These men just finalized a superb ad campaign. A bottle of the best." Spirited by the news from his morning meeting, Tom was in a great mood. He loved moments like this. His entire career, Tom had thrived on impressing the bosses. And impress he did. In turn, he celebrated with his team. Today would be no exception.

"Iced tea for me," Mark told the waiter. "I'm meeting with finance this afternoon. I need to keep my wits about me. I tell you, those numbers guys are too serious. Who schedules a budget review on Friday afternoon?" He said, winking at Tom, hoping he was off the hook.

"I'll have a Coke. With these darn meds, I can't have a drop for the next week," Jeff chimed in. It was early Friday afternoon, a little too early for him to start drinking.

"Suit yourselves. More champagne for the rest of us." The first quarter results were in, and, as usual, Tom's division was in the lead. His boss had hinted that with one more year as head of the top-performing division, Tom could count on a promotion. Tom could finally add the coveted VP title to his business card before turning 50. He was right on track, maybe even a little ahead of his plan to make Senior Vice President before retirement. He raised his glass. "To the best sales division in the country." The Brut champagne—dry, smooth, and bubbly—set him right.

By the time dessert arrived, Tom had noticed that Brian had a bit of a red nose and Ian was more talkative than usual. He enjoyed this camaraderie. With the constant pressure of landing new accounts, Tom prided himself on being a good boss to his team. He often treated them to these lavish Friday lunches. Sometimes accounting complained about the expense, especially when the boys wrapped things up with a good cognac, but being the top sales division had its perks. He had to keep the troops motivated, especially the younger ones. Both Brian and Ian were young fathers with a weekend of playing taxi driver ahead of them—ballet, soccer, and who knows what else. He was relieved that his kids were past that stage.

Tom wondered how these new superdads did it. He'd been lucky. Peter never was much into sports, and Carole always took charge of Sarah. Tom could drop Peter off for his guitar lesson, have a quick beer or two at the pub, and be home by noon for the ritual Saturday afternoon barbecue. He wondered how these guys avoided getting a DUI while spending all that time on the road between the games and playdates. Tom bragged to himself that he, too, would have managed. He could hold his liquor better than any of them. It took a lot more than champagne and a few beers for him to stagger or slur his speech. Tom could not remember the last time he'd been drunk. Carole always said how grateful she was that she'd never had to worry about him making a fool of himself. She had seen plenty of corporate wives embarrassed by their husbands.

Tom had a well-honed strategy: bread and butter and always a few glasses of water. It was an old trick that one of his motorcycle buddies had taught him when Tom had teased him for ordering bread instead of peanuts at the bar. "The fat absorbs the alcohol faster, and the water dilutes the effects," he'd said one afternoon when they were riding together. Tom wasn't positive it worked, but it seemed like a good habit.

When his wife went on her health kick last year, Tom cut out the bread and butter to please her, so he tried to double up on the water. She liked that he tried to keep hydrated. She always praised him when he did something healthy. He silently spited her in those moments. Did she think she could control him with a little flattery? He grabbed his glass of cognac and downed the last of it.

"Team, it's been splendid. Congratulations again," Tom said, standing up, high-fiving Mark, Jeff, Brian, and Ian in an exaggerated exuberance. They all laughed. He basked in the ease of the moment, knowing the evening barbecue would be less relaxed. "I'm going to call it a week. No point going back to the office at this point. Enjoy the weekend, boys."

Tom had carefully orchestrated his day to have one last drink by himself at that dark pub a few blocks away from Whole Foods where he was meeting Carole. He loved the city and all those corner-and-in-between establishments where you could walk in any time of day and be welcomed by the same characters who would never remember you. He enjoyed those dimly lit bars where big silent screens hovered above scattered patrons, mostly men, who stared at the bottom of their glasses.

Tom spent his strategic thinking sessions in such places. It was the new trend in corporate coaching: time away from the pressures of the office with your Blackberry turned off. Tom was happy to oblige. Lynn, his loyal administrator, knew that once a week Tom would disappear early at the end of the day to do some blue-sky thinking. She knew to call him if anything urgent came up, but she otherwise protected his time. With every promotion, Tom pulled Lynn up another rung on the support staff totem pole. They were a good team. She had his back in the same way that Carole had his health. Lynn never asked where Tom went, and he always made sure to step outside to answer her calls to suggest he was walking around the city.

After finishing his solitary drink, Tom dropped the exact change for his bourbon, plus a generous tip without waiting for the check. He nodded to the familiar stranger who was bartending, straightened his tie, and tested his feet. Feeling right, even jolly, he looked at his watch and thought he had impeccable timing.

Carole: Not seeing

Carole spotted Tom waiting for her in the parking lot. She loved that Tom was so dependable. How many wives could count on their executive husband to be on time to pick them up from grocery shopping? She appreciated his sturdiness behind the wheel of his red Jaguar, an early mid-life present to himself. His thick, black hair neatly parted on the left, his strong hands and his compact neck jutting out from his Herringbone coat. Tom was a man with a presence. She liked his broad shoulders supported by his dense but not flabby waist. As Carole approached the car, he didn't notice her. She saw his head twitch and told herself what she always did: *he must have had a tough day with that meeting.*

"Hi there," she said, smiling.

"Hello, sweetheart." he said as he took the groceries and put them into the trunk.

As he planted a kiss on her cheek, she detected the faint smell of bourbon.

"How was your day?" she asked.

"Usual meetings and a quick lunch with the boys to celebrate their new ad campaign. Happy it's Friday. I called Michael. He said he would be by around 6:00 p.m."

Before she heard at what time Michael would arrive, her insides twisted, and her mouth tasted bitter. She had to dig her nails into her thighs to control herself.

"Fine," she managed to say, busying herself by searching through her pocketbook for nothing.

Her emotions could flip so easily on her these days. As if some invisible hand constantly flicked the switch hooked up to her anger and sadness. She wondered if her sudden mood swings were a warning that she had an early onset of menopause. If so, it did not bode well for the coming years.

❋❋❋

Peter had left to drive Debbie home and dropped his sister off at her college dorm when Carole started the post-barbecue cleanup. Carole was thankful he'd left his beer half-finished without her having to mention he should be careful since he was driving his girlfriend home. Carole did not like the idea of Tom encouraging him to relax with a beer and disliked his uncle Michael regaling him with alcohol-soaked drag racing stories from college. Fortunately, Debbie was only 20, so she could not yet drink. She had so bewitched Peter that he would barely sip his beer for fear of not being kissed goodnight. It was sweet to watch tender first love. Sarah, for her part, had not even finished the glass of wine she had been served by her uncle Michael when she arrived late for the barbecue.

Carole had asked Sarah to stay so they could have breakfast together. Sarah said she could not stay with exams around the corner. Carole missed their morning mother-daughter chat over the Saturday lifestyle section of *The New York Times*. On those mornings, Carole willingly sipped coffee and drizzled maple syrup on her pancakes, forsaking her dietary no-no's in exchange for time with her daughter. She hoped that Sarah had made a wise choice with law school instead of pursuing design. Sarah reminded her mom that fashion was for fun, but intellectual property would afford her a better lifestyle.

With the kids gone, Carole was left to her kitchen duties with only Melody Gardot tunes to help her out. That was the deal. Tom grilled and she took care of everything else. She heard Michael laughing all the way in the kitchen as she stacked dishes. Although it was still early April, the unseasonably high temperatures meant the brothers could enjoy a cigar on the deck. She could not quite make out what they were saying, but it was easy to tell that Michael, all six feet and four inches of him, held court. He did not stand for long. Michael dropped into the chair with the agility of a gorilla or a man drowned in beer. She looked away; there was no point saying anything. Tom would reproach her for not cutting his brother any slack. He was so protective of his baby brother since the death of their parents. Thankfully, she did not have to worry about Tom. He diligently stuck to his one-bourbon-per-barbecue-except-on-holidays rule.

"Good night, boys. I have yoga early in the morning, so I'm going to head up and read for a little while. Don't let your brother keep you up all night, sweetheart. We agreed to tackle the garage tomorrow," she said, and just as quickly regretted it. She knew Michael would now make a point of keeping Tom up. Michael liked to flaunt his newfound freedom now that he was single. She increasingly felt he was trying to win Tom over to create some sort of brotherly bond that outranked her.

As she removed her makeup, she cracked the bathroom window open. She told herself that she enjoyed the scent of early spring; in truth, she wanted to eavesdrop. She listened for a few minutes. Unable to hear above the sound of the music, she closed the window. One more of the many things she disliked about Michael—his choice of music. When he wasn't around, Tom would listen to soft jazz with her. When Michael was there, she had to tolerate his hard rock. Michael told her it was "soft" hard rock. It was all the same to her: noise.

She lit a candle, slipped into bed, and opened *Eat, Pray, Love*, a good distraction. Every few pages, she looked at the clock. By the time it was midnight, she was exasperated. She thought about going down to make a cup of Sleepy Time tea, but that would be too obvious. She thought about turning the light off but doubted Tom would notice.

When she heard the front door close, it was 1:00 a.m. She quickly put her book down, blew out the candle, and pretended to sleep. Although she was relieved that Tom was coming to bed, she did not want to talk with him. She only wanted to feel the warmth of his body next to hers.

"Are you asleep?" Tom whispered as he undressed in the dark.

"Almost," she replied.

"That was a great barbecue. Thanks for the delicious salmon. I loved the marinade. Why don't you enjoy your class tomorrow and take some time for yourself? Go to that new tea shop you mentioned. I'll take care of the garage." He leaned over to kiss her, letting his full weight slump before he could pull himself up.

"You will?" Then she added: "Has Michael invited himself over? I thought we were going out tomorrow night." Not that she wanted to spend the day cleaning the garage, but the last thing she wanted was to let Michael make a habit of interfering with their summer. He was divorced and a free man. Good for him. He could go and enjoy his freedom elsewhere.

"Hey, get off Michael's back. He's not coming over tomorrow. I just wanted to take my time spiffing up my motorcycle while I cleaned the garage. Sounds like you might need an extra yoga class." He closed the bathroom door a little too loudly. She rolled over, knowing full well she would not fall asleep. She fumed to cover up that sense of insecurity she felt whenever Tom pushed her away.

She heard him gargle, the last step in his nighttime ritual. She pretended to be asleep. He slipped into bed, gently inching his way closer until she could feel his skin next to hers. He reached over and lay his hand on her bare bum. She reached for his hand and they intertwined their fingers. How could she resist? She loved him. She was attached to him above all, and she believed he was attached to her above all.

"Good night, sweetheart."

2006 – 2008

Tom

There is but one loyalty when control is lost.

Carole

When one refuses to accept what is, life rebels.

Tom: Impulse dominates

To say that the months and years following Tom's promotion to VP were hectic would be correct, but to say they were a blur would be more accurate. The well-established equilibrium Tom had maintained since his college days slipped away from him. His life now was a balancing act between who he knew he was and who he presented himself to be. Yet strangely enough, even the people closest to him—Carole and his brother—were blind to the changes. Tom questioned how they did not see the distorted image reflecting from the carnival mirror.

When Tom had tried to bring up his struggle in loose terms with his new executive coach, the man told him not to worry. It was common for senior executives to succumb to the "impostor syndrome." He described the phenomenon as a person unable to internalize their success who suffers from a persistent fear of being exposed as a "fraud." His coach assured him that he would eventually outgrow this stage.

Aided by this explanation, Tom either forced himself to ignore his discomfort or tempered it with a little vodka. He had grown tired of Carole's attempts to regulate everything he ate and drank in the interest of lowering the stress that accompanied his new title. As a countermeasure, he'd taken to carrying a little flask of vodka in his briefcase. It was the perfect solution for his growing list of troubles. He had no idea that jumping the ranks by one lousy title would carry such a heavy burden: longer hours, more demands to his schedule, more networking and hobnobbing events, more of everything. The only thing there was less of was what he enjoyed: less time to ride his motorcycle, fewer strategic planning sessions at out-of-the-way pubs, and fewer mid-week barbecues. No wonder he felt distorted.

Lynn understood. She saw his calendar, she took the calls, and she tackled his emails. She too had joined the executive admin ranks. She too had received a handsome raise. Although she had not made a big fuss about it, Tom knew it meant a lot to her. As a single mother with a son in a private school, this eased some of her worries. She repaid Tom by covering for him when he needed to close his office door and take a little breather.

That's when the little flask of vodka became his best friend. He would sink into the unoriginal black leather couch, as his daughter Sarah called it, put his feet up on the coffee table, and enjoy a few swigs. He would close his eyes for ten glorious minutes the time it took for the vodka to course through his veins and set him aright. After that, he could tackle any budget decisions, marketing plan, or call from his boss. He could think more clearly. He could concentrate and be at the top of his game. Lynn joked that only if she could get the same benefits from her cat naps, her weekends would be more productive. Convinced of the power of his naps, Lynn had presented Tom a decorative cushion embroidered with the words "power nap." She never suspected the vodka.

✳✳✳

"Good afternoon, Mr. Smith. Would you like water or champagne before takeoff?"

"Champagne, please. I'll have water as well." Tom loosened his tie, took a last look at his Blackberry, and mumbled, "Goodbye, world. Checking out."

"Do you need anything else?" The flight attendant asked.

"Yes, a vodka, please." Tom looked at the stack of budget papers on his tray table, then looked out the window at the ground crew working in the sizzling afternoon heat. He loved to fly, no matter how many times he did it. He loved to stare out the window as the plane traveled down the runway, but his favorite part was that moment when the plane took flight. He felt the thrust of the engines and the lift-off. Tom still relished the exhilarating and delicious sensation he always experienced as the plane gained altitude. His life was now in the hands of a stranger, and he was free to think about whatever he wanted.

✳✳✳

Road trips to sign big deals no longer offered the thrill of victory. The fancy offices, gourmet restaurants, and trendy hotels merged into one another, and the allure of Europe had morphed into routine travel. Tonight, as in many other nights, he played the time zone game. "Sorry, gentlemen. I would love to join you for after-dinner drinks, but I have to take a conference call." He would go back to his room, shower, put on the thick monogrammed hotel bathrobe, and dutifully call Carole before checking out the minibar.

"Hi, sweetheart," he said as he tossed his sneakers to the floor and kicked them into the corner.

"Hi, honey. How's Brussels?"

Same questions, same answers, and same requests. "You won't forget the Belgian truffles, will you?"

"Of course not. Good night, sweetheart. See you Friday night, then."

"Okay. I'll bake your favorite wild salmon. Don't eat that airplane food. Be careful when you run on those cobblestones. Your ankles aren't what they used to be. I love you."

These conversations served no other purpose than to provide Carole with the illusion that he needed to hear her voice every day. The chocolates and the welcoming home-cooked dinner were part of the same charade: pretending they were still romantically inclined towards one another.

The reality was different. The last time Tom and Carole even attempted to make love, some three months ago, his performance was so dismal that they hadn't tried again. Anyone with his amount of responsibility at work, two kids in college, and a yoga instructor for a wife would do no better, he convinced himself.

❋❋❋

Tom tossed another log onto the fire and placed the poker on the stand. The clang of the iron rod crashing on the tile floor startled everyone. His close friend Rob stopped talking and, in unison, Barbara, Mary, Ken and Carole looked at him with the same look of surprise circus-goers would express if the juggler dropped a ball. Tom began to reach for the offending poker but wobbled as the room transformed into a crooked fun-house-floor right under his feet.

Carole lurched from the sofa. "Let me, Dear. With your bad back . . ."

Tom crouched down and picked it up himself. He stood up triumphantly. "Got it." He saluted. His friends began to applaud. "Got you. Ha! Ha! You're all so gullible." Without giving Carole a chance to move, Tom exploded into the position of a fencer and turned the fire poker into his foil, raised his left arm, and shouted, "*On* guard!"

Carole, always quick to the ready, stepped in front of Tom and declared, "Everyone, allow me to present the 2008 national fencing champion in the 50+ age category, Mr. Tom Johnson. Congratulations."

Everyone applauded. The palpable tension of the group lasted less than two minutes.

"Speech, speech, speech!" Ken chimed in. Mary, Barbara, Rob, and Carole joined the chant.

"I'd like to thank the tournament organizers, my coach Carole and, of course, all of you, my fans. Champagne for everybody." Tom, still feeling unsteady, ceremoniously handed the poker to Carole, embraced her, and extended his arms in the victory sign. "On second thought: forget the champagne. Let's have another round of cognac instead." The applause resumed.

The camaraderie blended with the soft buzz he felt inside. He marveled that their friendships had survived their career changes and the moves to new homes and that the women had never fallen out with each other. The six of them had grown, yet their bond had remained anchored during all of life's moments: babies, car accidents, promotions, illnesses, and many parties. Thankfully, they were real friends, not like the kids' Facebook friends. Tom preferred it that way. None of their follies and misadventures were publicly documented. Carried by the reverie, Tom headed into the dining room to fetch the cognac bottle from the bar cart.

Ten eyes followed Tom out of the room. The enthusiasm dissipated the moment he was out of sight and earshot.

"Carole," Barbara was the first to speak. "Have you noticed Tom's faltering lately? He seems a bit more off balance and forgetful."

"Not more than usual." She swayed as she intentionally stumbled to her seat. Her attempt at regaining the lightness of the moment failed. She looked in the direction of the dining room while her friends scoured her face. The glow of the fire and candles softened the edge of her collarbone, but her shoulders were bonier; her posture less correct.

"One more round before we call for taxis," Tom called out as he entered. He crossed the short space that separated him from his friends without noticing the crack that had formed between him and them: the ever-slight fissure which begins to form when friends share a secret but do not include everyone.

Tom had always been the leader of their shared lives. He was the natural organizer of trips and barbecues, the backup crew for kids' moves, the cheerleader for any of their charities, the wise career adviser, and the brilliant stock picker. Tom simply had to show up among his friends and was propelled to the forefront of each moment. Like all groups, theirs had a dynamic that called on each of them to play a specific role. The mantle of leadership rested squarely on Tom. He enjoyed wielding it both at home and at work. He directed much more often than he listened. Carole had always been the conduit by which Tom heard of sensitive matters.

***

"Tom, you are going to this appointment. I am concerned. Nothing is more important than your health." Carole was shouting, demonstrating the futility of all that yoga and meditation of hers. Tom refused her the dignity of acknowledging her concerns. He could not explain to himself his sharp objection to the idea. Tom was not afraid of seeing the doctor. He'd spent plenty of time getting sutured up, poked with needles, and examined over the years. Something other than fear triggered his refusal. It was a primal instinct. It was a question of self-preservation.

"Breath, Carole, breathe. You're the one who needs to see the doctor. With all that shouting, your blood pressure must be off the charts," Tom responded, smug in his confidence that he did not have Parkinson's. He felt robust and in the prime of his career, more together than ever. It was a ridiculous idea. Who'd put this idea in her head? His mood swung from relaxed to irritated. He thought this was Carole's latest strategy to involve herself in his life. All this melodrama because he twitched occasionally.

"Tom, please. I've researched it," she insisted.

"You're a med student now? Oh, let me guess. You've been secretly studying when I've been traveling which explains why you're always awake, regardless of when I get home." He definitely was not being gracious with her.

"Tom, for Pete's sake! Listen to this. According to the Mayo Clinic, she read from her iPad, 'Parkinson's disease causes uncontrolled shaking that usually starts in the limbs, and a person's hands may tremble even when relaxed, says Mayo Clinic. Stiff, painful muscles that limit the range of motion may be a sign of Parkinson's. The disease causes changes in the speech that includes speaking rapidly or softly, slurring, hesitation and using a monotone.'"

"Well, that sounds like every senior executive I know. Wonder if their wives are forcing them to see a doctor," Tom interrupted.

"Tom, just listen, will you? It goes on to say that . . ."

"Carole, stop it. You're being ridiculous. That's called aging. All I need is a little more time tossing the ball to Buddy and a hell of a lot more time riding my Harley. It's called lack of having fun, not damn Parkinson's."

"Tom, your uncle had it."

"Carole, you're hysterical. He was my mother's half-brother. I just called him uncle. We weren't blood relatives."

"What's all the ruckus?" Peter barged into the kitchen as he mimicked Sherlock Holmes. He had taken to impersonating the character when Tom and Carole fought. Peter was the peacemaker in the family.

"Well, Detective Sherlock, this man here, known as your father— you might forget who he is as he only makes guest appearances in our family life lately—has all the symptoms of Parkinson's but won't get checked out." Carole played along, lowering her voice and playing to her son's sensibilities.

"Well, Dr. Watson, what are all these symptoms?" Peter asked, looking at his father with an exaggerated expression.

Tom, rolling his eyes, headed to the fridge intentionally dragging his feet to make sure his slippers scraped the tile.

"Enough joking around. Stop making fun of me. I'm seriously concerned. Peter, will you please tell your father to just go see the doctor. Is it so much to ask? Just one appointment to put my mind at ease and save his life."

Peter turned to his father, who was leaning against the counter, hiding behind the *Inquirer* and sending tremors down the newspaper every few seconds.

"Damn you, Tom. Don't expect me to nurse you if you won't even take care of yourself." Carole stormed out of the kitchen.

"Dad?" Peter asked.

"She's mad, son, just mad because of all my business travels. She'll be all right after her yoga class this evening. I'm fine, Peter, just a little tired. A weekend barbecue will take care of it. How's the love life, son?" Tom said as he hugged himself in a pretend lover's entangled kiss.

"Dad! Stop it. Debbie's a great girl. Besides, stop changing the subject. Why can't you just see the doctor if it will calm Mom down? I think she's very concerned about you. When you're gone, she's so moody. One minute, gushing love and the next, in a mad rage at your laundry. What's going on?" Peter's tone had traveled the distance of his emotions: peacekeeper, a frustrated child caught between his parents and frightened.

Tom's irritation surfaced. When had his family become such drama mongers? "Peter, it's just a phase. I think your Mom is suffering from that dreaded time—you know, the one we can't mention, M-E-N-O-P-A-U-S-E." Tom spelled out the word. Putting his arm around Peter's shoulders and tugging at him, he asked, "Do you really think I have early onset of Parkinson's?"

"I don't know, Dad." Turning away, Peter added, "but I've noticed that your hands shake from time to time. What's the harm in checking it out?" When Tom did not answer, Peter shrugged his shoulders and walked out of the kitchen.

Tom brought his fist crashing onto the cutting board reserved for vegetables. This morning was a complete disaster. He blamed Carole. She had brought Peter into this. What a stupid idea she had in her head this time. Parkinson's. Really? He was just exhausted.

He slammed the kitchen door behind him and headed straight for the garage. Cleaning and tinkering with his Harley was the best way to calm his nerves and steady his hands. He rotated the dial on his iPod to the maximum and blared a favorite tune, grabbing the buffer to polish his already spotless Harley. Maybe he should just skip tonight's barbecue and head off on his bike, let them fend for themselves. He could almost feel the air on his face, the grips under his leather gloves, the sweet sound of that Harley roar.

He opened the fridge and grabbed a Bud Light, looked at his steady hand, and slammed the door. He looked at the clock: still an hour to lunch. He reached into the toolbox, lifted the tool tray, and took out the flask. Its worn leather cover fitted his hand the way a glove ought to. He paused, the anticipation almost as satisfying as the large swig that followed. In the space of a moment, the time it took for the vodka to filter through his body, the adversity with Carole loosened, and the simplicity of the task at hand cheered him up. He set the flask back but not before indulging in another mouthful. He savored the exquisite moment of solitude.

After polishing up the gas tank, he turned up the volume on his CD player blaring his *Ultimate Santana* album. He straddled his bike, careful to keep the kickstand down. He imagined the open road. By the time Carlos Santana was singing "Black Magic Woman," Tom was humming along and swaying in his seat supported by his grip on the handlebars. He had some of his own "black magic." Tom felt the blues groove in his soul and the vodka in his veins. The moment was just right. He did not mind the control the music and drink had on him.

He dismounted his bike, reached for the toolbox, and refreshed one more time. He opened the key box, but his Harley keys were not hanging where they should be. He searched his jean pockets. Nothing. He hadn't ridden his bike in at least three weeks. He tried to remember what he had done with the keys the last time. He was a creature of habit and had a vague recollection of putting them in their proper place. He hated forgetting things, especially when it came to his well-established routine. Why did his memory keep betraying him like this? He refused even to entertain the thought of asking Carole.

The thought of his wife crushed the bliss he was experiencing. He'd have to figure out where his keys were before she discovered they were missing. Otherwise, it would be one more reason for her to harass him. His thoughts turned vulgar. Unable to tame the outburst of renewed animosity towards his wife or perhaps the sense of inadequacy he felt towards himself, he left the music blaring in the garage and wandered out to the garden to find Buddy.

Carole: The juggling act

"Peter, you look terrible. Were you chatting with Debbie all night?" Carole asked.

"Leave me alone." Peter grabbed his toast and coffee and turned his back on his mother.

"Peter, your Dad is ill. I know it's hard for you." Carole spoke quietly, trying to reach her son.

"He is? What does he have?" Peter about-faced his mother. His eyes showered her with anger, not concern.

"Well, I don't know. That's the problem. Your father won't get tested."

"You've got to be kidding me. Are you still going on with this business? He is going crazy from your nagging." Peter snapped and marched out.

Alone, she sat down across from Tom's untouched, perfectly set breakfast. She stared out the window, not seeing anything, not feeling anything, experiencing an abstraction of herself. It was her body, her kitchen, her son, but it was not her life. She wanted to be angry with Peter, to reprimand him for talking to her that way, but he'd exposed her insecurities.

Was she becoming the caricature of a menopausal wife? Would Tom trade her in for a trophy wife? Why had she become obsessed with this idea that he was ill? Carole no longer saw him, but his twitches haunted her. They became the very proof that she was right in hounding him. There were other signs: his forgetfulness and the way he stumbled over nothing.

Her thoughts were no longer her own. They latched on to Tom's existence, observing his every move, scrutinizing his words, and balancing the reality of how he was to the vision of how he should be. Her mind was continually evaluating whether each variation of Tom's behavior was a clue to an undetected illness or infidelity. Was he suffering from infatuation with a pair of young legs that caused him to be distracted and forgetful? She despised herself for hoping it was an illness, something curable, but a mistress, well, that would disrupt everything. How can a wife wish for her husband to be sick?

Her body created its own chaos. It refused to sleep. She lay awake at night in silent desperation, waiting for the relief of her dreams. They refused to appear and instead conceded the space to nightmares. Her insides were frayed. She wore her yoga outfits more out of habit than need. Salted caramel ice cream became her answer to everything.

Her soul no longer afforded her refuge. It joined forces with her body, rebelling and suffocating her spirituality. Her meditation practice became more akin to walking through a graveyard of happy moments buried beneath a thousand hateful communications. Her ability to rekindle the bright moments of their marriage was now weighed down by slammed bedroom doors and slurred verbal injuries.

She knew that upstairs, Peter, her docile, conflict-averse, eager-to-please, only son struggled with the changing forms of his parent. He was detaching from her much in the same way Tom was, distrusting her emotional outbursts. She saw Peter searching for an explanation of who she became in those moments. The furrow in his brow was too deep for such a young man. He was changing, too. They all were.

❊❊❊

"Carole, I don't know what to say," Mary said as she cupped her tea mug. "If the neurologist did not find anything and neither did his GP, I guess it must be the pressures of the job."

Carole struggled to quell the alarm that spread through her stomach and caused her to swallow hard to avoid falling apart in front of her friend. She bit the inside of her mouth to stop herself from boiling over. Why did everyone think Tom was the only one feeling stress? He certainly was artful at deceiving even their best friends. She had to calm down.

So far, she'd managed to contain her irritation with them. In the weeks and months before Tom's appointment with the neurologist, Mary, Ken, Bob, and Barbara had supported her concerns. They had closed ranks around Carole: the discrete nod in her direction when Tom struggled to get off his chair, the more frequent offers to drive when they went out together, and the extra hugs when they parted at dinner. Once Tom declared that he'd received a clean bill of health, their sympathies along with their worries dried up.

※※※

Any decision which required Carole to spend time away from the house or Tom caused her tremendous anxiety. The burden of her thoughts was crushing her. One by one, all the littlest details she'd noticed about Tom piled up. He hesitated when she asked what time he would be home. He shined his Harley more than he rode it. Carole also overheard the scraps of monologues when Tom played with Buddy. Then there were the early Saturday afternoons naps, the scattered coffee cups around the house, and the fewer football games he watched. He dwindled more time away with Michael. The pressure of all these observations amounted to nothing except the sensation that she was weighed down.

Carole decided she needed to get away. She would take Sarah to fashion week in Milan. She would make it her daughter's Christmas present. Sarah would faint with joy. All the glamour and drama of the catwalk would be refreshing to focus on unwearable fashion, futuristic hairdos, and exaggerated makeup. They could comment without discretion or sensibilities because everyone knew that these supermodels were there to be reviewed.

Life possessed this maddening way of undoing Carole. She thought that the decision to take Sarah to Milan would give her something to look forward to. Tom agreed, perhaps a little too quickly, that it was a fabulous idea. He was much less enthusiastic when Carole suggested that he might plan a European business trip at the same time so the two of them could have a little romantic getaway in Italia. He bluntly declared that February was too busy for him without saying why. Carole began fretting about the choice she had made.

She distracted herself by planning the logistics of the trip. She would leave the itinerary to Sarah. She looked up hotels, airlines, and excursions. Then it occurred to her that perhaps she could use some of Tom's points to upgrade her and Sarah to business class to make the trip even more special for her daughter.

It took her awhile to find the folder with their credit card statements. She wanted to do this on her own, not involve Tom. She realized how much he took care of everything when she opened the filing cabinet. The files were organized and labeled with his neat handwriting, but she could not figure out their order. It had been a long time since she'd pulled open one of these drawers.

Finances were Tom's domain while she managed their household. They had a system. She kept receipts and placed them in his top desk drawer. He checked them against the credit card statements, balanced the checkbook, and told her roughly where their finances stood. When there was a big purchase, they discussed it. Mostly, Tom talked it through and she agreed.

She located the MasterCard folder and scanned the November statement for the rewards program phone number. Her eyes stumbled over the entries. She flipped one page after another. There were numerous entries she didn't recognize. She flinched. They were restaurants and pubs. She looked through October, September, August, July. The closer she looked, the more she saw.

Why were there hotel and airport charges, too? Those should be on his company card. Was he having an affair? She sat down on the floor, her back against the filing cabinet. She scanned June to January. There was something odd about the charges, a pattern, but she couldn't figure it out. The hotel amounts weren't enough to be nightly charges, not at the Ritz or the Sofitel. There was also a reoccurring charge for $400 almost every month in New Jersey. Then it dawned on her; it was a liquor store.

The moment was sudden and horrific. There in all those numbers and charges, the reality was in plain sight. Tom was drinking heavily.

Tom: A single romance

Tom knew his father had romanced the bottle, but he was not like his father. He controlled his drinking, especially in the presence of his family. None of his family members or friends could pinpoint a moment when he'd been inebriated. That was the technical term he liked to apply when thinking about the matter as it related to himself. It was clinical, distant, and unemotional. It referred to the tip of the iceberg. One-tenth was visible to the world; the remaining nine-tenths were different—below the surface, hidden.

Tom could not quite remember when his trickery with vodka had started. Perhaps on that trip to France with his team for the annual Christmas party. He remembered how his colleagues sloshed around fine red wines pretending to be connoisseurs. He did not share their affection for the grape juice. It was too weak, too ceremonious, and too attention-seeking. He discovered, however, another French national: Grey Goose. The French and their fixation on geese: *foie gras* and Grey Goose.

There was, however, one problem with the Grey Goose. It lacked personality. Surprisingly for the French. Tom preferred bolder flavors that matched his bourbon, so he began to add more flavor to his day: Kahlua, for example, the Mexican liqueur. A little sugarcane rum and Arabica coffee, perfect to blend into his morning Columbian roast—multiculturalism at its finest. Later in the day, who could argue with a gin and tonic to brighten up that dull part of the day, the afternoon. He certainly would not quibble with a great mind like Winston Churchill's, a man who declared *"The gin and tonic has saved more Englishmen's lives, and minds, than all the doctors in the Empire."* It certainly had saved him from many monotonous post-negotiation chit-chats or dreaded neighborhood gatherings.

The French did redeem themselves with cognac. In this drink, they'd outdone themselves. Brilliant idea—keep that feeble wine juice on the wood longer to transform it into a rich caramel-colored brandy, then allow it to age just enough to create the great dame of liquor: cognac. Now, that was a beverage worthy of holding up to the light, sniffing, and gushing over.

Tom did not need the company of others, only of his thoughts. He liked to slosh his Remy Martin XO around his snifter, savoring his nightcap as much as his boldness. He'd smuggled a bottle and glass into his home office after the Paris trip. They fit perfectly in the expansion file he had neatly labeled "2004 taxes." He had shelved the folder next to the identical ones for 2005 to 2008, another part of the hidden iceberg.

January – February, 2009

Carole
Mystified by the realization, you consume yourself.

Tom
At last, the bottle subjugates you and relieves you.

Carole: Alone

Carole thumbed a few coins. No one spoke. An older man, visibly unhappy, nodded to Carole from across the room. She wasn't sure if he intended to stay either because he still wore his scarf, gloves, and coat.

The person sitting at the head of the table started to read. "Welcome to the lunchtime meeting of Al-Anon and hope you will find in this fellowship the help and friendship we have been privileged to enjoy. We who live, or have lived, with the problem of alcoholism understand as perhaps few others can. We, too, were lonely and frustrated, but in Al-Anon we discover that no situation is hopeless and that it is possible for us to find contentment, and even happiness, whether the alcoholic is still drinking or not. We urge you to try our program. It has helped many of us find solutions that lead to serenity . . ."

His voice trailed off. Carole came seeking a solution, a fix, and a quick one.

Carole might not have come to this meeting without the insistent advice from their marriage counselor that she attend. Dr. Marsh had held Carole back after the last session when Tom marched out at the mention that he needed to get help for his drinking.

"Carole, get yourself to an Al-Anon meeting right away. Tom can't control his drinking, and you can't control him," Dr. Marsh had said.

"You have no idea what's happening to you or him. You've been living with a disease. Alcoholism affects the entire family, not just the addict. Carole, just trust me, it will help you. Just go," Dr. Marsh had said.

The words "alcoholism," "disease" and "addict" had been too big. They had scared Carole into coming to this meeting.

Carole tried to focus on the next speaker, a man in his mid-70s. He introduced himself as Mike. He was one of the few well-dressed people, wearing a navy-blue suit, crisp dress shirt, paisley silk scarf, and Stetson hat. He looked like one of those old-time black trumpet players you'd find in an old Philly jazz haunt. When he spoke, though, his voice carried loudly. Mike was also articulate. "I've been coming to these meetings for over 30 years now. I still get something out of them each time."

When Carole heard that this man had been attending for 30 years, she knew she was in the wrong place. She stopped listening.

The chairperson once again turned to Carole and directly addressed her. "We like to give newcomers a chance to introduce themselves and say something. You don't have to, but if you want to say your name and something," he repeated, "or if you want, tell us about your situation, we're here to listen. No one will comment or interrupt."

A few seconds went by. No one spoke, including Carole. The silence felt unbearable. Carole stared back at Mark, angry, resenting the fact that she now needed to talk.

"Hi, I'm Carole. This is my first meeting. I'm here because my husband, who is a loving father, hard-working, and to whom I've been married for 25 years, drinks too much. I need to figure out how to stop him. Our couples' therapist said I needed to come here, so I'm here."

Carole let the last words trail off. Her defiance turned to hesitation.

"I'm obsessed with checking the bottles a hundred times a day, even when I know he's drinking vodka at 7:00 in the morning. I don't understand why I keep checking! I know he's hiding bottles too, but I don't know where. I've scoured the house from top to bottom, and I can't find his hiding place. It's driving me mad. I know he is drinking every night, but we are together all the time. I've checked the bathrooms, the garage, his closet—nothing! Where does he hide it?"

Carole looked up at them individually; she wanted someone to answer the question. She wanted to know where people hid their bottles. She wanted to find them and smash the damn things.

"He promised before Christmas that he would quit after the holidays. But then, he saw friends get drunk over the holidays. He wasn't staggering or being an idiot like them. That convinced him that he doesn't have a problem and that it's just normal to drink. But he can't see that drinking in the morning is not normal. The children and I, we need him to stop."

She hung her head down and folded her hands. She was done. Carole thought that if she had a pain meter, it would register red; and if their family had a damage meter, it would read out of control.

"Thank you for sharing," was all they said. A few people added, "Keep coming back."

✳✳✳

When the digital clock flashed 1:00 a.m., Carole realized a full week had elapsed since their shipwreck on the night of their anniversary. They had fought like alley cats. Tom had orchestrated an expensive night out. She had been unable to contain her emotions. They had ended up slamming doors instead of making love to celebrate their 25-year marriage. Time continued to move in a circle that came back to the same point: Carole looking at the clock and waiting for Tom to go to rehab.

Tom had committed to check into rehab by noon this Saturday. Not to her but to their couple's therapist. Not that it mattered. Carole had less faith in this promise than in her own to stop checking the inventory of bottles. Tom's body burned next to her. She snuggled up to him. His snores, long and deep, punctured the silence of the night. The only way to be together and not ensnarled was when Tom passed out. Sleep had become his other form of escape. Sleep had become her Holy Grail. The vigil continued: 3:00 a.m., 5:00 a.m., 6:00 a.m. She kept thinking of the Al-Anon meeting she had attended a few weeks ago but never returned.

By 6:30 a.m. that morning, she could no longer endure her sleeplessness. She lay there frigid, afraid to move or to upset the chain of events. It was too early to wake him. She would let him sleep until 10:00 or even 11:00 to avoid loosening his resolve. She'd been warned: The drinking usually increased dramatically before rehab, as much as threefold—a form of rebellion against a decision already made.

Guilt filled her sleepless nights with the sharp edges of her self-defeating acts. These were not acts of rebellion but weakness. Carole was disgusted with herself with each small act of violation—every incursion in his pockets, every peek at his emails, and every inspection of his briefcase. She was addicted to discovering incriminating evidence—a jealous wife, nurturing her anger.

Anger was more comfortable to handle than doubts. How could she have missed her own husband's unraveling? Why had it taken so long for her to see he wasn't sick at all; he was an alcoholic. No, the word was wrong, all wrong. Alcoholics were those bums out on the street, not her husband. He had lost control, that was all.

The alarm went off. It startled her. It read 9:00 a.m. Three hours to go. She could make it if she treaded lightly.

Tom rolled over, groggy from a hangover, his skin the grey of ashes, his face raw, his eyes stained. She could not connect this image of him with the assured man with whom she'd fallen in love.

"Well, last morning for snuggles for a while, honey. I must go. I don't know how I got here, I don't know what happened, but I have to go."

Three hours, Carole thought, *three hours to check him into rehab.*

Tom: The end of the romance

Tom stuffed underwear and socks into his suitcase, then took them out and started folding them and counting them. How many pairs do you bring to a rehab center? Stacking them by color, then thinking himself ridiculous, he emptied the suitcase onto the bed. His mind could not piece the puzzle together. He did not know what the image was. He went to his closet and pulled out five shirts. That was the limit on a business trip: five working days. But he was going away for 30 days. He reached for his dress slacks and tossed them on the pile, then a blue, black and brown belt. He was about to take a jacket off the hanger and stopped himself.

Who was he fooling? He was not attending an offsite meeting.

He had promised he would not show up at rehab drunk. He would show them who was in charge. But his head pounded from a headache. It felt like it followed him around from behind by the sheer weight of it. He decided he could handle a little vodka, just enough to take the edge off his hangover. This was his riskiest hiding spot: a small metallic flask between the mattress and the box spring on his side of the bed, far enough away from the edge so Carole wouldn't touch it when she made the bed. There was a thrill knowing it was so close, within reach, and almost close enough for her to discover.

He took one long, slow swig. His mouth could barely contain it all. Quenched, he went back to the closet and pulled out his Harley jeans and his sweatshirt smudged with grease. If they were going to treat him like a bum, he would dress appropriately. He was not going to shave either. The bed was now covered with clothes, and his suitcase remained empty.

Randomly, he pulled shirt, pants, and socks from the pile, intentionally choosing mismatched items. He shoved everything in his suitcase, tossed his toothbrush and floss in the zippered pocket, making sure to leave his expensive cologne behind. He chose the unopened Old Spice from the back of his drawer. Be less than average. Spite gave him courage.

He decided he did not need to control himself this morning. It was the end, so he finished off the vodka. This time he did not push the flask quite as far toward the middle of the bed. Let Carole find it when he was in rehab. He could validate her even when he was not there.

***

To any pedestrian peering into the local pub window, Tom and Carole were a couple sharing a Saturday brunch, except that the half-drawn tumbler of scotch might have indicated trouble. From the outside looking in, Tom and Carole would not have appeared so forlorn if they had not both been gazing intently out the window in the direction of nothing.

"I'm ordering one more scotch. My last. Then we will go."

Carole said nothing. What was there to say?

February 2009 – February 2010

Tom & Carole

When the stranglehold becomes unmanageable,
the only option is the courage to release its grip.

Carole: Check-in and check-out

Carole began the check-in process the way she would if she were signing him into an ER. She answered every question. She knew everything there was to know about Tom after 25 years of marriage. Tom came and went from the waiting room; he followed different men with different name tags. When they had to sit together in the waiting room, they made sure they were separated by empty chairs as they flipped through promotional materials fanned out on a coffee table.

When Carole had to wait alone, she was directed to make herself a cup of tea in the check-in guest kitchen. She steeped a chamomile tea bag, imagining the men struggling behind the door marked "in treatment"—likely men of all ages in rough shape, some thin, others bloated, all empty-eyed and jittery, each alone in their detox Hell. Carole shuddered. She reassured herself that there must be a few peers among the group at the current guest rate. Retired CEOs, professionals, perhaps investors who, like Tom, had clung to the bottle to deal with the stress of their careers, broken marriages, and lost children.

She had rehearsed their goodbye, scripted it. She wanted to fill Tom with hope and strength. She had played her role to the end, the dutiful wife. She had tucked 28 notes in his suitcase when he wasn't looking.

She had made bargains with the universe for this moment to happen. Now that it was here, she feared leaving Tom here. All he had said to her was "goodbye." All she responded was "goodbye." He never turned around as he walked away. She never reminded him that she loved him.

Carole and Tom: Unknowing

The 28 days that spread between mid-February and mid-March created the most substantial pause in Carole and Tom's 25-year marriage. They'd never been apart this long. Never had others dictated when they could and could not speak or see each other. Individually, they clung to a memory of who they were as themselves and as a couple. Time had forged this fantasy vision of their family fed by the "perfect" birthdays, anniversaries, and continual success.

The space and time that separated them from one another fortified their belief that they would recapture this vision the moment they reunited. That same space allowed each of them to return into the fold of their assigned roles. Carole cleaned the house, attended to their children's needs, and busied herself with social pretenses—behaving as if Tom had gone on a business trip.

Tom sat in meetings, slept in a bed other than his own, and led walks around the rehab campus as if he were attending an offsite meeting. Sarah and Peter, unaware that their parents' separation was not because of a business trip, went to class, did their homework, and responded to their mother's need to parent them.

On Sunday mornings, Carole drove to rehab instead of the yoga studio. Tom waited for Carole to arrive instead of Carole waiting for Tom to arrive. They walked around the designated trail well within view of the rehab common hall, holding hands and sharing weekly updates without ever mentioning where they were or what the future held. Their time together during the permitted family visits transpired in a bubble floating above the jagged edges of the reality of Tom being in treatment for alcoholism.

Tom was away for 28 days, and Carole was home for 28 days. They never talked about the invitation for Carole, Sarah, and Peter to attend the Family Education Program. They both knew that only Carole would attend. They both knew that her role was to sit silently and listen. Carole attended and performed marvelously. Tom was grateful that neither of them turned into the other ten sobbing messes who sat around an empty water cooler labeled "the bottle." Carole and Tom exchanged knowing glances, solid in their belief that when Tom came home, life would resume, and they would erase the past years and months from their family history.

✳✳✳

Day 28 occurred on a Wednesday: It was hump day. Carole stood at the door as she waited for Tom and his roller suitcase. At the appointed time, Tom came through the doors as if his flight had been on time. They kissed and walked to the parking lot out of habit from the hundreds of times Carole had picked Tom up at the airport. Both stared ahead and held hands in silence. There were no travel stories to tell.

Then something different happened. Carole put Tom's suitcase in the trunk. Carole opened the passenger door for Tom and closed it after he sat down. Carole sat behind the steering wheel. The difference was not that Carole was treating Tom as if he'd just checked out of a hospital; the difference was that each immediately felt entirely alone in the presence of the other. Silence was the safest form of communication.

Carole was a bundle of contradictory adjectives: happy and sad, anxious and relieved, knowing and unknowing. Tom was a string of passive verbs. He was being directed by Carole, he was being silent, and he was clueless about how to live the next moment.

Tom: Learning to walk again

In rehab, the treatment required Tom to examine and list "the people, places, and things" that could trigger his desire to drink. Although confident in his ability not to relapse, this phrase, above every other cliché, stuck to his rib cage. He had not inclined his will to "the program." Sure, he thought Alcoholics Anonymous was a good idea, a crutch for the guys he'd met in treatment. It was easy enough to see that willpower was not their strong suit.

Like his "band of brothers," his rehab cohorts, Tom had signed a treatment plan that called for "90 in 90"—the undertaking to attend 90 AA meetings in the 90 days after he left treatment. There were so many slogans: *"First things first," "Easy does it," "Don't take yourself so seriously,"* and the list went on. Tom reacted to these with annoyance. They rolled over him as so obvious. These clichés were an insult even to the maturity of a teenager.

Tom had formulated his own strategy: sheer willpower. Nothing fired him up more than short-term goals; his career was one long series of overachieved sales targets. That's what he knew and made him successful. He planned to win here too through dogged determination to add one day after another to his sobriety.

At night, in his shared room in the men's wing, deprived of his *Economist* magazine, CNN news, and budget numbers to read, his mind would obsessively return to "people, places, and things." People: his brother and his sales team were clearly at the top of the list. As for Rob, Ken, and their wives, they were not on the list. No one would be crazy enough to include their best friends on the list. Places: every pub on every street corner, airports, and hotels— particularly those with fancy lobby bars. Things: his Harley and his briefcase.

Of those, Tom did not have to deal with sales teams, airports or his briefcase for another 30 days. Against his best judgment, he'd agreed to tell his boss about going to rehab. Given Tom was within a few years of early retirement and had his coveted Senior VP title, they had negotiated a "sabbatical." He shouldn't be so sarcastic about it.

Eager to exercise control over his destiny and to liberate himself from the weight of "things," Tom knew he would have to handle the second set of triggers with one decisive act.

His Harley held power to seduce him. He did not even have to ride it. The emotional pull of blasting Creedence Clearwater in the garage and buffing his wheels would be enough. Without having time to think about it, he would reach for a beer. If there was none to be found, he had more vodka stashes in that garage than a squirrel has winter caches. His hiding spots were so devious that no one would have found them in his absence. The rapport between man and his machine and man and his drink were intertwined in Tom's emotional fabric. To be safe, the Harley had to be out of sight. He would have to store it for a while. Given it was only March, Tom figured he would be in charge of his cravings by riding season in late April and pull it out again.

❋❋❋

Tom paced the yard, talking to Buddy after lunch, and rehearsed how he would tell the kids that evening about his luxury stay at the "health spa." Buddy bounced around, fetching the ball, oblivious to his master's predicament. It was the best part of coming home. It was uncomplicated: Tom tossed the ball, Buddy fetched it, no explanations required.

Tom teetered between an apology and an announcement. If he offered atonement, he could explain the cyclone that had occurred in their home: slammed doors, yelling matches, and his belligerence toward any of their concerns for his health. The disease of alcohol had attacked him and made him lie, yell, and ignore them. But he had faced his demon. He'd gone to rehab and was sober. They could return to their family life and put this dark episode behind them.

Instead, Tom romanced the idea of an announcement. His mind conjured many brilliant schemes. He'd gone away to surprise them with the purchase of a second property in the sun—but after rehab, no chance. Treatment ate away a lot of play money. He'd gone to investigate the claim that he had a half-sibling who wrote to him after some DNA testing—but that would be a lie. He was interviewing for a job in Paris—he wished. He amused himself with all those scenarios knowing that the only real option with his children was the truth. Lightweight truth, he called it.

In the end, Tom apologized for not telling them before he went to rehab. He'd waited until now since actions speak louder than words. Their father stood before them after going 28 days without a single drop of alcohol or even coffee. He joked that the coffee withdrawal was worse.

For Tom, it was important that admitting the situation to his kids allowed him to report back to his sponsor and recovery coach that he was already working on Step Nine of AA's golden Twelve-Step

Program. "Made direct amends to such people wherever possible, except when to do so would injure them or others." Not bad for his first day out of rehab.

He tossed the ball harder, feeling more energetic. He rough petted Buddy's fur and looked into his dog's eyes.

"Hey, Buddy. I'll show them how a motivated senior executive gets things done. I'll knock out these 12 AA steps and these 90 meetings in 90 days like they haven't seen before. Yes, Buddy, I will put all of this behind. Watch me. I've got this thing."

Tom hated it when his options were limited. He realized that he could hide from everyone else, even his loyal admin, Lynn, but not from his children. Lynn. It was the first time she entered his thoughts. He wondered how much she knew and how much she'd guessed. She could be counted on for discretion either way. The card that accompanied the get-well flowers sent to his home was Lynn's way of letting Tom know his secret was safe with her. She would uphold the "health spa" story but was signaling him that she knew he'd been to the hospital. The gesture signaled her solidarity and eternal support. Her reward to him for pulling her up the company ranks. If she only knew what "kind" of hospital. Fortunately, Tom knew Lynn's discretion. She would never ask. Whatever she intuited, she would keep to herself and stamp out any negative water-cooler talk.

Sarah and Peter, on the other hand, would notice the changes: Tom's coming and going when he attended AA meetings, the AA literature and AA people he was supposed to incorporate in this life. It was best to tell them. He had no intention of providing the sordid explanations presented at rehab or telling them that their father had a lizard brain. They were good kids, not heavy drinkers—no way they had inherited the "drinking gene." With them, he wanted to be honest but keep it on a need-to-know basis.

He rehearsed a light version of events to share with them—his stress, work, travel, drinking more often, then too much. But now all was under control. Fortunately, he had avoided DUIs, managed to keep the family finances in check, and could not recall having embarrassed any of them. The beauty of being a "functional alcoholic," if there was any beauty in the matter, was that it allowed the family myth of external perfection to remain intact.

Given the social stigma, they would keep it a family affair. Tom would be careful to avoid referring to their pact as a "secret." That would be non-AA-compliant. In the short-term, he would follow the AA rules to keep his sponsor at bay. His kids were bright. They would understand the need for privacy and undoubtedly be relieved. He would officially nominate Carole, Sarah, and Peter his Three Musketeers: "One for all, all for one."

Tom wished he'd inherited a heart condition instead of this. Addiction had stigma written all over it. He called upon his Musketeers to guard their family's honor and maintain the sanctity of their family reputation. He would commend Carole for her strategic planning and invite her to share their plan regarding his concern. Colluding felt good. It renewed their bond.

Their mom had hatched a cover-up story and laid the groundwork with his friends and colleagues when he'd been away. Tom elaborated on the details, which were, in fact, broad strokes. Keep it simple, he and Carole reasoned, for the children's sake. Tom and Carole performed for them the plot and their roles.

Carole had devised this idea of a "spa" vacation for Tom for three reasons. One, their friends had been concerned about Tom's health and had repeatedly suggested he needed extended vacation. Two, a health spa insinuated that it was a medical rest, explaining at once why Carole was not with him. Three, and perhaps most importantly, the doctors at the spa prescribed medication for Tom, giving a reason, at least initially, why he was not drinking. Carole calculated that this alibi would provide Tom enough time to figure out how he wanted to deal with the situation.

Since Tom had decided he did not want the kids to see him in rehab, this was the same story Carole had previously told them. The counselors argued with them that they needed to explain to the kids. Tom insisted he would upon his return. Peter, lost in the fog of young love, had not questioned his mother further. Carole had told Sarah over the phone to make Tom's spa vacation sound normal. Tom agreed with Carole that Sarah had probably feared the worst but had toed the line, always concerned not to trouble her parents.

Tom's new medication required him to abstain. No details would be provided, only a vague reference to a family condition in Tom's family tree. They would test the kids when they were older, but there was nothing to do now. Best not to dwell on it and upset them. The doctor would monitor Tom's condition until they declared him in full remission. Until then, no sauce for him.

Carole and Tom agreed that after a few months, people would get used to Tom's ways and everyone would forget about it. Given all the rules and etiquettes surrounding privacy, this cover would work brilliantly at work. No one would dare to ask the specifics of his condition.

✳✳✳

Carole and Tom leafed through glossy travel magazines and the weekend section of *The New York Times* that had two kids looking at summer camp brochures and ads for stimulating tours promising fun and romantic times ahead. Tom had two more months left in his sabbatical. He wanted to have stories to tell when he went back to work. He had positioned his "sabbatical" as a "recharging of his batteries" to be ready for the last push before his early retirement.

Squished together on the couch, Carole and Tom compressed the space that separated them, believing for that moment that they were destined to travel and live happily ever after. They sorted through the pile of travel brochures, news clippings, and printed-out emails as naturally as if they had always approached their vacation this way.

It was part of the new unspoken pact, one they had not negotiated between them but one they both pretended to exist.

Tom noticed, without commenting on them, some of the options Carole had tucked in with the traditional winter escape brochures. There was the Omega Institute calendar tagged with Post-It notes on pages that offered couples' communication with the Borofsky method and Pema Chödrön's teachings based on her book *Smiling at Fear*. Tom had positioned his preferences: a house near the slopes of Elk Mountain and a cabin on Lake Placid.

They had not yet spoken about the practical realities of Tom's sobriety. It was the first weekend back and the first without plans to get together with Rob, Barbara, Ken, and Mary. Tom worried about reuniting with them. Would he lie about his time at the "spa" to his best friends?

When Tom had left the rehab, the women had reacted no differently to Carole's call informing them that Tom was at a "health spa" for a few weeks on doctor's orders than if she had told them he was flying to China for a business trip. None of their friends had yet called Tom upon his return. Carole covered for them by telling him, "Oh, they are waiting for you to call them." Tom was unaware that during his absence Carole had made two calls. The first was to let their friends know Tom was away for only two weeks. Then she called again to let them know the initial two weeks had been extended for another two. As a parting half comment, she mentioned that Tom had been prescribed some strong medication for internal pain. This last bit of information had scared them and resulted in no one calling anyone in the group anymore.

"Everything has to be counterintuitive from now on," Tom said. He had taken to using the AA slogans to fill the silence between them. At other times the slogans provided an answer to Carole's question with such finality it ended the conversation. For example, when Carole had asked Tom the day after his return whether he wanted to go on a movie date that Friday night, Tom had replied: "one day at a time." It closed the conversation in such a way that Tom cleverly avoided the question that would have followed: "Would you like to go for dinner first? Or shall we go to the late show after your AA meeting?"

"Yes," Carole agreed, not knowing what she was agreeing to.

Tom thought that using rehab jargon would reassure Carole. He had no idea if it was working. He spoke to her mainly by staring beyond her.

"From now on, I want to plan our vacations ahead of time. No more spur-of-the-moment, figure-it-out-on-the-fly, let's-go-to-Las-Vegas-tomorrow trips." Tom was attempting humor: they'd never gone anywhere spontaneously. Between Tom's work responsibilities, Carole's yoga classes, and two children, impromptu moments had revolved around dinner at the local pub versus cooking at home.

"Well, your travel agent will be disappointed, but it's fine with me," Carole countered with her own flat joke. They both laughed mechanically in slow motion.

"Let's stick close to home. I've traveled so much in the last few years. It would be great just to drive where we want to go, just you and I. Remember the early days of road trips? Let's do that again. Me, my gal, and a cooler full of iced tea. What do you think?" Tom offered. He felt smart at that moment, in charge as he had been. They would avoid airports and stay at roadside motels without fancy lobby bars—keep to people, places, and things under control.

Carole accepted all of Tom's suggestions because she was fearful of her own. Tom would not go down on her watch. He had just over a month to go. Then Tom would be the responsibility of his company. She planned to say yes to everything he wanted except time alone or alcohol. She prayed he would not want sex.

Three hours later, their calendars penciled in from March until the end of December, their mission accomplished, the husband and wife executive team were back in their groove.

"I have to get to my meeting. I lost track of time. It will be a good month, Carole. Ours. Then, when I go back to work, I'll be home a lot more without all the travel and dinners entertaining clients. You'll see. Everything will be different now. I'm the old Tom again."

"Yes. You go off. I'll make us some dinner." With those words, she left him at the kitchen door and blew him a kiss.

Carole believed him without the slightest doubt. She saw only his Herculean force. He would stuff his rounded figure back into his shapely Harley jeans—the ones that had buttons instead of a zipper to make him feel more hip. His muscled chest would show once again under his white shirt.

Carole imagined that Tom's forest-green eyes sparkled again, although she had not looked at him long enough to know this for sure. She told herself that his face had recovered his mischievous smile. Tom had smiled since he arrived but Carole wondered if he was happy or only moved his mouth to form the shape of a smile.

Carole: Her first 30 days

Carole wore brilliant blue, yellow, and red stripes about her midriff, feeling like an old-fashioned red top, the kind she used to be fascinated by as a child. She swirled gracefully into Tom's new sober life. She thought she could bump up against any obstacle and keep swirling without faltering.

Without knowing why or how, suddenly the exhilarating swirling stopped. Carole tumbled over, exposed on all sides. Motionless, she looked up, bewildered and lost.

✻✻✻

Perched on the kitchen stool facing Tom, Carole realized she loved these moments in the morning when she sipped the green tea prepared by him. He enjoyed his coffee. They chatted as he sliced

watermelon, oranges, pineapple, or ginger, creating a new juice elixir
for them. Tom used the phrase "counterintuitive"; she called it "role
reversal." He appeared to relish these morning rituals even more
than she did. For her, this time together removed the cup of loneliness that had choked her soul.

"Good morning, sweetheart. I love the smell of watermelon and
ginger first thing in the morning. I wonder if smelling healthy foods
makes you healthier?" she teased him. Humor was no longer alien
to them.

"I'm sure it does," Tom answered as he wrestled the supersized
watermelon on the counter. When he stuck out his tongue on the right
side of his mouth, he was focused. It encouraged her that he could
concentrate—no more twitching.

"Anything new going on?" Carole asked, swinging her legs back
and forth on the stool like a little girl waiting for a chance to lick the
chocolate spatula.

"No."

"You haven't heard from your brother yet?" she asked.

"No."

In the time it took for his response to travel through her ears into
her soul, trouble stirred her inner calm.

"Everything is different now. Everything is counterintuitive,"
Carole reminded herself. Maybe he forgot because he directed his
attention to the watermelon. Michael had left her a message that he
had tried to reach his brother but that Tom was not returning his
calls. "Progress not perfection," her inner voice offered. At times, the
AA slogan irritated.

"I'm surprised you haven't heard from him. He knows you've been
back two weeks," Carole pressed on. *He'll backtrack*, she countered her
internal voice.

"I haven't. I'm a little surprised too. I'm in no hurry to tell my
brother our family barbecue will be bring-your-own-booze," Tom
answered.

"What do you mean, bring-your-own-booze? We agreed, no alcohol in the house for the first year. Reduce the risk of relapse," Carole said.

"Relapse. Are you crazy? I'm not going to relapse. If I tell Michael he can't drink, he won't buy the medication story. Besides, you don't trust me. I told you, I'm done with booze. I'll have cigars with him. That's it." His voice pitched on the last few words. He never looked up at her.

Carole's internal voice went ballistic, "*So soon?*" His brother of all people. He'll taunt him, tell him a little cocktail of pills and whiskey once in a while will do him good. Otherwise, Tom will risk turning into some boring old fart. What's that phrase from rehab—*Watch people, places, and things.* Carole knew Michael; the deck and the barbecue fit all those criteria.

Didn't they tell him in rehab to stay away from heavy drinkers? For all she knew, Michael was probably an alcoholic as well. It would not have surprised her. She needed to act and fast. She was the lead Musketeer.

Just like that, they fell through the time vortex and landed in their old dynamic. Carole asked Tom why he was playing with fire. He denied he was. She told Tom that Michael had left her a message asking why Tom was not returning his calls. Tom fired back that a message was not a conversation. He had not talked with his brother. She said she had asked if he had heard from him, not talked to him. Tom accused her of splitting hairs. Tom stormed out of the kitchen. A few moments later she heard the bedroom door slam. Fortunately, Peter had left for school already.

Welcome back to reality, Carole yelled at her internal voice and headed straight for the meditation corner she had set up for herself in the attic.

❋❋❋

Carole knew long before her exit interview with the rehab counselor that she needed a new therapist who specialized in addiction. Al-Anon helped, but sharing with strangers could not repair the punctures in her soul. Carole wanted explanations, timeframes, reality checks and, most of all, answers. She hated the Al-Anon 12-Step process. The program had been conceived for alcoholics. In her mind, it had been copied for the "loved ones" (another phrase she hated) as an afterthought to make the family feel involved. She thought it was more akin to arming the recovering addict with a reason to argue about the behavior of others. She was not convinced, but being the dutiful wife and mother, she attended. To say she participated would have been an overstatement.

The first therapist she met flunked. She sat across from Carole in her jeans, among boxes, explaining she'd recently moved into her office and was still settling in. If it took her a week to unpack a dozen boxes, how many years would it take her to unravel Carole's jumbled emotions?

The therapist, who insisted on being called Pattie, talked without pausing to take a breath. The informality of the name bothered Carole. She wasn't looking for a friend. This woman had no tact. She could tell a client the time in the same tone and absentminded language she would diagnose them as clinically depressed. One thing Carole did not want was another label or more jargon.

Nonetheless, it came. Pattie finished the session, which to Carole was an interview, by issuing her pronouncement.

"First, your husband's behavior is pathological. What that means is that he is a compulsive liar."

Carole stared at her defiantly.

"Second, alcoholism and recovery are both narcissistic processes. The first because the world around the alcoholic systematically collapses, and the second because recovery requires every ounce of energy to stay on track. "It will take at least," she continued— stretching the words "at least" for maximum effect—"five months to even start trying to understand whether he is a pathological narcissist or whether it is the alcohol that made him egocentric. He may have a chance to emerge from his self-absorption, if . . ." (Again, she stretched the "if") . . ."if he works his program consistently every day and stays on the AA path."

Carole remained silent and incredulous. The distance between the two women grew with every syllable that Pattie uttered. The luxurious purple corduroy couch intended to make Pattie's clients feel at home felt to Carole like the hard, wooden chair in a time-out corner.

"Finally, it will take at least 18 months to two years before you can start to trust him again. That is assuming he works hard at his recovery."

Carole fired Pattie, although she hadn't hired her. Carole expelled Pattie's diagnosis from her memory the moment she closed the door with the purple sign, "Dr. P. Harding, Addiction Recovery Specialist."

No one had the right to judge Tom without having even met him. That woman was out of her league. Carole already trusted Tom, she told herself. They would get through this by the end of summer, not two years.

❋❋❋

Carole counted the days before Tom returned to work in much the same way she'd counted the days before he went into treatment: with anxiety. She wanted him to go back to work. His presence in the house was too all-consuming. Her mind followed him wherever he was, heard every sound, checked her memory bank to determine whether the sound was natural or subversive. She had no idea whether she'd found all the hidden bottles. She evaluated every moment of the day against the possibility that relapse was imminent. It was exhausting.

Carole also lived in a parallel universe in which she pretended to herself, her children, and her friends that this madness, illness, episode, whatever it had been, had ended. When she operated in that universe, she looked at herself from a distance. She acted out a script, embodied the role, but lacked conviction. The post-rehab honeymoon was over. They had both picked up their roles as wounded spouses playing nice for the sake of the children.

❊❊❊

Tom snatched victory from the enemy. He counted his first 30 days of post-rehab sobriety. He crossed the days off on his home–office calendar. Carole wrote the number in big letters in her journal. Nothing was said. Both looked over the horizon to see if they could spot a sun or tempest.

"Carole, you're not broken. This isn't just about Tom's drinking. It goes much deeper, doesn't it?" said Lisa seated cross-legged in her living room sofa chair. Her apartment lined with purpose—books strategically placed and paintings checkered on every wall with the precision of an accountant. Carole swallowed hard and stared at the Kleenex on the coffee table; she was determined not to use them.

Carole preferred to inventory Lisa's living room that doubled as an office and was very smart. It made sessions feel more conversational—two friends, sharing afternoon tea—except there was no Earl Grey tea or scones. Instead, there were a lot of raw emotions. Each session, Carole noticed a new detail previously overlooked. Today, Carole concentrated on the selection of books neatly arranged across from her. They revealed more about the therapist than she, the client, wanted to disclose about herself. Carole found comfort in the familiarity of the titles: *Atlas Shrugged* by Ayn Rand, *Smiling at Fear* by Pema Chödrön, and one of her current favorites: *The Joseph Campbell Companion: Reflections on the Art of Living.* The books were far more familiar to her then Lisa was.

The family photos particularly distracted Carole: studio family portraits, posed smiles, perfect hair, lovely outfits. Carole populated each room of their home with such photos. She also added ones of splashes in the lake, frozen expressions on ski slopes, and toothless grins in front of the Rocky steps. Each family was so identical in its joy and also shared the same darkness.

Carole inspected each detail of the unfamiliar religious icons scattered around Lisa's living room. She busied her mind weighing whether they inspired Catholics or Russian Orthodox followers. The Tibetan *mandala* next occupied Carole's attention. Her eyes slowly traced the contour of the white figure sitting cross-legged on a white lotus throne. Carole capitulated to the need to scrutinize each brush-stroke. She herself was not worthy of the same attentive examination she bestowed on the white figure.

Her eyes moved on to the closed rolltop desk. What confidential notes were hidden there? Perhaps an evaluation of each client. She imagined the entry:

> "Carole Johnson: early recovery, obsessed with husband, quiet on the surface raging inside, unwilling to focus on herself. Damaged child, parentified, perfect mother syndrome, frigid . . ."

As if Lisa divined her thoughts, she interrupted Carole's inspection of her living space by asking: "Why don't you start by telling me how it feels physically?"

Conveniently, Carole's inner voice picked up the conversation. *Stop wasting your time. You're not here visiting a friend. You're here to move out of this morass. Go on, answer her question.*

"Well . . ." A long pause, filled with the hope that Lisa would pick up the threads and lecture her on some Al-Anon principle, sparing Carole the need to expose herself. Silence. Exhausted from all the silences at home demanding her contribution, Carole conceded, assuming this space was safer.

"I feel this knot in my stomach wound so tight that it feels like I've been stabbed there with a sharp knife. It sucks all the energy from my body and turns it into some nervous gob that gets stuck in my throat. I feel noxious all the time."

"What do you think this gob is?" Lisa asked kindly.

Carole looked down and noticed that her brown shoes needed polish, scuffed from the salt in the Whole Foods' parking lot, at the dry cleaners, in the ice cream parlor, and from every other errand she completed alone.

Tom's unwillingness to wait for Carole as he once did was now on the list of "counterintuitive" changes that baffled her. At times, she wondered whether this slogan permitted Tom to dodge his share of the household chores.

Carole focused again on her shoes. She inventoried the shelf in the laundry room at home to recall whether she needed to stop on her way home to pick up some brown polish or some leather spray.

"Carole, is it something you're afraid to say or something so familiar that the thought of it makes you feel sick?" Lisa insisted.

"Probably the last."

The question hung between them. Carole was in no hurry to answer. Lisa waited, staring back at Carole. The technique so basic, every mother mastered it. The art of asking and waiting in the face of your child's discomfort until they blurted the very thought they were trying to hide from you. Carole knew that whatever she uttered next would be labeled as some unconscious revelation. She resented the examination of her private thoughts and emotions, their dissection to find some hidden meaning. Why spend all this money on Lisa for this purpose? She would have preferred 28 days at a health spa of her choice.

Carole decided to throw out the pain of her childhood, a stew of emotions requiring many sessions to digest—a counter-technique. Thicken the broth.

"Lisa, I thought I had healed this part of my past with my father— the rejection. The dutiful daughter who brings home the A+, the gold medals, the trophy for the best athlete. Jumping up and down to tell him 'look over here, over here, I exist! Look at what I've done. You can be proud to call me your daughter. Spend some time with me!' I thought I was over all of that. I have hundreds of pages of journaling and hours of meditation to show all the efforts to get over that needy child."

"Why does Tom have the right to stir up all these old memories? He seems to have some slogan for everything. An easy answer to what I spent my entire adult life unlearning. Should I have just gone away for 28 days and come back with a book full of clichés? He justifies his behavior by these slogans. Why don't they apply to me? I think it's an easy way for him to do just what he wants, to avoid what he doesn't feel like doing and stay in his own little world. Then he can look at me from the height of his sobriety. He is the hero who is now the authority on my troubled past."

Carole blurted out a mix of an old hurt that no longer seemed her own and her current frustration with Tom's lack of progress. Carole turned to the grandfather clock. Fifteen minutes left in the session.

Lisa's insistent silence irritated Carole. She paid Lisa to say something, not daydream in her presence. She distanced herself from Lisa, reclining into the sofa and hugging the velvety beige pillow like a buoy. Carole perceived her complaints as a failure of character. She joked to herself that she'd failed the entrance exam into maturity. Clearly, she did not possess the talent to rise above her little problems. Her years of focused attention on her family never dissolved her need to receive validation from others.

Lisa tilted her head, softened her face, and smiled gently—all indications that she was about to reprimand Carole for her selfishness.

"Carole, you have healed. Just think of it as an old forgotten injury. Think of an old knee injury. You hardly remember if it was the left or the right one. But occasionally, maybe on a rainy day, you feel a little tinge. It's gone before you give it much thought. But then, one day, you're out on your bike. You fall and that same knee hits the ground. You've damaged a ligament. You realize right away that this spot was tender once before. In a sense, your new injury causes you to feel your old one again. The pain feels more acute. Often it's hard to tell which is hurting more, the fresh injury or the compounded one."

Carole caressed the pillow. She traced a circle in one direction and then in the other, focused so that no fiber popped out of place. The pattern mattered to her.

"Carole, tell me about the old injury."

"I used to have this old movie playing in my head. It took me a long time to pry the CD out of the DVD player and pack it away for good. It's a series of snapshots. I was in grade 6. I was the only student in my entire school who won the Medal of Excellence awarded by some state department to students who beat the highest standards on a series of physical fitness challenges. There were many silver badges given out, a few gold ones, but I was the only one who earned a Medal of Excellence. It was gorgeous and it sparkled like a real Olympic medal. I still have it packed away in my basement. It had a swirly gold symbol embroidered in the middle of a red circle with bronze, silver and gold-threaded stars above it. I was so excited and proud of it. I couldn't wait to show it to my Dad. I couldn't wait to tell him I'd even beat all the boys."

"The day I took it home, I waited until my mother had set the table for dinner. I carefully laid the badge on my dad's plate. I was sure he couldn't miss it that way. I prayed before going to sleep, because that's what I did back then, that he would be home for dinner that night. I prayed that in the morning he'd come to the breakfast table, look at me and crack a great big smile, maybe even hug me, tell me how proud he was of me and that I'd always be his princess. I was so anxious for him to come home, I listened for the garage door opener until I drifted off to sleep."

"But it didn't happen that way. When I woke up in the morning, he was gone, or maybe he hadn't come home. My mom told me over breakfast that he had seen it and was proud of me, and was sorry he had an important meeting to attend. I could tell by the redness of her eyes that she was making it up. It happened so many times with report cards, writing competition ribbons, and track and field medals. It was like cheap TV reruns, the same script, just different set designs."

"Then there are lots of scenes leading up to my mother leaving my father—too many. They're all the same dysfunctional family stuff. The screaming matches over my dad's mistresses, the black days of my dad's depression when our house was quieter and more somber than a cloistered convent, and all the disappointments of broken promises from an absentee father. Then there are others that I could never make sense of. Like the time I overheard him yelling at my mom that if she left him, he would kill us all. A few weeks later I walked in on him in the storage room and surprised him as he was putting away a rifle. I was scared and pretended I hadn't seen anything. I'm not sure if my mom believed me when I told her. I have no idea why he had a gun. He didn't hunt, but he always went on about the right to bear arms. I always thought it was just talk."

"When we finally left—I should say when my mom left him—we needed to hide. We were afraid of his rage. We were fugitives staying with relatives or my mom's friends with no fixed address for the three years it took for the divorce to be finalized. My dad never got over it. It's the story of so many kids today. But then it was a disgrace. No one talked about it. No one's mothers left their husbands. The kids without fathers were rare."

Carole checked the time.

"The rejection didn't stop there for you, did it, Carole?" Lisa prodded to move the storytelling along.

"Not really."

"Carole, we have time. Keep going, let's get through this."

"It was a difficult time. The thing is, I was still a child trying to make sense of this. I didn't understand how someone could lose sight of their children. I was too young to understand adult pain. When the court granted my dad a visitation weekend, my brother was excited to get to spend a weekend back home. I refused. My mother forced me to go, asking me to look out for my younger brother.

"I remember this moment so clearly, Lisa. My dad pulled up to the lobby in his big, shiny red car, dressed to the nines, proud as a peacock. My brother walked up to him; my dad gave him a big hug and ushered him into the passenger seat with a big grin. He put my brother's bag in the trunk and closed it shut. I was standing pressed against the building's glass doors holding my bag. My Dad walked over to the driver's side of the car. Then yelled over to me, "Tell your mother I'm just taking your brother. It's not your weekend."

"I remember just standing there for a long time as people came and left the building, wanting to walk into their lives. I thought it had to be better than this. My weekend never came. I made sure of that. Each time my brother returned from a visit with my father, he carried a mountain of toys. The sight of these bribes, which my brother was too young to realize were not signs of love but of manipulation, strengthened my resolve never to go back to my father's house, our former home. I never did, ever. That one hurt the most."

"Why?" Lisa pried.

"Because he was still my dad. Why wasn't I good enough to be chosen?"

"Tell me more."

"What's the point?"

"To acknowledge the old wound."

Carole returned her attention to the pillow and fingering different doodles. She gathered another pillow and drew the same pattern.

"Why don't you just list them. You don't need to explain everything in detail," Lisa said.

"I applied to college but never went. Instead, I took a string of part-time jobs, anywhere, just not within driving distance of either of my parents. I managed to make ends meet with part-time jobs until eventually, I met Tom. My dad never congratulated me on my engagement. Never came to our wedding. He doesn't know his grand-children. I guess if I wasn't good enough for him, children issued of my womb are doubly cursed."

"How's your relationship now?" Lisa asked.

"About ten years ago, I finally made my peace with it. Sometimes I still grieve for what could have been, the things my dad never taught me, the fatherly love I never experienced. But it's in the past now. I accept that. Today we have a polite relationship. I continue to be the dutiful daughter sending birthday cards, calling him once in a while, but we never see each other. He grew into an old, embittered man living in the fantasy of a recreated past to soothe his conscience. When he talks about the past, I don't recognize the story he tells. It's as if he's a stranger."

"That's a deep injury. The roots of your co-dependency were set a long time ago, Carole. You're looking for the validation you never received from your father. You may have forgiven him, but I'm not sure you've healed."

"What's that have to do with Tom?" Carole fired back.

"Nothing. It has to do with you."

"I don't understand. I'm upset because of the way Tom behaves. How is that related to my sense of self-worth?"

"Here's the analogy that codependents hear all the time. I think that's what is at play here. It's as if the person you love just had a terrible life-threatening accident. You rush them to the hospital, wait there patiently during the operation, and pray for the success of the outcome, stay up all night through the surgery, anxiety-ridden. Then the doctor comes into the waiting room and tells you the operation was successful. You naturally want to see your loved one. The doctor then looks at you and says no. You must wait in the waiting room until he's well. Thanks for getting him here though. Now it's under control and we'll handle it from here. Just wait."

Carole did not grasp the analogy.

"You want to go into the recovery room, check up on Tom, make sure the nurses and doctors are taking care of him. You want to see the healing for yourself. But instead, you're told to take it on faith that it's all progressing well. You just have to wait for a year or so. That's not what you want. You want Tom to behave like he did when you were first married. You want him to tell you that everything is better, that he feels good, alive. You want him to express his gratitude to you. Most of all, you want him to let you in, to trust you, to share all his feelings and thoughts. When he doesn't, you feel left out, rejected."

"That's your old wound, your healed knee getting hit again, feeling the old injury mixed in with the new one. It triggers your sense of self-worth. You should have done more; everyone seems to be able to help Tom but you. It's not about Tom; it's about you.

"Carole, you must focus on you. We have to work on your self-worth."

Carole shot Lisa a look.

"This is sounding more and more like I have to do all the work. Again. Tom's off the hook and it's my fault. Again. When does this end? When will someone just recognize that I've been supportive, stood by him, and I just want a little acknowledgment? What's so wrong with that?"

"It's normal to want to be appreciated. The point is, whether Tom appreciates you or not shouldn't change how you feel about yourself. Your self-worth has suffered so much that you need someone to tell you that you are a good, worthy, talented person. You don't believe that about yourself unless someone else confirms it. You're constantly trying to prove yourself, setting higher standards for yourself than anyone else. No wonder you're exhausted."

❊❊❊

Carole turned over the empty glass bottle in her hand. The strokes of green and blue with faint tones of purple painstakingly applied by some Italian artist in some workshop in a village celebrated for its Italian liqueur, Grappa. Italian things seduced Carole; they were fine, elegant, and handsome. These attributes, combined with the flirtation of all those stretched vowels: *te amo*, che bella. *I love you. How beautiful.* Familiar, yet charmingly captivating in what the unknown words suggested. Italian things offered the possibility of discovery and adventure. But this Italian thing, this object bore none of those interests for her. In fact, it frightened her.

She had recognized this glass bottle in an instant, although she had long ago forgotten about it. The odor was still faint, brandyish but slightly perfumed. Not a screw top but a cork, one that was now missing. Sticky to her touch. She recalled the gift was from Mary and Ken after their Tuscan adventures.

Carole had overlooked this liqueur bottle in her house cleanup while Tom was at rehab. It was not stored in the bar but added to souvenirs of dusty ceramics, silver emblazoned spoons, and other knickknacks they kept in the name of friendship. Carole displayed these travel keepsakes in their TV room until they could be replaced with new ones without offending any of the gift givers. It was silly how they always exchanged these tourist-trap gifts. No one quite knew what to buy, but the tradition of bringing something back was ingrained in their polite manners. This Grappa bottle, because of the artistry of the hand painting, had not been intended for consumption but for display. Left uncorked for a decade and relegated to the back of an *armoire*, Carole had not regarded it as alcohol when she had detoxed the house.

Now, the sight of this bottle triggered an immediate, catastrophic response because it was empty. It should not be empty. And it should not have been at the back of Tom's night table where it did not belong. Carole's calamitous thoughts exploded in an uncharacteristic stream of chaos: "*Fuck, fuck, fuck.* Where's my phone? What a fuckin' surprise!

He's at some AA weekend with the boys, and this is what he leaves me as a present! They are having a grand time, thumping each other on the back, damn heroes of sobriety, probably reading the goddamn Bible, feeling angelic. Where's my phone? Let me give him a piece of my mind. I am so fuckin' tired of this addiction nightmare! I *CAN'T* do this anymore!!"

By the time Carole stomped down the stairs, the peace of her home had been shattered. With each step, the expletive that was never uttered anywhere except in her head—and there it was seldom— was suddenly a very audible shout. Aware that Peter was not home, Carole did not self-censor.

Where's my fucking phone? It's enough. I don't care if he's attending some AA thing. It's our life; this is my damn life, too. Enough is enough with all the program rules. It's my house, and I won't put up with a fucking relapse.

The pronouncement of the word "relapse" out loud stunned her. The one word that held more nightmares than any other. Saying it betrayed her relief. There, it had happened as predictably as every warning she had refuted since Tom arrived home. Now it was over like a dreaded phone call past midnight that your kid has been in a car accident. The knowing of it somehow made it more tolerable.

Another weak voice entered the edge of her awareness: Nora's voice from the Tuesday Al-Anon group. Not intended for her, but for the rooms, Carole had heard it but quickly classified it as not applicable to her and Tom. The voice message came back to her during her rage of looking for her phone.

"I regret threatening my qualifier to leave him if he relapsed. I now realize that I should never have threatened to leave if he relapsed. After he was sober, I thought it was okay to give him ultimatums. I believed that he was responsible for his choices the moment he walked out of rehab. He was so scared I'd leave him that he never told me when he had cravings, he never told me when he was fragile. Yesterday when I came home, my suitcase was on the bed. He sat in the corner chair with an empty beer in his hand. He looked so small. The only thing he said was that it wasn't worth it. It was his last beer ever. I know I shouldn't believe him, but I do. The look on his face—it wasn't the crazy drunk one from before. But I had no choice. I threw a few things in my suitcase. I shouted, yelled, and denigrated him. All the while, I wanted just to start again. But 'life on life's terms,' right? I had to keep my word that I would leave if he relapsed. But all I want to do is go back. He doesn't deserve for me to give up on him."

Carole remembered how confused Nora had been. She remembered how she thought Nora did the right thing to leave her husband. He had to learn his lesson. That's how she felt now about Tom. Maybe Nora regretted it, but Carole would not. She had not threatened to leave Tom, so she did not have Nora's dilemma. She had been nothing but exemplary in her conjugal duties.

"Living life on life's terms" meant the asshole had to feel the consequences of choosing to drink when he was sober. All this navel-gazing, meetings, and not doing his share around the house was over. It was back to rehab for him. Carole would tell everyone what had been going on—forget about his precious little pride. Their friends had to know what she'd been enduring. They needed to know she was the hero of this story.

Carole felt as if Tom had stabbed her in the back. It blocked her ability to think through the next step: the betrayal, lies, and play-acting. Tom went to this retreat as a fraud because he was drinking again. Carole's anger turned histrionic when it occurred to her that they knew. Those men and women of AA knew about the relapse before she did. Tom would have told them. This went beyond betrayal of Tom and Carole's pact to face this addiction together; this was treason against their marriage.

Carole grabbed her favorite Japanese teacup and threw it against the kitchen wall. What once appeared so solid shattered on impact. The broken ceramic sprayed across the floor, a symbol of serenity no longer.

"Do you have a few minutes to talk?" she texted Sandra. She sat in the midst of the broken pieces feeling just as fragmented, relieved to feel the pain of the ceramic shards in the back of her leg. She reached for another piece, about to run it across her thigh when her iPhone beeped back. She let the piece go.

"Sandra, he's relapsed!" Carole whispered. The words heavy, gloomy, foreboding all the pain ahead. She picked up the ceramic piece again, gently pressing the sharp edge into her leggings. Numbness replaced the flood of anger from a lifetime before. Her sense of nothingness so complete, she did not feel the sharp edge puncturing the cotton and gently scraping her skin.

"*Shit!*" Sandra's words exposed the reality, normally so poised and gentle.

By the time Sandra's cursing reached her, Carole had wholly disassociated herself from both her emotional and physical pain. She saw herself from outside her body, seeing this female creature sprawled among smashed bits of ceramic. She looked pitiful. Her anger suddenly converted into numbness.

"The worst is that I thought I'd feel angry, but I lost all emotions. I don't have any more feelings," Carole said as she continued to press the edge of the ceramic on her leg.

"Are you sure? About the relapse."

"Yes."

"He told you?"

"No, of course not. I found the empty bottle."

"What? Where?"

"In his night table. Does it matter where? I guess I thought Tom was different from the others, that the odds didn't apply to him because he is so *s-p-e-c-i-a-l*," she said, stressing the last word.

"Are you sure it's recent? I mean, the bottle."

"Of course it is. Don't you believe me? The smell of it is so pungent. It reeks. It's recent, trust me." She was unsure of why she needed to be trusted amid Tom's deceit. Why did she need the reassurance?

"What exactly did you find?"

"You won't believe it. Probably the only bottle I did not clean out because I did not see it as alcohol; I saw it as a souvenir. It was a gift from our friends' trip to Tuscany. A hand-painted bottle of Grappa that's been there for a decade. He must have been desperate." Carole was ambivalent about what to pity most: her husband's inability to master his liquor cravings or the self-repulsion he must be experiencing. Tom, the successful senior executive, brought to his knees by a tiny, tacky, touristy bottle of Grappa.

"Wow. And you found it in his night table? That seems so risky?"

"He's started journaling, and I told him I would never read it; he is entitled to his privacy. He must have figured I wouldn't look in there because it's where he keeps his journal. But I did look. He just left. It's Friday, for Pete's sake. I was angry to be left to another boring TGIF. What happened to my life? Anyway, I decided to look for his journal. He's gone, so I figured I was safe. I was testing myself; I wanted to see if he left his journal behind. I don't know if I would have read it. Old habits die hard. I was used to checking for bottles, so why not see if his diary was there? But I had doubts, so I sat down next to the bed. When I opened the night table, I didn't see his journal, but I did see a bottle, a goddamn bottle, peering at me from behind some Kleenex." Carole banged her fist into her leg. She felt nothing.

"When does he get back?"

"Sunday. How poetic. He relapses, and I get to find out when I'm alone. Lucky Tom. I get to calm down for a few days so I can be mindful of how I talk with him. *The hell with that!*" she yelled at the empty kitchen. "Who knows? Maybe he's not even at this retreat. Maybe he's having a bender somewhere and he just gave me this excuse so I wouldn't phone him. I'm so fucking tired of it all, Sandra. *I CAN'T DO IT ANYMORE!*" The cursing tumbled out of her mouth, unaccustomed to the rudeness of it. "Sorry, Sandra, I don't usually swear."

"That's the least of your problems right now. What are you going to do?"

"I'm going to phone him until he picks up. Maybe I'll tell him Peter's been hurt, and I need to speak to him. Get him worried for a change, and then I'll read him the bloody riot act."

"You're not going to do that. You need to focus on yourself. Let's meet for a coffee and figure this out. You need to get out of the house. Get your Al-Anon book, and just go. I'll be there in 20 minutes max."

"Sandra, I am so exhausted, I am so bloody exhausted. I don't care about the relapse, only that he's lied to me. *I CAN'T TAKE THAT*. He promised me he'd tell me."

"Carole, he's an addict. He hasn't recovered. You know that. You've told me yourself! He's just sober, that's all. Just do what I say. Meet me now before you do something you'll regret. Whatever you do, *DO NOT CALL HIM*. You're not ready."

Carole hung up. She stared at her phone, resisting all temptation to call Tom. It was greater than her. She had to dial. She had to call someone. She could not be quiet at that moment. Lisa, she thought. She phoned her without caring that it was Friday, without caring that she wouldn't get answered. She needed to do something.

"Hi, Lisa. It's Carole. Tom has relapsed."

There was silence before she said, "We should meet to talk about this. I have a cancellation at 3:00 p.m. today. Can you come?"

"Yes."

"Carole, breathe and focus on yourself. Read the literature and do nothing. Just breathe and feel what you're feeling," the detached voice directed her. Carole received the instruction. She wanted to be told what to do. She'd done enough for that day. She'd managed to remove the blindfolds that were preventing her from seeing how broken her life was. Seeing is knowing. Now she knew.

Tom: Going back to work

Tom reached for the folders neatly organized by deadlines on his desk in his home office, relieved to be going back to work but also nervous. The challenge that concerned him most was how to juggle his new mantra, "Everything must be counterintuitive," yet retain his former self as a successful senior executive. Since he left rehab, he obsessed about how he'd be able to perform with the new chemistry in his brain and the smothered fire in his belly. Who was he now?

He struggled with the image of himself being shaped by AA. The idea of powerlessness frayed his self-confidence. The idea that he was medically diagnosed with a disease softened the blow. Control had shaped him into the person he was. To appease Carole and his recovery coach, he assumed the role of a dutiful patient, following the prescribed course of treatment: meetings, therapy, and recovery readings. His sponsor was both his ally ("fake it until you make it") and his foe ("his illness cannot be cured but it can be kept in remission by your program").

It had taken some negotiation with his sponsor not to reset his sobriety date after the Grappa incident. Tom had argued that it was a slip. Three small swigs from a touristy trinket bottle was not a relapse. He had made a lot of progress but he was not perfect. That very momentary loss of control had made him realize the risk of relapse. He had not had anything since and had no intention ever to try again. Carole had accepted the decision made by Tom's sponsor to keep March 19th, the day he left rehab, as Tom's sobriety date. He also knew that Carole's agreement did not include her forgiveness. That would take more time.

Tom continued to rack up extra AA meetings against his "90 in 90" target. He attended two meetings a day the last two weeks before going back to work. He compared it to peak season in sales: you rake in all the deals you can to stay on track to make your numbers. He devised a strategy to double up his meetings on weekends as well. He would be able to deliver the goal but give himself some days off. The slip was a thing of the past; he had to focus on work.

❊❊❊

Alone in his bedroom, he ran his fingers over the merino wool of his newly dry-cleaned suits. He organized his freshly ironed dress shirts: all white, thin blue pinstripes and less formal ones. He polished his laced black and brown wingtips. He sorted his belts and noticed they needed some attention as well. He was pleased to see he could pull them in a full two notches now. He sifted through his color-coded sock drawer and amused himself deciding which pairs matched which shoes.

"I've never seen you interested in your clothes before. Am I losing my job as fashion coordinator?" Carole teased as she brought toilet paper into their master bedroom.

Her presence irritated him. Ever since the slip, Carole seemed to be that winter fly. She appeared out of nowhere and out of place. "Can't a man choose his own clothes?"

"Sure, but that means he is then responsible for washing, ironing, and doing the thankless job of preparing them, too." With that zinger, Carole left the room.

Her attitude towards him was akin to tropical weather. In the course of a day, it could be cold like a morning breeze, unpredictable as a rainstorm, rarely steamy, and mostly humid, clingy, and uncomfortable. Tom preferred to keep his distance, tired of the sudden downpours. It was depressing.

❊❊❊

On Wednesday, before his eminent return to his "real life," Tom logged into his company email for the first time. His inbox overflowed with emails from friends and colleagues checking in with him. On

Lynn's advice, each of their queries had received an out-of-office reply. He checked off all the emails from February 20th onward and, with a click of the button, erased them. Fresh slate.

Tom only wrote to Lynn. He would not use the expression "baby steps." That was too demeaning, so he turned to the slogan "easy does it." He wrote:

> Dear Lynn,
>
> I look forward to seeing you Monday. I'll get my own coffee from now on and please no more donuts, I am trying to cut down on sugar.
>
> I plan to go to the office this Sunday to look over reports and any important memos.
>
> I thought I would give you a head's up on my new scheduling requirements—doctor's orders. No worries. I've just been advised to ease back into things. So:
>
> 1. Please set up individual meetings with my team for Monday and Tuesday so they can bring me up to speed—Mark first, if possible.
>
> 2. I have to do some follow-up physio, so I need to leave the office by 5:00 p.m. on Mondays, Wednesdays, and Fridays.
>
> 3. For now, let's not schedule any meetings over lunch or dinner. I don't want to bore clients with my new diet.
>
> 4. Keep Fridays clear of any meetings unless you check with me first. I look forward to using my power nap pillow again.
>
> See you Monday,
> Tom

A sense of satisfaction overcame him after he hit the send button. He had this. Setting boundaries was easy. You just told people where to stand.

One thing gnawed at him: how to be authentic and lie about his addiction.

***

Tom sat in his office on Sunday afternoon. It was the same as always, but it was hardly the same. Lynn had fluffed up his power nap pillow. The reports were chronologically organized on his desk, much the same as cascading cards, while the memos were stacked in four piles, each with a purple Post-It note: *Budget, FYI, For your approval,* and *From HR.* There was something dull about it all.

Tom felt the absence of the tinge of excitement he usually felt when he arrived at his office. In the past, it was his domain and dominion. He would waltz in, aware that he was at the top of his game. He sat in the corner office, and all those people were his staff. Tom imagined that everyone noticed and cared that he'd worked late or sacrificed his beloved family barbecue to close a deal. Tom projected into their consciousness a great awareness of him.

Today, he saw the empty cubes. He was aware of them: the people who occupied space at the edge of his office, the people whose lives existed beyond the company. Resentment bubbled to the surface just above the heaviness pressing firmly against his rib cage. Everything looked so ordinary.

Tom shifted his gaze to the painting above his credenza. He knew nothing about the artist. He had chosen it because the expensive fuzzy red and orange splotches called modern art were the rage among senior executives. For the first time, Tom felt like he connected with the painting. Just like the brush strokes, perhaps his thinking and his emotions were smudged.

In the rooms of AA, Tom had heard about the bleakness that followed the pop of the pink cloud. But Tom did not believe in the concept of having a high or a low post-rehab experience. He had not felt rosy with enthusiasm in early sobriety, and this was not a low time. It was not a big deal. He just felt listless, much in the way a man feels when confronted by passionate plea to take action for a cause he cares nothing about.

He got up, walked to his filing cabinet, and pulled out his flask. The thought of what he was doing was two steps behind the actual execution. The habit was playing out before his mind grasped what he was doing.

What flashed before his eyes was the scene with Carole when she confronted him on his Grappa slip. Three small swigs had destroyed the trust, his pride, and set their relationship back so far that he did not know if it would recover. He flung the flask at the canvas. He looked at it bounce back almost straight at him. He jumped out of the way. He stared at it on the floor. Then he stamped it, jumped on top of it. He tried to crush it with all his might. He slammed his right leg down on it once, twice, over and over again, losing count. The stupid bloody thing, it still controlled him. He hated it. He cursed it. He wanted to destroy it. It was not going to win this time. No way.

Feeling spent, Tom dropped to his knees, not moving his eyes from the flask. He looked at it. How could something so inanimate and so insignificant have such an incredible and magnetic hold on him? The flask had a life of its own, and if Tom waited any longer, it would strangle him. The magnitude of the mistake he was about to make for a second time scared him shitless.

He grabbed the flask and held it at arm's length. He marched through the labyrinth of cubicles, down the hallway, turned at the water cooler, flung the fire door open, careened down the stairs to the basement, and hurled the flask into the dumpster. The ping of metal hitting metal reverberated all around him. He about-faced and returned to his office just long enough to grab his car keys and call Carole. There was only one thing for him to do: go to the one place he both needed and dreaded the most, the Sunday AA 12-Step meeting.

Carole: Alone again

It was a warm spring day in mid-May and they were sharing breakfast. Carole conceded to the odd *espresso*. Tom swallowed the green concoction on Mondays, Wednesdays, and Fridays. They negotiated the rest. Tom ate English muffins with jam, peanut butter, and anything sugary. Carole ate gluten-free Chex with blueberries.

The calm still fractured easily between them.

"Shall we have a family dinner on Saturday?" Carole asked.

"I'm not ready," Tom replied.

"Why don't you just tell your brother what's going on?"

"You mean, why don't I tell the guy who drinks too much and has a loose tongue, don't you? He'll tell everyone, and then we won't have to keep this dirty little secret."

"Tom, that's not fair. I just think it will be easier to tell him than to keep giving him excuses about why we aren't having our weekend family dinners."

"I'll just tell him Peter's away, so we're skipping the family shindigs for a while. I know you think he drove me to this drinking problem, that it's his fault."

"Tom! I'm not going to lie for you. Peter is here. He's in his room. What if he hears you want to lie about him? Is that going to rebuild his trust? Also, I never said anything like that about your brother. Aren't you supposed to be telling the truth?"

"You can't tell me you didn't think it. That's worse. Thinking it and not having the courage to say it. How's that for building trust—lying about your thoughts?"

"I'm not going to have this conversation. I understand you're angry, but don't take it out on me."

An unnatural silence settled between them, Carole uncertain of whether she was putting up barriers or setting boundaries. She hated the way Al-Anoners grabbed at the word "boundary" with the same desperation as relapsed smokers stuffed gum and chewed-up pens in their mouth. The result was the same, a poor substitute that left you wanting.

Carole screamed at Tom as often as she screamed at the voice in her head, the one that shamed Carole for her undeniable truth: Tom was more fun when he was drinking. This thought obsessed Carole and frightened her. She guarded it with the same hypervigilance as she had Tom's bottles. The idea was equal to a felony for which she should be imprisoned.

She was sure that no other wife in the history of recovery could possibly have been as selfish as her. How could any wife seeing her husband kill himself with drink wish for him to be drinking again? She was supposed to believe that they could create a better life in sobriety. She did not. She wanted to share fine wine in little cafes with her husband again. Carole relished the idea of an after-dinner drink while telling stories with their friends as they used to, and she wanted their life to be normal like before. This is where she needed to apply the concept of boundaries: to separate herself from the shame and guilt of her honest feelings.

On the good days, Carole performed with ease the dutiful role of the loved one supporting someone in sobriety following a script she had not auditioned for. She politely declined invitations for dinner, gave away orchestra tickets, and passed on attending fundraisers. She focused on the surface of living. Carole wondered if that was all that remained of the life of a mature widow.

On bad days Carole quickly blamed herself for going off-script, apologized, and doubled up her efforts to stay in character.

"Sweetheart, I'm sorry. I didn't mean to push you. We can wait. I'll just tell your brother this isn't a good weekend. We don't need to explain. Just let me know what you want to do for the weekend."

"What I want to do doesn't matter. What I will do is attend three meetings on Saturday and Sunday. That way I won't have to sneak out of my office every day afraid that someone will figure out I'm attending AA meetings. I want to nail these 90 meetings and be done with it. My sponsor says I need to do 90 in 90 "The Program" way, which means one meeting per day, not my way."

"Sweetheart, I know you like to feel in charge." Carole tried to reason with him.

"It's just math as far as I'm concerned," Tom interrupted. "If I attend 90 meetings by June 17th, then I've met the goal. I'm not some junior manager who needs to be micromanaged. I'm a senior VP who knows how to deliver results on target, and that's what I'm going to do. How I do it is up to me. I'm staying sober. That's the only thing anyone needs to worry about." He turned away from her.

The tension in Tom's voice increased as he went on: "I want to get together with my brother like old times, but what I have to do is stay away from people that trigger me—and that includes my one and only brother."

Carole stepped towards Tom, placing a hand on his shoulder. Before she could say a word, he moved away from her. Still not facing her, he added sharply, "Don't 'sorry' me. You don't get how everything has changed. And please don't tell me it's for the best."

Without kissing her, he grabbed his suit jacket and was out the door. She stared at the melted butter on his toast, the opened raspberry jam, and the full pot of coffee. She sat with her hands planted on the placemat to keep herself from diving below the surface. She stared ahead at the absence of Tom. She willed herself just to breathe. She expanded her lungs with exaggeration and exhaled noisily. She repeated this until enough space opened within her so that she could begin to eat breakfast by herself.

Carole's perspective shrank the moment Michael's name appeared on the caller ID. She let it ring. There was a tiny place inside her heart that did fault Michael. The way he drank with reckless abandon angered her. She knew alcoholism was a disease, but the idea that Michael was to blame for Tom's condition still held power over her. To make Michael guilty was to relieve Tom of his failure to control his drinking. And there it was again, the ugly thought that the issue was one of will power.

She slumped in her chair. It would have been so much easier to deal with Parkinson's. A disease everyone understood and would empathize with. Not this: a condition of the mind that was shameful and had to be kept secret. That her husband was sick with a stigma made her sick. She twisted and manipulated the thought, but there was no logic that could undo the fact that Tom suffered from a substance use disorder, not from the harmful influence of his brother. Blaming Michael was no more useful than hanging on to the romantic illusion that Tom had been misdiagnosed and that life would return to normal.

"Normal," she scoffed to herself. The photos scattered throughout the house depicted a happy family: her son with a missing tooth on the beach, the awkward proud smiles at her daughter's high school graduation, group ski photos with their best friends Barbara, Rob, Mary, and Ken. And their anniversary trip to the Grand Canyon. It had all seemed normal.

Now all that was left was the weight of the last three years. Heavier than all the memories of their life together. Carole doubted the happiness of the photo gallery. She studied Tom's face in the photos one by one, looking for a clue that she missed. Had he been happy, or was he just playing at being husband, father, and friend? What was real and what was make-believe? One thing was certain; Tom had put on weight and looked more haggard.

Carole slipped below the surface of her thoughts. The people who knew the truth about Tom's condition did not question her. She asked herself instead: "How could I have not seen Tom's slide?" He almost slipped the whole way into the graveyard. She was blind to the changes in the man she had vowed "to love in sickness and in health, 'til death do us part." The photo screamed at her: *accomplice!* How could she have missed his drinking? How could she not have seen what Tom was doing to himself?

She'd remained in love with the image of Tom, not the reality of Tom. How could she forgive herself? How could he forgive her? And the children?

Carole picked up the uneaten breakfast and tossed it in the trash. She didn't even make the effort of keeping the blueberries or drinking her cold green tea. She looked at her watch. If she hurried, she could still make the Al-Anon noon meeting. She hoped they could help her grieve the loss of 25 years of marriage. It was over. Tom and the bottle had buried it a long time ago. All that was left was for her to grieve its loss. She needed to lay some flowers on the gravestone and let it go.

Tom: Standing alone with his brother

Tom's forehead creased with the effort of composing his day with as many distractions as possible. The more he occupied his mind, the less he suffered temptations. Idle time was his mortal enemy. His mind refused to padlock the past in the attic of his memory. It insisted on replaying the moments he was most ashamed of in vivid slow-motion color. He fought against the refuge of naps to ease the pain. He lived in an unsolvable conundrum. A sober present longing for the ease of his distant past while his recent past, full of the horrors of drinking, stuck to his present. No place was safe except for the future, and he had to wait for this.

❈❈❈

Dr. Cohen, unimpressed by Tom's 90 in 90, chose instead to poke at Tom's edges to rouse his emotions. Tom shunned his feelings. He equated them to excitability. He preferred to detach, sit on a perch observing the swirls around him. At the sight of any emotions, Tom's internal voice retorted how childish or how weak. Tom recoiled as he recalled his last therapy session. When Tom failed to articulate his feelings while answering some absurd questions about his childhood, he'd snapped at his therapist. "Any five-year-old can tell you how he feels because he's ruled by his impulses to be praised by his mother, to play with a toy, or to eat a chocolate cookie. A teenager will go on and on about their frustrations because they know it all. Young men ruled by their hormones are in a constant state of craving sex. So all of them spend too much time emoting. But once we become adults, our job is to grow up and control our emotions. I feel what I want when I want to, and nothing more."

Dr. Cohen, undeterred, prodded some more. Frustrated by the pointlessness of the exercise, Tom had defaulted to his old habits. He had lied. He had said he felt fine with the events of his boyhood days. His parents had brought him up in a typical middle-class family. Unimpressed by Tom's answers, Cohen had assigned him extra homework. Faced with such obvious attempts by his therapist to conjure up some Freudian connection, Tom reacted with his second most reliable technique: silence. Internally, he fumed at the waste of time and money and promised himself he would show this therapist who was in charge. He would return to the next session with a journal full of meticulously detailed minutiae of his daily emotions.

❋❋❋

By mid-June, spring bounced around Rittenhouse Park. People draped their coats over benches while couples used them as blankets in the grass. The dog population tripled by lunchtime. Tom noticed that everyone laughed in turn. It seemed to him that some hilarious joke was being passed around but the people kept skipping him. He observed the scene from way above, detached from the charm that warmed the park goers.

The leather-bound journal lay open on his lap. He coddled his coffee mug with both hands. It was Friday afternoon, and the pages remained blank. His determination to upend Dr. Cohen had dissipated. He excused himself, pretending to suffer from writer's block. Even if he didn't have the slightest idea of how it was relevant, still, he liked the idea because it implied that he wasn't responsible. He simply lacked a muse. Most famous artists called their drink an inspiration. As quickly as the thought occurred to him, he chased it out of his mind.

He looked down at the damned page and forced himself to concentrate. What was he feeling? He tugged at his thoughts, pulling hard at them to see if any emotions would tumble out. Nothing. He recoiled. He hated failure. It was the most basic of failures, his inability to experience his feelings.

Carole was always telling him what she thought he felt. After 25 years of marriage, he'd given up trying to figure out if she was right or not. It had become more comfortable just to ask her: "Should I be angry at Peter for this?" She always replied without asking him what he thought. If she hadn't always been so sure of what Tom was feeling, maybe he would not have lost touch with himself.

He fingered the cigar in his breast pocket. After he wrote just one page, he could have it. *Always reward performance*, he sneered to himself. Ten minutes later, his pen still idle; he turned to his reason. He told himself that relaxing was known to release tension and allow feelings to surface. He decided to have a cigar now and write later. It was his second cigar of the day.

Tom unwrapped the Romeo and Juliet, snipped off the tip, sucked the end, sniffed the freshly cut tobacco at the other end. He held it between his fingers. He cocked his head and looked at it. Once, twice and thrice, he lit the cigar, rolling it gently with every flame. Holding it at arm's length, making sure it was evenly lit. After watching it burn for a few seconds, he brought it to his mouth and finally inhaled.

The hot smoke in his mouth tingled. He let the puff sit there for a moment to enjoy the taste of the smooth quality of the tobacco. He didn't want to release it prematurely. He anticipated with glee the impact of the sensation. As he slowly exhaled, watching the smoke escape his lips, he waited. A few seconds later, the reward came. His brain registered the experience. *"Damn fine."*

Tom eased into the moment. At Parc, Devon, and Rouge, patrons squeezed around every table. Elevated trays were overflowing with oysters and prawns, cheese boards and drinks, lots of martinis and wine, and a few *espresso* cups. Tom wished he didn't feel so separate from them. All those smiling and pretty people were connected in a way that left Tom on the outside.

He slammed his journal shut and capped his Mont Blanc pen. Like hell, he was going to write down his feelings. It was one thing for him to stop drinking, but they were not going to turn him into some granola head. His sobriety did not give anyone the right to play inside his head. He tossed the expensive leather-bound journal in the trash can.

❋❋❋

"Hey, bro, what's up? You have me worried about meeting in a coffee shop. You trying to throw someone off your scent?" Michael said as he plunked down onto the sofa across from Tom. Michael's knee practically hid his face. The worn leather couch had lost its spunk a long time ago. It was no match for his brother's weight. He hadn't lost any weight since Tom had seen him three months earlier. Michael sat up, putting his elbows on his knees to re-center his weight.

Michael looked around and nodded in the direction of a young woman in tall brown boots and a tight pink sweater which complimented her pink hair. The edges of her pink bra and cleavage in full view had attracted his brother's attention. Tom noticed the roughness of Michael's facial skin, a scrape on his chin probably from a quick shave, and the thickness of his neck. Michael turned his attention back to Tom and winked.

"She's too young, bro. Grow up," Tom said with a noticeably annoyed tone.

"Hey, what's with you? I haven't seen you in ages. Carole's like a prison guard. Can't get past her, and you don't return any of my calls." There was a sharpness that revealed a blade of hurt.

Tom looked away to gather his courage. "Michael, we have to talk." He paused. Although he had rehearsed this conversation a dozen times with his AA sponsor, everything felt wrong. He felt neither of them fit in at this place. Michael picked up coffees at Dunkin' Donuts to chase his hangovers, not to have conversations. Tom felt like a parent every time he walked into a coffee shop. They all seemed populated by tech-savvy college kids with more devices than common sense. Any adult that did not take away their coffee was usually counting time in early retirement pretending to be enjoying their book or some new-age, yoga-attired woman picking at some vegan snack.

"Okay, but if you want a real heart-to-heart talk, let's go to a bar and get some beers. You look like you have some bad news to share. And if you want to tell me here, it's really bad, so I'm going to need a cold one," Michael said. He busied himself, picking some dirt off his jeans, his fingers rougher than his face.

The sight of his brother looking so lost triggered a memory Tom did not want to remember. Michael reminded Tom of this man at rehab called Paul. The memory haunted Tom. Paul wore a frumpy but tailored merino wool black turtleneck with Armani jeans and dull but elegant Italian loafers. He exuded chic even out of his business suit. Not that Tom had seen him wear one, but he easily could imagine it. The Mediterranean genre with a neatly shaved beard and sleekly combed back hair. He would wear a mauve silk handkerchief to accent his suit with the confidence of a man, son of immigrant parents, who now owns the town.

Paul's silence had been as evident as the red stains in his eyes. He sat there day after day, scratching at the seam of his jeans just like Michael was doing right now. Tom could tell Paul was coming undone from the inside. The emotional bleeding was bubbling up into his eyes. The frameless lenses of his candy-red glasses made his pain the focal point of his face. When Paul's silence grew intolerable even to himself, he began to cry.

Tom knew that everyone in that room was scared by that moment. Paul screamed, "I need a drink." The counselor asked him, "Why?" Paul sobbed on. "I couldn't save my daughter. I don't care if alcohol kills me. I don't want to live." He got up, grabbed the steel-framed folding chair, banged it against the floor and walked out. That day Paul packed his Gucci leather bag and left.

It was the self-recrimination in Paul's voice that infested Tom's mind. Tom had worked so hard to prevent that same searing red lava from exploding. After that day, it was as if each man waited for their insides to blast open, covering everyone with that life-stifling black purulence of emotions. It did happen again. Every so often, another man would erupt. Some shattered, some collapsed, and some frag-mented. But no one else left. Everyone was there to face their demon, but everyone was afraid of losing control. Tom had not wept, not even in the darkness of the night. Not once, during or after rehab. Tom was determined to get this conversation over with and not let Michael trigger an explosion.

"Hey, bro, what do you say? Let's get out of here," Michael repeated.

"No. I have something to say, and you need to listen. Don't inter-rupt me," Tom said.

It took all of fifteen minutes for Tom to tell his brother that he'd been to rehab, that he had not had a drop of alcohol for over two months, and that they would not see each other for a while.

Michael quickly became confused, defensive, and angry. "You let those pricks convince you that you needed rehab so they could charge you through the nose. I've never seen you drunk once in my life. Who put this idea in your head? Carole? You're not going to start preaching that AA cult stuff to me now, are you?" Michael, agitated, stood up and said, "This is ridiculous. I'm going to grab a beer to cool my heels. You coming?" Michael towered over Tom with his height and emotions like a schoolyard bully.

Without getting up, Tom calmly replied, "No," and waited.

Michael's face grew red. He shoved his hands in his jean pockets, lowered his head, and said in rapid-fire: "Goodbye, Tom. Good luck to you. You always had to show how much better you are than me. We have nothing in common but blood. Have a nice, sober life." Michael struggled to free himself of the confining space between the coffee table and the sofa. He never looked back at Tom, not even at the woman in pink. He just walked out, shoulders hunched, like a rejected lover.

It had happened exactly as Tom's sponsor had anticipated. He had prepared Tom by role-playing. Somehow, he knew that Michael would be angry in the end. Tom had expected his brother to be relieved, happy for him, not bitter. His sponsor had quietly reminded Tom that addiction was a family disease. It distorts every member's perception of themselves and their role within the family unit. Sobriety threatens the very fabric that unites a family suffering from addiction. Tom should expect denial from his brother, mainly since he was a heavy drinker himself.

Tom ordered a coffee and sat by himself. He examined the outline left by his brother on the couch. It dawned on Tom that everything was different. In the past, he sought his brother's presence to fill the empty spaces around him. Now Tom needed his brother's absence to get in touch with what was inside of himself.

Tom acknowledged that he felt something, but he hadn't the faintest idea what it was. Fear that he would not see his brother again? Relief that the conversation was over? Hurt that his brother walked out on him the way he had on their parents? Why did it have to be negative? What was the point of that?

Could he not just be happy? Yes, he decided. He felt happy. He did not want to feel sad or hurt, and he chose not to. With that decision made, Tom picked up the business section of *The New York Times* that had been left behind. As he read the headline he remembered one of the AA slogans: *Stick with winners.* Proud of himself, he promptly forgot about his brother and turned to the stock market news.

Carole: Still more Al-Anon

As Carole walked toward the community center in a neighborhood of South Philly, she noticed that the trees were nude, and the September light was already dull in the early afternoon. So much time had passed since her first meeting that a VAP store had replaced her favorite tea shop. She missed sitting there before her Al-Anon meeting. Cities sometimes changed faster than their residents. She slowed her pace and felt her shoulders release to their natural position; the muscles in her neck relaxed, and her rib cage loosened to welcome the late fall air.

It had taken her months to find a home meeting. After all the church basements, this community room in the church attic felt more welcoming. The natural light peered through the large stained-glass windows providing much needed cheerfulness to the room. The three couches were in complete disharmony: a rounded, purple-flowered couch clashed with the narrow Irish green plaid stripe divan next to it, which in turn accentuated the wear and tear on the burgundy crescent leather sofa. The starched white dusty linen tablecloth looked at once too formal for the corner table and too plain for the oversized fake floral arrangement of carnations and forget-me-nots. The fatigued wooden chair was reserved for the person chairing the meeting. The blue and bright pink area rugs stood out like newcomers. Everyone tried to ignore them, but their eyes eventually fixated on them. Al-Anon literature was stuffed into a stainless-steel pamphlet holder that was in turn stuffed into the abandoned fireplace. Someone had stacked a few discarded black leather Bibles in the corner to avoid offending any sensibilities.

Noreen chaired the meeting. She was crossed-legged, sitting correctly with the well-worn black binder holding the Al-Anon meeting script on her lap. Stress emanated from her rigid position. She smiled out of habit at Carole, softening her expression for an instant before returning her concentration to the meeting notes. It surprised Carole to see Jeff sitting on the burgundy couch looking at his running shoes. Although attendance was voluntary, the regulars kept a mental tab when someone had missed a few meetings without warning anyone. Then there were the people who only attended when their lives crumbled or crisis was imminent. Jeff was a long-term member of this group, but his presence was intermittent. Tall with soft, reddish-brown hair that fell gently to his ears, he reminded Carole of a St. Bernard. Always ready to help a lost soul, but in need of hugs himself.

Bob sat on the purple-flowered couch—as always with his pressed shirt, stylish pants, and shoes. Today he wore a sports jacket. Although Bob needed as much comfort as anyone, he spoke wisdom. Carole guessed that behind his confidence, which was not arrogance, was the experience from having spent more time in these rooms than she had. If he hadn't grown more comfortable with this family disease, at least he'd learned to live with it. Both his daughter and his wife were sober. Carole thought that was an unfair burden for one man to carry. The only other person present was Pat: an older gentleman who was quite ordinary looking, of average height and weight. Unlike Carole's husband, Pat could easily be ignored when he walked into a room. He often shared his feelings about the stigma of alcoholism. Carole thought he'd learned how to make himself invisible.

Noreen opened the meeting with the usual serenity prayer followed by all the sequential readings. Although this group never counted more than a dozen attendees at best, it never occurred to anyone to diverge from the established meeting format. At some point during every meeting, Carole looked forward to the day she would graduate from Al-Anon. She had no intention of staying on after she'd worked through the 12 Steps. She fervently believed there was a tipping point where the camaraderie of fellow codependents outweighed the depressing effect of listening to the same stories of broken lives. The universe could hold just so much identical pain.

"The meeting is now open for sharing," Noreen announced.

"Hi. My name is Pat. It's good to be here today. I'm struggling with my daughter right now. I know I have to get out of her way and let her make her own choices, but it's so hard. I just want to go and fix everything all the time. That's what I do: jump right in and just try to take charge."

"She's moving, and I think she's not going about it the right way. When she told me where she was moving, right away my mind started running in circles. That's a stupid place to move. It's farther from her work. I don't think she's got the right roommate either."

Carole looked at invisible Pat. She saw him. She connected with his story. It was her story in different clothes. She immediately put up her hand. Noreen acknowledged her.

"Hi, I'm Carole. I struggle with my mind, too. It never ceases to amaze me how quickly it goes from absorbing one piece of information and within a matter of seconds, goes through a whole series of associations and connections that take hold of my thoughts. Then I start spinning my wheels, wasting energy, and triggering unwanted emotions."

"Now that he's in recovery, I thought this would change. But I still often see my train of thoughts run wild starting from a pleasant thought and within a few degrees of separation, I'm rehashing an old grievance with the addiction."

"Just now, when Pat was talking, I had a real visual of what my thoughts look like when I don't take charge. This weekend my husband and I were visiting some friends for dinner. They took their miniature Schnauzer upstairs while we ate. He's one year old and they named him Clooney."

"Somehow, he escaped from the room and charged down the stairs to where we were. Before anyone of us realized what had happened, this innocent grey pound of puppy energy grabbed the toilet paper roll from the powder room. He made a mad dash for it and ran all over the room, up and down and around the sofa and coffee table. Within a few minutes, he'd woven the living room into a monster-sized white nest of fluff. He was completely out of control. Just like my thoughts. They grab hold of that toilet paper roll and run like a frenzied Clooney."

Stoic Bob and invisible Pat burst out laughing. Then Jeff joined in, roaring even louder. For about two minutes, they all just laughed.

Noreen regained control of the meeting and nodded to Jeff to share.

"Hi, my name is Jeff. Well, Clooney's in charge of my head today!"

"All right," Noreen intervened before laughter consumed the room again.

Carole experienced a noticeable shift that day. Laughing at herself while that room full of co-dependents laughed at themselves had planted some hope. Maybe she would tell Tom about the story, and they could laugh together and at each other with the same lightness.

March 2010 – Summer 2016

Tom & Carole
Unshackled from the influence, their heart-work could begin.

Carole and Tom: On the roller coaster

"Tom, just hold off before you start the laundry," Carole yelled up the stairs.

Tom stood by the washing machine, obedient and wound up. Carole's voice sounded like a monkey screeching a warning. The pitch irritated his nerves.

Carole approached him, unraveling some bath towels. She handed them to him without noticing Tom's mood.

"I can't take this anymore. I have to be my own person," Tom stated with such force that Carole took the towels back. She lowered her chin and squinted as she eyed him. The statement was so incongruent with the moment that it felt like the cartoonist had put the wrong comment in the conversation bubble.

"I'm sorry, Tom. Were you talking to me?"

"I said, it's enough. I need to be my own person. I can't be told what to do anymore," Tom said.

Carole looked from the washing machine to the towels to Tom's face.

"I'm my own person. This is going too far," Tom repeated.

"You want to choose the wash cycle?" Carole asked.

"Don't make fun of me, Carole. It's serious. Everyone keeps telling me what to do, how often to do it, and how to do it."

"You've found a better way to do laundry?" Carole asked, unsure what they were talking about.

"Damn it, Carole. Forget the laundry! I'm talking about me. Can't you see? This isn't me—all this therapy, antidepressant pills, and AA meetings. It's been a full year now. It's enough."

Tom described hours upon hours of the treatment he endured: the endless questions prodding into his past relationship with his mother, trying to unearth some deep childhood trauma that simply did not exist. Hours of listening to men who could no better handle their razors than their vocabulary, recounting painful memories. All the stories sounded like repeats of a bad sitcom. Tom felt they could get unstuck if they stopped repeating themselves and went out and lived their lives. Everyone had cravings. You just had to get on with it. Cravings would not disappear; you had to learn to put up with them.

Carole listened to Tom with poise, intending to appear sympathetic as she mentally reviewed the grocery list. Tom behaved much in the same way as the AA members he complained about. He repeated his displeasure at the way he had to account to everyone for how he spent his time to get them off his back. When Tom reached the subject of antidepressants, Carole snapped back to attention.

The entangled dance played out. Tom wanted to stop taking antidepressants. He felt fine and hated the way the drugs absconded with his sharpness. Carole reminded him that he felt fine precisely because he was taking them. Tom replied that she preferred him lifeless because she could boss him around. Down and down, the spiral they went.

"Tom, give it time," Carole pleaded. Tom, without antidepressants, morphed into a bar brawler who took offense at every look and believed that any snippet of conversation hid some double meaning. The experience of Tom off his antidepressants exhausted Carole as much as the tension of Tom as a functioning alcoholic. That truth festered within her and when they argued it unleashed ugly words that she always regretted.

Not knowing how to change the script, each of them stepped into the same costume and rehearsed the role they knew best. The scene always ended with the same exit: slammed doors. Each withdrew to separate bedrooms until the one with the most guilt trumped the other. Apologies were then exchanged, and they awaited the next rehearsal, unable to improvise new lines.

✳✳✳

Just as Tom's frustration overflowed, his sudden charm rekindled her hope for their relationship. Carole tugged at her strand of pearls. She sprayed on a little Givenchy perfume, slipped on her crayon-blue heels, and took a deep breath. The designer silk dress hugged her shape perfectly. She experienced the *cliché* of butterflies in her stomach. She skipped down the stairs with manufactured enthusiasm and genuine nervousness.

"You look so elegant. I love your sense of fashion. I'll have the hottest date in town," Tom winked at his wife.

Carole fidgeted with Tom's handkerchief and tapped him on the shoulder. "Pretty dashing yourself, Mr. Johnson." She noticed Tom was wearing the suit he'd bought for Sarah's high school graduation. She glanced at the graduation photo on the coffee table. Tom looked healthier now, and the suit fit him even better. She thought he even looked younger.

"So, what's the surprise? Why are we all dressed up?" Carole asked.

"We're going out on the town. A date night for my gorgeous wife and me," Tom responded. His eyes gleamed the way a young mischievous boy looks up when he knows he has the perfect plan.

Words failed Carole at that moment. She batted her eyes at him exaggeratedly, the way a cartoon belle would in a bar scene. She racked her brain, searching for which character role she'd been cast in tonight: dream girl or guardian angel. A date night seduced her. It had been almost a full year since they'd dined out on the town. Trendy chefs had changed decors, cuisines, and locations without as much as one visit from the Johnsons. Were they ready for their first public appearance without a rehearsal and the chaperone?

The black town car arrived before Carole spoiled Tom's enthusiasm with doubts. Tom helped Carole with her coat, opened the car door for her, and slipped into character. If Tom was nervous about this evening, he didn't let it show. He reached for Carole's hand, looked into her eyes and said, "We're going to town, Baby." He laughed out loud. It caught Carole off guard. The sound was familiar to her, like a tune from the past you remember but can't quite place.

Carole fought not to spoil the gentle affection that Tom directed towards her. It was a déjà vu from a moment they had liked before they owned a house and started a family. On their first date, Tom in the driver's seat had looked at her with the same eagerness and the same unknowing.

The evening unfolded with cinematographic perfection. Carole and Tom sat at a discrete stamp-sized table, covered in a pressed white linen tablecloth, cascading white flowers, and votive candles, their backs to most of the other guests. The room was at once lush with grandeur and intimately romantic.

Carole, engrossed by her husband's charm, felt the drinks arrive before she saw the waiter carrying the crystal champagne flutes. Her face transformed itself into a mask. Her eyes and mouth kept smiling but her face flexed. Tom reached for the flute. Carole braced herself pushing her hands into her thighs under the table to ground herself. She had not been this close to champagne since their last cruise with their best friends. It felt like an eternity ago.

Glass in hand, Tom lifted it and said, "To my dear wife, the most incredible woman of all. No husband can be luckier than I. You've gone through hell with me and supported me through it all. Thank you! I love you with all my heart."

Tom noticed that Carole had stopped breathing. He'd planned the night so meticulously and secretively to surprise his wife. The impact was so complete that Carole appeared mummified. He traced her eyes to his hand. She was now gasping.

"Carole, it's ok. I've got this," he said, laughing.

She remained transfixed, without a word. Afraid for her more than for himself, he continued. "Carole, sweetheart, raise your glass. I've taken care of everything. I am drinking ginger ale. And you, my dear wife, you deserve champagne."

A red glow replaced the ghastly white on her cheeks. He motioned to her to clink his glass. Her hand jerked as it reached for the glass, her eyes engaged his. He saw the fear of a woman looking down into the Valley of Death.

"Relax, sweetheart. I phoned the restaurant a week ago. I ordered our drinks, our meal and our dessert. My dinner is whole-fat and alcohol-free. Yours is à *la carte*." He clinked her glass again.

Carole lightly touched her flute against Tom's fearing its contents more than the fine crystal. The champagne tickled her mouth and rose into her nose. She expelled a small cough. Tom laughed again.

"Has it really been that long since you had champagne?"

Carole may have recovered her color, but her tongue was still held hostage. She took a long gulp of water. She felt the champagne travel the length of her. The bubbles moved slowly but thoroughly through her body. She tested her self-control by releasing her shoulders first. When nothing happened, she released her back and relaxed into the elegant chair. Only then did she breathe again. Her eyes fixed on Tom's face.

Tom beamed with pride at his cleverness. Carole spontaneously decided to honor him with trust. She squelched the voice in her head and ignored the tremor inside her skin. She met the moment with what was required. She held her glass up and said, "To my handsome husband who never ceases to amaze me. You are my hero: brave and determined. Thank you." She winked at him and continued, "And might I add, very sexy in that suit. You know you make me melt when you get all dressed up." They toasted again. She took a cautious sip. She did not want the champagne to go straight to her head.

Carole floated through the evening. She permitted herself the glass of Pouilly-Fuissé that Tom had the sommelier select for her to accompany the *escargot pistou*. She sipped it slowly so that it accompanied the grouper *Grenobloise*. Although Tom suggested she enjoy another glass with the entrée, Carole politely declined. That had been the only awkward moment of the evening. The silence had perched itself atop the flowers and lingered a little too long. The waiter, sensing the discomfort, appeared and cheerfully announced the cheese course. Tom motioned to the sommelier. Carole shook her head no and studied her serviette. The silence insisted on keeping its position.

Carole looked up at the waiter, less inquisitive about the next course as to plead that he remove the intrusive silence that was about to ruin the evening.

"Perhaps Madam would prefer a *profiterole* with our own pâtissier's *ganache* sauce?"

"That is a lovely suggestion. Chocolate is my greatest weakness. Well, after my husband, of course," Carole said. With that, the silence flew away and the evening regained its lightness.

Carole savored each flavor. The refined dishes satisfied an unmet want for gourmet living that had grown since Tom had gone to rehab. This meal swept away the countless salads, sandwiches, and comfort foods eaten in all the coffee shops. Carole preferred tea shops to warm her soul with pearls of jasmine tea or flowering tea buds in quiet and solitary contemplation with her journal before or after yoga classes. She abhorred the coffee shops with all the college kids absent but connected with their online friends. Dining out was an experience: a meal prepared by a chef and sous-chef to levels that you could not, yourself, achieve in the kitchen. She had missed going out for grown-up dinners in places Carole felt she and Tom belonged.

Minutes after the driver dropped them at home, she tossed her heels off and dropped her dress to the floor with abandon. She paraded around the bedroom in her black-laced lingerie covered only by Tom's admiration.

"Tom, thank you for being so sensitive to my needs tonight." He reached for her. She went to him, not out of habit but because she hungered for their intimacy.

❋❋❋

"No, Tom, I won't have it." Carole stood firmly between Tom and the car trunk.

"Carole, we can't do this for the rest of our lives. I'm ready," Tom said.

"I can do this." Carole insisted.

"I know you can, but it's time for me to start being a man again."

"Tom, you are a man! You don't need to carry the bottles of wine into the house to prove that to me. Besides, it's not about you. It's about me. I am not ready to see you handling the wine."

"Carole, we've gone through this a million times. If I want to drink, I can go to any pub. It's been a year. I think it's time you trust me."

"This isn't about trust. It's about protecting you and our lives. It will be a year this weekend. After the party. Don't get ahead of yourself." The pitch in Carole's voice increased with every response.

"What are you saying? I'll relapse before I can tell our oldest friends what's going on? That's what you think of me? I'm not a child that needs protection, damn it! You still don't trust me, do you?" Tom's pitch matched hers.

Trapped by her fears and Tom's self-righteousness, Carole wanted to bolt to the house and hide in her meditation room. The anxiety that ravaged her since she'd agreed to host this dinner party with their best friends as a coming-out evening had reached an intolerable level. Tom always outsmarted her with his negotiation skills.

Wearied by all the complicit excuses she'd tendered to her best friends for over a year, Carole felt Tom was betraying her loyalty. He wanted to clear the air and tell his friends about his sobriety and do away with all the invented medical conditions that excused his not drinking.

As Carole selected recipes without alcohol, not an easy task, and found substitutes such as vinegar for white wine, she fretted about the meal. It was not, in reality, the challenges of cooking but the fact that she'd be exposed to their friends. She assumed that in front of Tom, they would first express concern and then shower him with praise for his accomplishment. In private, when they stacked dishes, the wives would pepper her with questions and express their indignation that Carole had not confided in them.

Everywhere she stepped, Carole was trapped. Whether it was her concern for Tom or her need to take care of herself, the dividing line always placed Carole on the outside. She wanted a circle, actually a series of them, where she and Tom were in the middle together with rings extending beyond them to infinity.

How would any of their friends understand? She could barely understand the concept of a family disease herself. Aside from revealing that she'd chosen Tom's needs over their trust, she would have to expose herself to the breakdown of their family. They might as well strip her naked, peel away the skin and muscles, tear off the nerves, and splay her heart to see if they could find her principles.

"Tom, it's not you. I do trust you. Just understand, it's a big step for me to agree to serve wine in the house. I know you can drink if you want to. I just feel guilty," Carole said, expressing her feelings instead of mouthing off pretenses.

"Guilty?" Tom asked. He saw her. He felt curious rather than defensive.

"Yes." Carole answered.

"I'm sorry, Carole. Let's go inside and talk about this. The wine can stay in the trunk for now." Tom placed his arm around his wife and led her into the house.

This was new: their awareness of each other, their understanding of the need to slow things down. They reached for each other instead of pushing each other away. The border between them grew softer.

Carole and Tom: Adrift after five years

Carole stretched into Eagle, Warrior, and Goddess pose to search for her self-confidence. She recited mantras and filled pages of her journal to surrender to her Higher Power. Spirituality insinuated itself into her existence without the word "God" ever falling from her lips.

The more poses she conquered in her yoga practice, and the more journals she stored away, the more she questioned whether she'd reached the limits of her therapy. Although her marriage remained caught in the wind's fickleness, she found herself repeating the same stories to Lisa.

"Lisa, I know I have a reflex I need to slow down when Tom does something that triggers my sense of abandonment. I recognize the twist in my stomach. I've slowed my reaction time. I've learned to give Tom his space and let him work through his recovery. I don't always get it right but I know when it's time to call a friend or go to yoga class." I feel that we've reached the limit of what you and I can accomplish at this moment," Carole said. It was part of setting boundaries.

Lisa sat motionless in her chair. Carole looked at her but did not examine her for a response. She no longer needed Lisa's approval for her recovery. It freed her to be responsible for herself. Carole had no idea whether her marriage would make it, but Lisa was not the determinant in that outcome. She was.

"I've been coming to see you for the last month because I was afraid that if I stopped my therapy, Tom would stop his. Then we'd never get to the point of our joint therapy. I've reflected on this for a while now. I need to stop my therapy and let Tom do what he will do. For the moment, I am done."

Lisa closed her notepad, leaned towards Carole, and extended her hand. "I agree with you, Carole. You have my number if the need arises. Just remember, it will take Tom a long time still. I don't think you fully grasp how much time. My wish for you is that you take care of yourself."

***

Six months later, Carole entered Lisa's living room office, accompanied by Tom. Carole had returned to Lisa in the depth of the winter unable to see the spring light. Tom had fired yet another therapist. Their marriage drifted into one tempest after another until amid the perfect storm, Carole had threatened to leave Tom unless he went with her to see Lisa. Carole hoped that Lisa could save their marriage.

"Tom, do you love your wife?" Lisa asked.

'Yes," Tom answered and glared back at her. He was hardly there of his free will. He was trapped by all the estrogen that had ganged up on him in this room.

"Carole, what do you need from Tom in this moment?" she asked.

"I need him to see me. I can't do this anymore. All his anger. He is so self-centered."

"Carole, that is not the question I asked. What do you need at this moment?" Lisa interrupted.

Carole looked at Tom's profile. He hadn't removed his coat. He was examining his Starbucks coffee cup as if it were a Rubik's cube needing to be solved. Tears rolled down her cheek in the grooves of her face that had developed over the last many months. Preferring to look at Lisa in defeat, she said, "I just need him to hug me and tell me we will work through this."

"Tom, can you do that?" Lisa asked.

Without an answer, Tom turned around, wrapped his right hand along with the coffee cup around Carole's shoulders and stared across the room.

"Tom, do you want to do this?"

"Yes."

"Then give Carole the hug she wants. Put your coffee down."

Tom rolled his eyes and put the coffee on her table next to the Kleenex box. Rebellious child, he unbuttoned his overcoat one button at a time. The clock ticked in the background. He rose, removed the coat, folded it and sat back down. He turned ceremoniously towards Carole and wrapped his right arm around her.

"Now, put your left arm around her," Lisa said.

Tom moved his left arm and moved his face to the right of Carole without touching her.

"Look at Carole." Lisa's voice maintained a neutral tone.

Tom stared at his wife.

"Now, breathe and keep looking at her." He took three long, forced breaths.

"Keep looking, Tom," Lisa insisted.

Carole saw the stiffness dissolve from Tom's eyes. The stranger disappeared and Tom emerged. Their breathing joined and they inhaled and exhaled at the same time. No one spoke.

"Thank you, Tom," Carole said, holding back tears.

Tom sat back.

Lisa led Tom through a series of questions. Then she closed her notebook. Carole didn't want to leave the protection of Lisa's living room. She had no idea whether anything Lisa had said to Tom mattered, whether he'd heard all or none of it, whether he would call on the new therapist Lisa had referred for Tom—number five in five years.

❋❋❋

Tom wrote another series of checks. It was 2015 and therapist number five. Tom refused to add up the amount of money he'd spent post-rehab on therapy, psychiatrists, drugs, and personal growth workshops. The amount surely would be equivalent to or higher than what he'd spent on rehab. Independent Blue Cross had reimbursed him a token $3,000. He could own a sleek convertible Jaguar by now. That would have been a much more rewarding late mid-life crisis expenditure.

After four sessions of Tom stretching out the details of his journey to rehab and the disaster of his marriage, Robert, the new therapist, asked Tom, "Do you want to be here?"

"Yes. I think I'm ready this time. I've fought it long enough. It's time I figure it out. Not for Carole, but for myself."

Tom permitted Robert to explore the childhood issues he'd refused to reveal to the other therapists. They discussed his father's alcoholism. Tom told Robert about seeing his father hit his mother late at night as he hid behind the bathroom door. He spoke of his guilt towards his brother Michael. He never cried, but he reconstructed his childhood for Robert. Sometimes it took him weeks to recall the color of his parent's bedroom. Sometimes he raged against Robert.

Tom discovered that even a city guy like him could enjoy the solitude of nature. He had started fly-fishing when he and Peter had taken a lesson as a father and son thing. Peter was too young and busy with his new career to keep it up. But Tom stuck with it. It gave him time to think about life and feel the breeze in his ever-disappearing hair. It's also where he made a lot of decisions, such as deciding to mentor young boys. It was time for him to give back and stop worrying about quarterly earnings.

✳✳✳

"Robert, I hugged one of the young boys I am mentoring when he fell apart after he lost the sailing race." Tom said.

"Go on." Robert prodded.

"I told him I felt sad too when I was not good enough. And then it struck me. I was feeling sad for him and me. Robert, I was there with this kid at that moment. I wasn't afraid to be sad or to share his sadness." Tom said. The doorway to his emotions cracked open wider.

When Robert announced to Tom four months later that he would be away on the conference circuit for a few weeks, Tom decided it was time for a break. He told Robert that between his sponsor, fly fishing, and his family, he had all the support he needed. Tom wrote Robert his last check.

Tom and Carole: Living a healthy relationship

"Carole, I've decided to retire. It's time for us to have more time together and I want to enjoy my Harley." Tom announced. He expected her objections, but they didn't come.

Carole winked at him. "Let's celebrate! It's time that the old crowd meets our new friends. We'll invite everyone." This time Tom and Carole eased gently into this significant life change.

When summer came, Tom went fly fishing with his AA friends. A few weekends a month, he took the young boys sailing in the Poconos. Even Buddy was in better shape from all the balls he fetched in the yard. Tom and Carole took up hiking on Saturdays. Sunday brunches gave way to Sunday barbecues with Sarah, Peter, and Debbie, who now wore an engagement ring. There were water hose fights, plans for European travels, and talk of learning to snowshoe. Carole did not stand still. Her yoga practice became a springboard to teaching. Once a month, she ventured into near-strangers' homes when she attended her book club night. Freed from her constant buzzing around Tom, she made new friends. She introduced Mary and Barbara to Patricia, and the four of them had a standing girlfriends' night out.

When Carole needed surgery, no one worried about Tom being alone. Carole never considered that Tom wouldn't be there for her. Tom bought a new set of dominoes so they could play in bed while she recovered. The ebb and flow of their discussion evolved. They now looked forward to their time alone. Once awhile, they even told the kids that they were turning the lights off in the house. It became their family joke, the euphemism for "Mom and Dad want to be alone."

2019

Tom & Carole

The gift of recovery, walking together united by a healthy bond of love.

Carole and Tom: Marching in the recovery walk

Tom wore a purple sash as they walked down Columbia Avenue. He held Carole's hand, who held Sarah's, who held her brother's, who held his wife's. Debbie was part of the family now. Behind them followed what they later found out was 27,000 people to mark the 2010 Recovery Walk in Philadelphia. Three years into retirement, they'd found their stride together, individually and as a family. Their immediate family was whole except for the absence of Michael, who was still not talking to them. Tom wished his brother had been there with them on this day. It was the annual recovery walk he and Carole attended. This year marked ten years of recovery for Tom and his family. The purple sash with "honor guard" in bold gold letters identified all the marchers with ten years of sobriety.

"Dad, I'm so proud of you." Peter said. "Maybe we will name junior after you." He added, winking at Debbie.

Sarah was the first to react. "I'm going to be an aunt!"

"Well, that calls for a ginger ale toast after the walk." Tom said to Debbie as he hugged her. "I'm going to save my best cigar for this one." Tom said to Carole.

Their lives were still full of ups and downs. Recovery had not immunized them to life's challenges. Recovery simply meant they could live life to the fullest. Like this moment, life was full of surprises. Although the AA and Al-Anon meetings were few and far between these days, Tom and Carole knew that their remission wasn't guaranteed. This is why they walked every September: to remember the long journey.

PART III

✳

True Stories of Couples In Recovery

The core of recovery is becoming a person increasingly capable of functioning in a healthy relationship.

—Ernie Larsen
Stage II Relationships: Love Beyond Addiction

The Essence of a
Perfect Relationship

[David & Leslie]

David and Leslie enjoyed a harmonious relationship in their comfortable colonial home and were anticipating their empty-nester retirement years with glee. Their living room, infused in earth tones and accented with bold floral chairs, welcomed all friends. There were no musical-chair games here. Over the years everyone had commandeered their favorite spot. Their children hung out in the family room where the blue leather sofa was slightly distressed by the constant flow of friends and the dogs that had accompanied the kids' rites of passage into teen hood.

Life was fun. Their neighbors were fun. Travel was fun, even when David gently nudged Leslie out of her comfort zone to visit South America. Their children's scratched knees, broken hearts, and college experimentation had tested the metal of Leslie and David's wedding bands. Also, David's hand surgeries were not fun. They were no strangers to the stress of careers in corporate America. Still, all in all, Leslie and David had a perfect relationship. Their life together resembled tales told in old-fashioned storybooks.

Leslie was not prepared when the storyline began to stray from the "happy ever after" ending. Leslie's life with David was predictable, and she liked it that way. She was looking forward to the grandchildren and the bouquets at the end of the rainbow.

✳✳✳

David was born and bred in the generation that worked hard, paid their taxes, raised a family, and played by the rules. David's blood-line could be easily traced from his grandfather to him without any hesitation. David learned to stand tall, work in the yard for extra cash, and get up when he fell. If he hurt himself, he kept on going. He never expected others to help, and he carried on without complaining. This was not "tough love"—that concept did not exist back then—it was simply what was expected of you and what you were supposed to expect from yourself. David's upbringing was as solid as it was ordinary.

Procter & Gamble had built his hometown: good schools, team sports, and jobs for those who wanted them. A work ethic ran through the community along with upright values. Kids in high school pushed their luck; they drank what they could nab from their parents' wet bars and smoked a little pot here and there. David joined in. It felt cool to flirt with girls with a joint hanging from his mouth, offering a not-so-discreet nod with your beer. David preferred the joints to the beers, dabbled in a few light drugs, but nothing stuck. Being cool outweighed being high.

David tested his own wings by attending a university in New Orleans. Faced with racism, crime and economic disparity, his frame of reference was rearranged. Unlike other freshmen he had partied in high school and had no need to test the boundaries of his new freedom with booze. The college years were a stream of part-time jobs bartending and shelving books at the library to satisfy his loan requirements, sweating it out on the basketball court and football field, with hours of attending classes beginning at 8:00 a.m. and ending whenever he crawled back to his dorm.

Two weeks after graduation, David upheld the legacies passed down from his grandfather and father: he began his career with Procter & Gamble.

✻✻✻

Leslie's trajectory into her perfect life was marked by a few minor deviations. It started with a Fonzie-type guy: handsome, fun and a little wild. He derailed Leslie's studies at George Washington University in DC. He symbolized everything a mother recognized as bad for her daughter. Twenty-year-old Leslie ignored her mother's advice. Instead of walking to the podium to claim her degree, she walked down the aisle with a growing belly to take her wedding vows. Little Nicholas filled her life with joy and possibilities while her new husband dragged her from innocence to the edge of criminal activities. Leslie wanted no part of it; she divorced him and moved in with her parents.

Extroverted and in need of an adult life, she worked in a hotel. She flourished. There were people to take care of, people to work with, and people to socialize with. The hotel barely paid her, but the darkness of her failed marriage quickly faded. She regained her lightheartedness.

"You are cute, but you are married," she said to one of the hotel suppliers she dealt with. "Do you happen to have a brother?" she teased.

"Yes, I do, as a matter of fact. My brother David has just been transferred from New Orleans to Washington. How about a chaperoned date?" the cute man said.

She accepted and soon met David. In a flash, the romance that would bring Leslie decades of joy ignited. Her version of athletic, dependable, and all-around perfect manhood fell in love with her and Nicholas just as quickly. David took charge and righted Leslie's life. He married her, moved them to his hometown in Ohio, adopted Nicholas, and fathered John and Caroline. On cue, David earned one promotion after another under the protectorate of Procter & Gamble.

✻✻✻

David eased into every new job position with gusto. Having both captained the college football team and led the marching band with his trumpet, he knew that hard work was the key to success. The pressures at the summit of his career, however, far exceeded that of calling a play to score the winning touchdown. With more respon-sibilities, he reported to more bosses. The Head of North America had one agenda, the Head of Marketing wanted more turf, and the CEO counted on him to implement his vision. David decompressed from the pressure cooker with a few weekend martinis. Occasion-ally he skipped the fancy elegance and straight-out overindulged in drinks. No one noticed.

The storybook ending to his career naturally fell into place. After 31 years at Procter & Gamble, with a snug profit-sharing plan, and satisfied with his achievements, David maneuvered into a comfortable early retirement at the age of 52. Well done, he thought to himself. A few consulting projects would perfectly occupy him until it was time for him to grandfather the next generation of his family.

The one snag in the otherwise seamless transition to the second chapter of his life was his health. The body that had carried him so marvelously throughout his life began to hurt. Following his fore-fathers, David handled his agony with the same genetic fortitude. He would not let pain get the better of him. The herniated disc, however, refused to heal. Uncomfortable with his physical weakness and mounting pain, David relied on a little vodka here and there to get up and go. Procedures were recommended. First, it was back surgery; then he needed hand surgery. Not one to believe in pain medication, after swallowing two pain pills he tossed the meds out.

When medical treatments interrupted his consulting work, David's interest in the flow of his projects waned. Often on his own, with too much idyll time and physical pain, David turned to vodka for companionship. Unchallenged by either family or friends, David's illusion of being in control of his life remained intact.

❋❋❋

"Darling, I know you are in a lot of pain. You need to see your doctors and figure out what is happening. All that twitching and forgetting—it's not you."

"Hey, brother, what's happening? You can't hold a glass of wine. Must be your post-surgery meds. Maybe you should take a little holiday from the pain medication."

"Dad, I'm worried about you. You seem tipsy a little too often."

"Ma'am, is your husband okay? He's not himself. His eyes are glassy and his head is twitching."

❋❋❋

After another fruitless night racking her brain, Leslie still could not understand what was happening to David. Unable to tolerate the restlessness any longer, she went down to the kitchen. As she entered the dimly lit room, she saw David stirring his orange juice as he pocketed what looked like a small vodka bottle.

"Sweetheart, it's 7:00 a.m. You can't be spiking your OJ this early in the morning."

She immediately regretted the blaming tone she had used. The kitchen swirled around her as she went through the motions of preparing a large cup of coffee, hoping the caffeine would help her figure out what was happening. David did not bother responding, he walked out on the porch. She tried to remember when they had stocked small liquor bottles. They were too easy to hide. She experienced the uncontrollable need to do something. She searched the liquor cabinet, the cupboard where she kept the cooking wines and liqueurs, and the basement where they stored extras. Nowhere did she find other flasks. David must have bought this mini bottle of vodka without her knowledge. What pain was driving David to drink like this?

A few weeks earlier, Leslie had confiscated the car keys when she found David staggering around the house. She thought he surely would get into an accident. His balance and reaction time were way off. He could not even catch a football in the backyard. Or was she exaggerating? What kind of doctor had she failed to consult?

Alzheimer's scared her to death. She was afraid to do the laundry in the basement if David was not on the first floor. How would she deal with an absent-minded husband sitting in the living room who forgot she was even in the house?

She abandoned her search and joined David on the porch. She studied his hands, scarred by the operation. The orange juice was sloshing around the half-empty glass. David could not hold it steady with his shaking hand. It hit her all of a sudden with extraordinary clarity.

"David, is this your first drink today?" she asked.

"No, it's not," he said.

Oh, my God! How could I have missed it? He has been drinking. He has been self-medicating with alcohol. How could I be so blind? Married all these years, and I missed it. It has to be the pain. He's never in his life had a drinking problem. He's not an alcoholic. He is a man in pain.

"David, sit down We need to talk, Sweetheart." She led him to the kitchen table, and they sat down.

"We can take care of this, David." She reached for his hands and held them with the confidence gained from years of mothering. She could handle this. The doctors would adjust David's medications to manage the pain, and she would make sure he took them. The image of the pill bottles in the bathroom trash can flashed before her eyes. Leslie had thought David was over the pain, but she had missed a beat. He was never one for pills so he had switched to vodka.

Relief spread over Leslie. She could get David back on track. In a few weeks, the doctors would figure out the right meds. She would be strict about David attending all of his physio appointments. No more excuses. They had three beautiful kids, an elegant house, and a perfect life. It would not take long to fix this. It energized her to have a real course of action after the last couple of miserable years. Leslie would get her life back and soon.

✳✳✳

Neither of them had gone through anything like this. The doctors could not prescribe a quick fix. The pain had morphed from a physical one to an emotional one. No one could help. The bottle had David.

In the midst of the Ohio winter, from January to March, Leslie dutifully drove David to out-patient services at the Lindner Treatment Center. An hour there and an hour back, three times a week, Leslie played out her role as the dutiful wife. From 6:00 to 9:00 p.m., in the frigid darkness of winter, Leslie occupied herself in downtown Cincinnati, pretending she had a normal life. Ultimately, the counselors at Lindner and the sponsors at AA were powerless to sever the bond between David and the bottle. He had beat cholesterol with low-fat dieting and a strict exercise regime. He had rehabilitated his back after surgery and his hand, too, through sheer dedication to recovery. Leslie and David were both mystified by David's inability to quit drinking.

✳✳✳

During these endless commutes Leslie teetered between reminding David what an intelligent, loving gentleman he was and berating him for all the pain he had caused her. The anger she experienced swelled into rage at everything around her. David sat in the passenger seat, unresponsive.

Full of shame from diminishing the noble legacy of his grandfather, David isolated himself, white knuckling three weeks of dryness between visits to Lindner and a few AA meetings. Then he could only manage two weeks without drinking, and then one week, until he could not even manage one day. David was not getting up after this fall, no matter what he had been taught in his childhood. He knew he needed help but had no idea how to ask for it.

Each time he failed to say no to the bottle, he loathed himself so much that only the vodka itself could numb the shame. David knew he was genetically trained not to ask for help, but he was not aware that he was also predisposed to battle alcoholism. The combined effects of his ancestral lineage ensnarled him so completely that he failed to see the helping hands extended in his direction.

❄❄❄

Leslie morphed into detective Colombo. She hunted for all of David's stashes, convinced that if she could keep the house dry and keep David at home, he would eventually come to his senses. She amped up her efforts to find every secret spot. The more bottles she found, the less empathetic she became, and the more she yelled.

"David, you have to be kidding me! What will the postman think? That we've lost our sanity! How could you hide a bottle in the mailbox? This is outrageous. Don't you think the neighbors will see you drinking out there? Why can't you just go to more meetings? Why do you not love me enough to stop? Just stop drinking! It's not complicated. Just don't put any bloody alcohol in your mouth! If you don't want to do it for me, at least do it for the kids!"

"David, you cannot, read my lips, you CANNOT deal with your hand pain with alcohol. Take the pain meds and stay away from vodka. This has to end or else . . ."

At first, Leslie did not have the courage to finish her threats. As she walked the full length of the misery path, back and forth, her verbal abuse gained momentum.

"David, you are ruining our lives, you are destroying me, you have no backbone. And you lie to me over and over again without any remorse, telling me you have not had a drop, and then I find this!" Leslie held up a bottle of Grey Goose, pointing to the sky, her body reverberating with anger as she shook the culprit. She walked over to the sink, poured out the vodka, and slammed the empty bottle in the recycle bin with all her might so it would crash. It would not be salvaged and refilled.

She walked over to David and shoved him against the wall. "You have to stop this insanity. Stop it. STOP! Do you hear me? Stop it or—" She looked him straight in the eye and finally said it: "Or I am leaving you!"

But she stayed.

✳✳✳

David knew he couldn't control his drinking but resisted full in-patient, go-away-for-28-days rehab treatment because, in the words of AA, he had not hit the infamous "bottom." The therapists at Lindner had explained that it was difficult for people like him who are "high functioning alcoholics" to grasp the danger of their disease because they often don't hit "bottom." David did not mind being referred to as high functioning, after all he had been high achieving. He had heard men in his AA meetings sharing about their "low" or worse "rock" bottom, that turning point when they finally could start getting up because they had lost everything, their jobs, family, health and dignity.

Saved by Leslie's hypervigilant supervision, he'd never had a DUI because she took his keys away. Procter & Gamble's profit sharing insured his financial security. Surgery on his back had corrected his health. His life-long friends visited less regularly, but their lives were so intertwined with his family that they never disappeared. Between the kids' activities, the tools they borrowed, and Leslie's social agenda, David saw them often enough.

David had been fortunate to benefit from an enabling and supportive circle, which unbeknownst to them, had helped him sustain his addiction. They had kept his life from collapsing while he slowly deteriorated.

The challenge with HFAs, the therapists had repeatedly explained to him in different ways, is that externally they appear to lead a brilliant life with all the trappings of success while privately they intermittently lose control of their drinking. Inevitably, they are more often out of control than in control. Until one day, they reach a "high" bottom, the point at which they lose something or someone that they cherish. Perhaps they are asked to "retire" early, or their wife leaves them, or they embarrass themselves so thoroughly that they cannot salvage their dignity or their self-esteem. Successful executives, they told him were the hardest people to intervene with because they have such "high" bottoms. Low bottoms are easy to identify as a person basically falls off a cliff and barely escapes alive. On the other hand, the high bottoms which push people over the hurdle of self-denial to seek full in-patient treatment are most often trouble with one of the three L's: Legal, Liver, or Love.

David felt secure with all his L's.

David lost track of when he was sober and when he was drinking. He lied to his counselor, he lied to Leslie, he lied to his daughter, he lied to his friends, he lied to his brother, and most of all he lied to himself. They knew the truth of his drinking. They lived with it. They saw him sitting alone at home.

On one ordinary Wednesday night, in the intimacy of Leslie and David's bedroom, David discovered that the L's were creeping up on him. Leslie sat on one edge of the bed as he sat on the other with their backs to each other. He turned toward her, ever so slightly, trying hard not to push her over the brink. David noticed that Leslie looked haggard. His well-kept gorgeous wife could not, or no longer would try, to cover up the sagging bags under her eyes. The perpetual worrying had creased her face with premature aging. He slowly reached across the bed, too far away to touch her back, knowing she felt his gesture because she felt everything these days, the slightest hint of something. Nothing escaped her. But she did not respond.

He felt her tugging at her wedding band until it came off and heard her gently open the drawer of her night table, carefully place it in the back, and close the drawer. She then turned off her night light and slipped under the covers, hovering near the edge. For the first time in 29 years, Leslie fell asleep without her wedding band.

***

"Please, Leslie, please put your wedding ring back on," David begged each morning. For one week she had walked out of the room every time without responding. Her initial resolve fueled by their cancelled trip to the Bahamas waned when she saw him in this pitiful state. Yet her resentment refused to die. This seesaw of emotions exhausted her. She wanted her damned umbrella drink on the lounge chair of the cruise ship deck.

But Leslie and David had been "disinvited" by their friends. Leslie felt betrayed by them. David's brother had shamed them into choosing between David and his health and Leslie and her need for a holiday. All agreed that a cruise would tempt David to indulge in even more drinking. Leslie fumed at their insensitivity to her need for a vacation. No one seemed concerned about her. What about her sanity? She'd needed the cruise. Not just the sun or the luxury of it, or even the time with friends, but the illusion that she still had a good life.

When soaking in her tub, Leslie realized that in her friends' absence she and David were now alone with each other, and she panicked. Was she living up to her wedding vows? Was she abandoning him when he most needed her? If she failed to stand by him, how could she expect him to do the same for her if illness befell her? These questions jolted her.

For a long time, she sat at her bathroom vanity tracing the wrinkles that she had lost interest in covering. She reached for her foundation cream and spent more than an hour making herself up. When she felt whole again, she chose that favorite little black dress that made David wink at her. She opened the drawer and slipped on her wedding band. Come Hell, or not, failure was not an option. She would figure this out.

Leslie sat in the living room without any lights on and said quietly to David, "I can't do this anymore."

In the absence of a plea or even a question, David simply responded, "Okay. I can't do it anymore either."

✳✳✳

David finally succumbed to the fact that he couldn't do it alone. He threw in the towel. He recognized he needed to attend in-patient treatment. The fear of being away from Leslie was only matched by the shame of having to tell his mother.

David surveyed his mother's kitchen as if there might be an escape door, an Alice in Wonderland kind of rabbit hole that he could drop into. The silence between them grew so awkward that he sat down and lowered his head, unable to look at her.

"Mother, I've been drinking too much," he began.

"Your hands hurt a lot, don't they?" she asked, staring at his surgery scars.

"They do, Mother. But it's more than that. Now, I drink too much not because of pain but because I cannot stop drinking." He rubbed his hands together.

"It's normal, David. We all have our limits with pain," she empathized.

"No, Mother, it's not normal. I've lost control. I need to go into treatment," he said and hid his face in his hands to avoid her eyes.

He felt the light touch of her aged hand upon his shoulder. "Get up, David. Let's go into the living room." She walked over to a photo of her father and his father hanging in a traditional silver frame. She caressed the image of her father slightly.

"David, your grandfather, he liked his whiskey. He was a serious man, worked hard at P&G. He took care of us. He was a family man, like you. But there were times when he stumbled into the hallway, his dress shirt hanging out of his pants, his tie all crooked. These times, they were more often than you can imagine. And his father, your great-grandfather, he pushed your grandfather to succeed. Maybe in the same way we pushed you." She looked at him with a shadow of empathy and the distant look of painful childhood memories. "Your lineage of men has done us proud. You've dealt with your pain as best you could," she said. She reached for his hands, held them and said, "You go take care of yourself, David."

David would always remember that moment as the family revelation—something he'd never suspected.

✳✳✳

David only knew how to overachieve. He packed his bags for in-patient treatment at Lindner. After the first ten days, his counselor asked David whether he wanted to stay for another 30 days or go to a treatment center that focused on alcohol addiction. David chose to stay. At least he would be close to Leslie and his friends. He could see if she visited him wearing her wedding band. She did.

When David completed the 30 days, the medical team recommended he attend further treatment. He would have to go elsewhere. They recommended 60 days at the Caron Treatment Center in Reading, Pennsylvania. They appealed to his sense of success and responsibility by explaining that he wasn't ready to take on this disease by himself. He needed a stronger foundation that only a treatment focused on alcohol recovery could provide him.

David struggled with the choice. During all the years of their marriage he had never left Leslie for a long time, and certainly never as much as 60 days. It scared him that she might not be there when he returned. He also battled his own strong will and the stubborn belief that now he could handle this problem on his own. He had not had a drink for a full month. He was back in control. It was his AA sponsor that helped David complete the first of the twelve steps. But David finally admitted to himself and to his sponsor that he was still powerless about his alcohol use and his life had become unmanageable.

Leslie refreshed his suitcase, and David left for Pennsylvania.

❋❋❋

Leslie stared at the burnt-out recessed ceiling light. At first, she ignored it. Then it obsessed her. Everything that was wrong in the world was right above her head. At five feet, she needed a ladder to reach that light bulb. This was David's job, not hers. In 30 years, she hadn't had to deal with this. Now David was away at "summer camp," what she called rehab at times like this, and the responsibility of everything rested squarely on her shoulders. The thought horrified her.

That task symbolized all her loneliness. Leslie always considered David the brain in the family, but now hers was fixated on words to describe her state of non-being: melancholic, doleful, and dispirited. No. Those were not her words. She was sad—sad and lonely to the core. Her perfect marriage had sunk to the bottom of a bottle. How much sadder could life be?

She attended a few Al-Anon meetings hoping to fill the abyss in her chest with some answers. It was no use. It was too much work, all those steps, listening to people blabber about their broken lives.

People were nice and helpful, she told herself. Yet her internal voice agreed with her brain. Nope, not doing that. Too hard. Not investing my life here. I have too much to live for. Won't be manipulated into spending my time this way. Not my area. Leslie attended her last Al-Anon meeting during David's first week away.

Leslie went back to changing light bulbs and doing her time. Sixty days of loneliness punctuated by weird visits to Caron watching men, grown men, walking around in their pajamas. She attended the Family Education Program expecting nothing. She and David had been dialoguing for 30 years, what more was there to say?

Leslie stood her ground against her mother-in-law's insinuations that festering marital discontent was the root of David's drinking.

"Dear, you do know that it's not uncommon for successful men to become alcoholics as a way to deal with their bad marriages," her mother-in-law had stated matter-of-factly. No, Leslie would not endure the sabotage.

"I want to reassure you that David and I have had a perfect marriage, as perfect as any marriage can be. We love each other. We never fought."

"Until David lost control of his drinking," Leslie silently added.

❋❋❋

Leslie welcomed David home to their fairy tale life. Sixty days absence made the heart grow fonder and forgetful of the pre-rehab frigid romance. Leslie gushed with the ardor of a newlywed. David appeared to float between a state of bewilderment and simple happy-faced joy. Leslie keenly interpreted it as his joy to be home.

The "we never fight" argument she had so emphatically declared to her mother-in-law did an about-face and became a "We frequently fight" admission. The battles became so intense that they finally did what other couples they knew did: they went to see a therapist.

Leslie, nestled into a cozy couch facing a far too well-compensated therapist, glared beyond Ms. Gucci at David.

"What does Leslie do that upsets you?" the therapist asked.

"Leslie wrote a $75 check to Diane," David replied.

"Why did this upset you, David?" the therapist asked.

"Are you out of your mind?" Leslie interrupted. "You want to approve everything I do, down to buying Girl Scout cookies?" This is what they were paying Ms. Gucci for? After 30 years, this was beyond ridiculous, Leslie thought.

"Why does this upset you?" the therapist continued.

"I just want to know. That's all," David said.

"Do you want to write a $50 check to some charity, David? Is that what this is about?" Leslie jumped in, her tone rising to match her anger.

"David, tell Leslie how you are feeling," the therapist coached David.

Leslie was thinking, "Is this what we are in therapy for? After three children, two major operations, and one executive career, we need a stranger to walk us through a $75 charge? This therapy is crap."

Out loud, she said, "Listen, Doctor, David and I are nice people. We do not fight over these types of things. We give each other lots of leeway. If I'm going to make a big purchase, I check in with him and vice versa. We're a team. What are we doing here?"

These conversations spilled into their drives home. They swelled to arguments in the kitchen and finished with doors slamming.

"David, this is NOT helping us," Leslie screamed. "I'll go as long as you want me to. But this woman just wants to milk us. If this is what I have to do to support you, I'll keep going. But this isn't doing us any good," Leslie said, more quietly.

David settled their invoice after five visits. The fighting stopped.

✳✳✳

"The gentleman at the table to the right, the one with the red pocket handkerchief, sends you his regards," the waiter said as he placed two tall flutes of champagne before David and Leslie.

"Mike, please tell the gentleman that we're much obliged and send him wishes of good health. And then can you slip me a new glass with that sparkling alcohol-free wine you served me last weekend," David said with a wink.

"Of course. Shall I keep the second glass chilled for Leslie?" the waiter said.

"Perfect idea, Mike. Bring it out with the stuffed porcini," David said.

Leslie observed David—her David, always the gentleman. Only two months out of rehab and he knew how to handle himself with charm. How they had struggled for three years in this tumultuous upheaval and now, just like that, he elegantly handled himself.

"Here, Sweetheart, enjoy. It's fine. I'm perfectly happy sitting here with my gorgeous wife. A toast to us."

The rich sound of the crystal tingled in their ears. Life as they once knew it was not over, it just had nuances. The fun was in not clinging to what they were drinking, but to the lightness of being.

✳✳✳

The August heat stuck to the walls of the house. It was well above 95 degrees outside and felt like 110 degrees inside. After 17 years of staying in hotels to visit their grandchildren, David and Leslie had finally purchased their leisure-retirement property. But like all such golden dreams, it had to be earned. The house's electric wiring turned out to be a disaster. Leslie and David needed to cover and tape up the furniture, paintings, and mementos before the tradesman arrived. To add to the stress, the air conditioner broke. There was no choice. They needed to check into a hotel along with all the sky watchers who'd congregated in the town to witness the "Great American Eclipse."

Leslie fretted about every inch of furniture, every photograph, every bit of everything in the house.

"Sweetheart, we have to slow down," David said.

"David, the guys will be here tomorrow. We still have the master bedroom, the living room, the—" Leslie told him, frowning with agitation.

David interrupted her, saying, "Leslie, I can't let this get to me."

"What?" Leslie asked pulling at a piece of tape that was mangled and fraying her nerves.

"Sweetheart, I can't do this. It's too much stress. It's too hot. If I don't stop, I'm going to drink. If I drink, I'm going to die," David said.

Leslie turned to face David. She hadn't heard him speak like this before. The abruptness first startled her and tickled her anger. But as she looked at him, as she saw his eyes, she recognized that something new was happening. She slowed down and took notice. David was expressing his vulnerability when in the past he would have puffed his chest, ground his teeth, and put up with it. She took a deep breath as she'd taught herself to do when she felt the groundswell of anger. Then a second breath, and she relaxed that spot at the bottom of her neck where her anxiety lay. She softened her gaze and engaged David's eyes.

"What's up, Sweetheart?" she asked.

"Life on life's terms. I have to accept this mess. I cannot fix it all at once. We need to take a break. Let's start again in the morning," he said.

Leslie paused long enough to take it all in. David was sharing his truth with her. He was expressing his fragility. In that moment, their relationship healed a little more. As much as she wanted to finish wrapping everything up in the house, she wanted to protect David more. She dropped the tape.

"I think it's iced-tea time," she said.

"With mint ice cream?" David asked.

"With lime sorbet," she answered.

✳✳✳

Leslie looked over at David sitting in their friends' living room. He'd sat in that same chair for birthday parties, after baseball games, for cocktails before a night on the town, to plan a party cruise in the Caribbean, after golf games telling tall tales of shots, and through all the heartaches of their kids' growing up. She'd always been the more talkative of the two, the more gregarious, the more opinionated, and the most in need of the friendship. David had often hummed, nodded, chuckled, and mostly been ever-present.

Tonight, Leslie felt awkward, too focused on David. She was spying on him, looking for the telltale sign that he'd reached his limit, and it was time to make an escape. She only half heard the story of their friends' recent trip to Florida, of the shopping for the cute sandals and of the near-Michelin restaurant experience. She pasted a smile on her face while her insides disintegrated into small devastations.

These friendships would never be the same. Sure, everyone cared for David and respected his new sobriety. Drinks were more restrained, fewer were passed around, and Leslie made sure they were always a little late to arrive. She looked for that perfect pair of earrings, calculating that her friends could have a round of pre-dinner martinis before they arrived. She could tolerate these little ruses to allow their friends time to drink more freely before she and David arrived. What woman does not want extra time to get ready before going out, she told herself.

What she did miss were the post-steakhouse nightcaps with their friends, those late evenings that turned into early mornings when they shared parental wisdom and stories that were only to be repeated within the intimacy of their tightly knit group, those carefree conversations that often turned to laughter until their eyes were tearing, allowing themselves to be kids with adult responsibilities. Many ideas for their shared lives were born during those idle moments of unwinding without the concerns of office or club politics.

Even with David's best buddy, Leslie saw that things were still a little off. Not exactly strained, but now there was an awareness, a certain caution. Out of respect, Leslie presumed, his buddy carefully measured his own drinks and chose to avoid vodka, knowing that David loved it. This new dynamic of minding their own behavior for David's sake both fortified Leslie's belief in their friendship and indicated a shift that was likely immutable. They would never be that carefree again.

Leslie wondered whether letting go of all the fun wine stuff was the same as aging prematurely. She loved visiting vineyards on their double-date trips with their friends: the anticipation felt as they read articles about different vineyards, outdoing each other in the most authentic experiences they could find, right down to the squish-the-grapes-with-bare-feet challenge; the endless conversations about which winery they would visit, in which order, and then how every trip one of them grew sentimental about an undiscovered cellar. The effort to ship cases of wine back from California, France, and then Italy resulted in endless stories that grew with every telling: the anticipation of the delivery, the uncorking of a red wine from the Loire valley along with a confit of duck made from a recipe book carried back from the same town.

Leslie tiptoed around her resentments, careful not to trigger their potency. She had to remind herself that a sober David was worth a lot more than a longing for the past. If it had turned out that David suffered from anything else but alcoholism, she would have willingly embraced her caretaker role. Her vows of "until death do us part" lie at the foundation of their entire relationship. They could call it codependent all they wanted in rehab. Every caring wife ought to look after her husband.

Leslie remained vigilant. When she noticed that David no longer responded to the conversation about the country club's next fundraiser, when his gaze drifted beyond them into the fireplace, or when he twitched at the sound of ice cubes in a glass, Leslie would call it a night.

"Sweetheart, I think it's time to head home. I'm a little tired," Leslie would offer. Their friends would nod. David would agree. It was their new unspoken pact. After 30 years, David would never fail to help her put on her coat. The way they treated each other, that was grace.

✳✳✳

The crux of their situation, as Leslie perceived it, was not that their relationship was immune to the realities of addiction but that they had survived them. Leslie had cursed David more in the last three years than in the previous 26. She had at once hated him—for his detachment from her and the kids and his failure to control his drinking—and now profoundly admired his courage to face his demons. Leslie loved being married to David more than anything else in life. They were an old-fashioned couple in the same way that apple pie was American. He earned the money, and she raised the family. He looked after their investments, and she bandaged the scraped knees. Clichéd, yes, but also happy, solid, dependable, healthy, and perfect.

During the last few years of chaos Leslie had developed one very strong conviction. The one person that was in charge of David's sobriety was David. Full stop. It was David's task to figure out what demon had propelled him to the bottom of that bottle and to slay that dragon. It was not her job. She believed in dividing responsibilities.

Her duty was to dissolve the recent resentments that had piled up. Leslie knew that time would do the trick, along with the redecorating of the house. A fair trade-off: his rehab costs and her renovations.

They could afford both. The visits with their granddaughter, the new fishing stories, and the bowls of Ben & Jerry's eaten in their pajamas would soon be the topic of their cuddles before bed. One day at a time was not a book cover for her, it was a way of life built up over 29 years of living.

The high-wire act, as David saw it, was manageable. In his career, he'd learned how to walk the tightrope. He knew how to read the winds of change, when to rush in and capitalize on a deal and when to patiently wait. Experience brings with it self-confidence, a sense of knowing, without the filter of analysis; a reflex that emanates from the gut and doesn't get tangled up in the brain. With a little practice, what once seemed new and tentative in a new job became just another day at the office.

Sobriety was not the career change he had planned. That was life. He hadn't been able to plan everything, but he always came out on top. David knew he could handle life; the process was always the same. Slow things down, learn first, integrate, and don't let your gut run the show. Make a plan and stick to it. Throughout his career, during his battles with surgeries and even during detox, he knew that the key to his success was to let Leslie in on his game plan. Once she knew what his intentions were, Leslie rallied. She was and always had been his best champion. Addiction had eroded the trust between them, but sobriety was steadily reinstating it.

When David told Leslie he was off to an AA meeting, he could predict her response.

"Good. You have a full-time job now. It's called sobriety. Retirement is over for you, mister." The irony did not escape him. He was back at work, and she held the fort. Their division of labor remained untouched even by the storms of addiction.

David learned that his weaknesses were just as plain vanilla as everyone else's in recovery: unstructured time, guilt over his high bottom, and celebratory occasions. These were the red-flag moments to be mindful of to ward off relapse, but not to obsess over. He knew the corporate equivalent well. It was a bit treacherous. It went like this: here are your numbers for the year, and if you make those, there is a stretch goal with a fat bonus attached. What Type A+ personality would not fixate on the stretch goal? Yet if you became obsessed with the bonus and did not pay attention to the basics of your business, you could easily mess everything up. So you learned to focus on your year-end numbers.

The unstructured time he easily addressed with AA meetings, projects at the Charleston house, and some safe socializing. The construct of recovery as a full-time job favored his success. Planning meetings and projects came naturally. Leslie clung to the notion that life as she knew it would eventually return. This created some dissonance between them. She reminisced over the good old times while thoughts of the past increased David's anxiety.

"Do you have everything you need, Sweetheart?" Leslie asked David as he walked into their bedroom.

"Yes, I am running a little late. I want to head out so I can take my time driving through West Virginia. The fall colors are out. It'll be gorgeous." He kissed her forehead and headed out the door. Three glorious days of fishing on North Carolina's Outer Banks with his AA buddies awaited him.

"Hey, mister. If the guys get boring or the cooking is not up to par, or you just decide it's a little too long on the boat, give me a call. I'll be there in a flash and we can enjoy the Charleston house together," Leslie said with perhaps a little too much stress on the word "together."

David turned around and looked at her. He slightly rolled his eyes. Why on Earth would he want to cut this trip short? Good fishing, good weather, and no temptations.

"You will be fine, Sweetheart. It's only two nights. See you at the house on Monday." He winked and headed out to avoid any further conversation.

"Yes, but three days." She said to his back with that little tinge of neediness in her voice.

"Have fun, Sweetheart," he heard her call out when he reached the bottom of the stairs.

All that togetherness over 30 years had formed her expectations of not being alone. The kids teased their mother. They called her "the scaredy-cat." Leslie was the run-up-the-stairs-at-night kind of gal. She hated going into the basement for anything if David was not on the main floor.

Leslie had managed better when David had traveled on business trips. Recovery may have been his new job, but his brief absences with his AA buddies irritated her for some reason. Yet by the time he pulled up to the house with a fresh catch for the barbecue, Leslie would be fine. She was, and always would be, his gal.

The guilt of knowing he had not hit rock bottom because Leslie had protected him, on the other hand, was a tricky one for David. At the AA meetings, he experienced a tug-of-war between gratitude and guilt. Without Leslie, he would've landed a couple of DUIs for sure. She'd saved him from the embarrassment and the tragedy of a fatal mistake. For that alone, he owed her his vow of "until death do us part." But the people in those rooms who struggled with the loss of everything, with the three L's that had brought them there, what could he tell them? With his well-polished penny loafers, his well-buffed car-of-the-year, and a roast lamb dinner waiting at home, he wondered why he'd been so fortunate. What could he do and what should he do to make up for the fact that he'd had such good fortune? He figured that by the time he worked his way through the 12-Step Program he'd be able to answer that question. For the moment, he'd make sure guilt did not tear down his gratitude.

Weddings. Those were his biggest challenge. Because all the kids in their extended circle were reaching marrying age, there were many celebrations. Drinks would flow, the toasts would become more emotional, and the dancing a little wilder. The New Orleans and Texas weddings—these weddings quickly tested his resolve.

"Welcome everyone to this evening of love. I see you!" he said as he turned to his daughter, the most gorgeous woman in the room in her wedding gown. And he did see her. And tomorrow he would remember his not-so-little-but-always-little-to-him, sweet Caroline looking at him, their eyes locking. He would remember that strand of hair that was always a little wind-blown and falling a little over her eye. He would remember his son-in-law winking at his daughter. He would remember it all.

Tears formed as he stood before his family and friends. It took David a moment to find his voice. "Caroline, my daughter," he began his father-of-the-bride speech present to the significance of the occasion for his daughter and for himself. David would forever cherish toasting his only daughter, his precious little girl jewel, embarking on her marriage. The knowledge that he would remember every little detail of this evening and share it with Leslie as they grew old together was the gift of a perfect marriage. That was the gift of sobriety.

The Boundaries of Wow

[Luke & Nadia]

*Water and denial permeate a surface in much the same way,
mainly undetected, until the floorboards collapse.*

Nadia tossed her college graduation gown over a chair in the corner
of her family-owned restaurant and walked over to the bar to please
a stranger who would haunt her life for the next 15 years. "What's
your favorite beer?" she asked him.

"Labatt's Blue"

From then on, the restaurant's bar was always stocked with Labatts.
Within a few months, so was their kitchen fridge. The empties accumulated and so did the wounds. Parties were seasoned with mari-
juana. The refrains of their dialogue echoed from one evening to the
next: "Where were you last night?"

"With friends."

"I work, and you hang out with muscle guys?"

"No, I was with my girlfriends."

"I don't believe you."

"But I'm telling the truth."

"Bullshit. You're lying, I can see it in your eyes. You lead them on."

"I don't, I swear."

"You don't even have the good sense to know. You're worthless."

✳✳✳

His words accused her; they slashed and burned. Nadia pleaded her innocence but then fatigued by it all, she conceded to him that he was right. She felt guilty of everything he accused her of. She extinguished her soul and bloated her body. She accepted her misdemeanors as proof of her inadequacy.

The household volume seemed to have only two levels: off or ear-shattering.

"Ma'am what's all the racket?" the police officer asked.

"No idea, Officer. I didn't call."

"No, your neighbors did."

✳✳✳

As the patrol car visits multiplied, so did the places to hide the empties. To avoid the trash can bearing witness to all the drinking, beer cans and vodka bottles were tucked away behind the couch, under the bathroom sink, and in the bedroom laundry basket.

Nadia looked away. The progression from repulsion at the sight of the containers littering her home to passive to her acceptance occurred simply and quietly. Her will to confront Max slipped away. Yet, the interrogation she conducted every morning of the person in her mirror intensified with relentless attacks. As she smudged more makeup to liven the eyes that were dying, she obsessed about the little being that insisted on growing in her womb. She didn't know whether to believe it could change the course of their relationship. Was it intentional or accidental? Perhaps this sprout could coax from his father the respect she couldn't out of her husband. Perhaps this tiny person growing inside of her could unclench her father's fingers from around his bottle.

❈❈❈

Nadia stared harder into her reflection, knowing that the distance between Max and her would grow faster than her belly. Without her gin and tonic in the evening, or maybe two or three, she would no longer be able to shape Max's beer-soaked behavior into affection. Her strategy to outdrink him would no longer be an option. It would have to be the baby or Max.

The choice terrified her more than she could admit as the long shadow of the first miscarriage had never quite lifted from her soul. It had mixed in with Max's persistent attacks. Nadia had to prove to Max that she could bear a child, that he was wrong about her.

Still more troubling was the burden to convince herself she was worthy to be called "momma." She knew Max would have no problem being the absent father, whether at home with a little vodka to ease the tension of crying fits or on a pharmacy run for diapers extended by a beer at the pub. With each passing week, she improvised mental scenarios teetering between fairy tale romances of their little family blowing out birthday candles without party drinks and the more likely dish-breaking screaming matches drowning out their newborn's colic. In Nadia's mind, only black-and-white options existed.

Neither the pregnancy nor the marriage came to full term. Both ended abruptly.

❈❈❈

In Nadia's experience, ballet and being single resembled one another. One moment you are twirling in this perfectly controlled elegant pirouette. The next finds you on the floor in a pile of bones and muscles covered in sweat and pain. Released from the egocentric whirl of her first marriage she spun wildly into the bachelorette dance. Her years of structured ballet classes had prepared her well for the transition to modern dance. But her years of early marriage to an alcoholic had not prepared her for the freedom of flying solo. She partied hard and collected her own string of reckless first dates.

Nadia derived a sense of security when she turned to online dating to control cocktail-infused bar scene choices. Before long she was hooked on the distance of online intimacy.

***

Luke knew what it meant to be a man: you were old enough to chug down a beer, then another, until you became enraged or stupid. It was the moment your falseness could be excused or ignored because you'd relieved yourself of the responsibility of your own existence through alcohol. The falseness was everywhere. No one rebelled against it, although a few did argue with it.

When his time came, Luke was neither ready nor unready. A lazy afternoon, an outboard motorboat, two fishing rods, an uneasy silence between his Dad and him, the mundane moment.

"Well, I guess you're old enough now," his Dad said without hesitating as he handed his Molson to Luke, who took his first sip at 12 years old.

The bitter taste lingered in his mouth all afternoon. By the time they got back to the dock, his Dad had piled a bunch of cans in the bow of the boat. He'd also drifted off in his own thoughts. Luke, initiated in the boat, testing the boundaries of his new manhood, pulled a beer out of the kitchen fridge in plain sight. It became a habit.

His mother carried around the steady rage of her own drug and alcohol-soaked life, until she ended it. Luke numbed his physical abuse from his explosive father the way his mother did—with drugs and alcohol.

Luke carried the ancient cycle of addiction into his own life with such ferocity that nothing could alter his trajectory. Although he felt different from others, he was not acquainted with himself or anyone else sufficiently to know whether he was. His path was littered with losses—lost days, lost jobs and relationships, and eventually his loss of freedom. No one cringed at his goings and comings to and from jail, his stints on the streets. He was damnable.

Luke passed on the suffering to his two sons. How he briefly cared for his eldest son while his ex-girlfriend paid her dues in jail for her own crumpled life, he hardly recalled. The vulnerability with which he burdened his sons clawed at his gut until the edges were too raw to dull with cocaine. Each time he returned his sons to their mother, Luke experienced an overwhelming relief that he was no longer responsible for their basic daily needs for regular meals, activities, and bedtime. At a distance, Luke could better pretend to himself that he was a loving and stable father figure in their lives. He never wondered which of the two of them would inflict less pain and fewer scars. He thought only of his own need to be away from people.

The rebellious son that had walked away from his own abusive father still held enough negotiating power with his soul to extract a promise from himself to not become like his father. Other than putting a loaded gun to his head, Luke knew of only one other way out: the place his father had not dared to go. Luke would face it on his own. He'd done jail often enough; how tough could this place be?

He showed up at a rehab center in North Bay, picked from an ad. They could give a try and see if they could rearrange his insides. Perhaps it would be less painful than all the bar fights and drug scrapes that had frequently landed him in jail.

For 28 days Luke threw out his shame and guilt as though he was throwing a fishing line back into that lake where he'd become a man in his father's eyes, trying to catch pieces of himself that had been irretrievably stolen from his boyhood. In the widening space between his drunken and sober selves, he decided to separate from his past.

Released from treatment, with the enthusiasm of a re-cast man, he determined to forge a new beginning. With six months of sobriety behind him, Luke moved to Ottawa where his aunt had offered him a bed and a chance to start over. Alone in a relative's home in a solitude invaded by his ever-present ego and self, he ached for a relationship to relieve him.

To stare down his past, he promised himself that he would speak the truth to any woman who dared smile at him. Living a "life on life's terms" meant owning his legacy. "Easy does it" meant online dating would slow down the immediacy of new intimacy. He was hanging onto the slogans from AA, but not committing to the process. The voices in his head were too loud to admit the presence of other people's burdens. Too much pain and too many faces, constant new faces. No, he needed only one new contact to translate between himself and the world; this needed to be a woman.

❄❄❄

When Luke suggested it was time to meet in person, Nadia looked in the living room mirror to confirm whether she could see herself. Could she define her boundaries with Luke without the escape hatch of the logout button? The next online chat comforted and alarmed her at once.

"Before we meet, do you have an issue with the fact that I'm in sobriety?" Luke typed.

"Well, your past is your past. I had a pretty beastly past, too. Where do you want to meet?"

Of all the matches that occurred on Plenty O' Fish, she'd managed to connect with an alcoholic. At least this one was in recovery, she told herself. A strange adrenaline coursed through her veins, confusing her instinct of flight or fight. She stayed in the conversation, but she didn't fight.

❄❄❄

When Luke set eyes on Nadia on Parliament Hill, light burst into his heart. The heat he felt from within surpassed that of the centennial flame reflecting on Nadia. For once, certainty was on his side. He knew his isolation had ended.

✲✲✲

One month after her first date with Luke, they moved in together. A few months later, they conceived a child. The ghosts of the past crept in on Nadia. From the pangs of early love, she drifted into the known territory of past anxiety. Familiar battles took shape, and the fear of another miscarriage haunted her. Not trusting herself to be alone, she entrusted herself to Al-Anon and her Al-Anon sponsor.

By early December, the fury of the snowstorms cast premature evening darkness into her living room and dumped snowbanks at her doorstep. She swayed to Bonnie Tyler's *Total Eclipse of the Heart*. The volume grew louder: *We're living in a powder keg . . .*

Left with Luke's shadow and a bottle of tequila, and rolled up on the couch with a blanket to cover her tummy, she hid from herself and sang with her friend Bonnie. By mid-song Nadia hit her stride, she was nearly shouting out the only too familiar refrain of her life: *now I'm falling apart.*

It may have been 1:00 in the morning or 1:00 in the afternoon that she rebelled. "What the hell! There's nothing I can do, and there's nothing I can say? What's this, an Al-Anon meeting?" Nadia listened to the lyrics repeatedly believing for a moment that Bonnie was her friend, talking to her, showing her the truth of her own situation.

Pathetic, pathetic, pathetic. How seamlessly she'd fallen into the same role. Luke might not be demeaning to her, but he wasn't sober either. The strand of bad choices hanging around her neck was about to choke her. No! She grabbed it and threw it on the floor. Enough! She may be able to drink, but what choices did she make with a glass in hand? Bad ones.

First things first. She'd done this before, pouring liquor down the drain because of others. This time it was for her. She was done. Next, it was time to sleep. Tomorrow she would figure it out. She attempted to push her way past the thought blocking her way to the bedroom. Luke.

Once more that evening she shouted to no one except to herself. *If Luke thinks he can handle a few drinks, that's his decision, not mine. They tell me I can be happy even if the person I love is drinking. I have no choice. I must be happy. I have a baby on the way. Now, get out of my way.* She shoved her thoughts aside and marched to her bedroom. With perhaps a little too much rage, she thumped her book of daily reflections, *One Day at a Time*, and cuddled it in bed. Not today, but tomorrow.

❋❋❋

It took a few months, but Luke did find his way back to her. She'd weathered the storm. She deleted Bonnie Tyler's song. Their laughter reappeared. Nadia basked in their physical intimacy. As her belly grew, so did Luke's lust for her. She gave his hands permission to trace the growing lines of their unborn child. He took to pleasuring her more calmly, more shyly. The new life form within her freed their desperation. They believed in their ability to begin a new family tree, one without all the broken branches.

❋❋❋

Charmed by his new life, Luke forgot the torments of his private scorched Hell. He forgot the all-consuming ruthlessness of the bottle. He held his old life at bay by keeping a distance from people.

AA meetings were too crowded both with people and stories. It took Luke too much effort to navigate these complex vibes. Without the alcohol, a room full of people and a walk through a haunted house were about the same: distorted people, images, and sounds mired in unexpected screams that embedded cries of fear into your soul. No, thank you. He was still learning to distinguish between David's cooing, gurgling, and grunting. Nadia's signs of trouble were equally confounding to him.

The beeps, chirps, and screeches of his metal detector took shape in his head in a way he understood. That was his calming universe. The goofy headset and his Hunter tracker exiled the world. No lyrics, no images, no people. Just him with his sounds, his feet, and the comforting swing back and forth of the tracker. It transported his brain to a space that was entirely his. He didn't even think; he just focused on a sound that could be heard, analyzed, and classified. Better than what any AA meeting could do for him. It provided him peace.

On a blue-sky day, he permitted a thought to enter the safe space reserved for his metal detecting. In the park, children on their sleds, the cliché hit him. He was walking on sunshine feeling the real love. David was six months old, and he still loved Nadia. Joy, it felt great. He picked up a beer.

Within a few days Luke had crawled back into his old skin. He forgot about his dignity, his word, and his soul. He slipped into the frenzied world of booze, cocaine, and lies. The boys at the construction site welcomed him back into the fold. They didn't care about his hangovers or his injured back; their party buddy was back in town. Let the good times roll along with the punches and the gambling dice.

The bottle had dislodged David and unhinged Nadia. Luke had once again crossed the threshold. He floated down the tributary towards Hell, the current gaining momentum and dragging everything and everyone along with him without getting caught on any of the broken branches.

❋❋❋

Six months after the birth of David, her belly remained bloated, not with the seeds of life but with the crimson of anger. Nadia had waited 15 long years for her first child. This perfect little creature had arrived into her life in full form as her life turned into unexpected misery.

"You've ruined everything, Luke!" she hurled at him. "You promised me sobriety. You've messed everything up with your stupid addiction. Why did you have to go and relapse—again! Was the last time not enough? Why? Why now? How can you do this to David? Haven't you damaged your other kids enough? You want to do the same to David? Will you ever hit rock bottom?"

Luke said nothing. He stared at his newborn child. Nadia looked at Luke looking at David and searched his face for answers. He walked out of the bedroom, grabbed his jean jacket from the hallway hook, and quietly walked away without bothering to close the front door. The frigid, minus 20 Celsius air of February couldn't match the Hell that Luke had walked out of.

Little David began to wail, throwing his tortured ancestral roots into the argument. He screamed and punched his closed fists, defending himself against a past he didn't yet own. The piercing tone of his shrieks touched Nadia's maternal instinct if not her rational self. She held David in her arms. Embracing or perhaps simply hanging on, Nadia and David's breathing slowed. Each tried to soothe the pain embedded in their bones before childbirth.

At 4:00 in the morning, when Nadia's rage had settled, she retrieved the memory of Luke standing before their son. In the dim light of her soul, she recognized that Luke could not provide the answer she wanted to the question she'd hurled at him. "Are we not enough, David and me?

Luke had forsaken his sobriety and surrendered to what would always hold him hostage, the bottle. Luke had not failed them; he had failed himself. Luke was not enough for Luke.

She realized, perhaps for the first time that not drinking and being in recovery were not the same at all. For a moment Nadia grasped the magnitude of Luke's demons. She could say "no" to that drink.

He could not. She hadn't had a drink out of choice for months. She felt better, but he did not. He had simply been white knuckling, as her sponsor had suggested might happen early on.

Luke had been taken down by the force of happiness because he hadn't yet constructed his new self. He needed to heal his personal trauma. *"Progress, not perfection."* Her compassion for him was elusive. She exploded into furor once again. There was no "we"; there was only a damaged "I" called Luke. She felt acutely aware of her impulses to wail at the world about the injustice of it all. *Don't vent your anger*, she pleaded with herself.

It was too early to phone her Al-Anon sponsor. She would have to face her wretched agony by herself. Spent by the effort of it all and the shame at her loss of control, she sat in the corner of her bedroom yielding to darkness. She lied and promised Heaven and Earth that she would be the best mom ever. She had to make the promise to stop herself drifting away from David. All she wanted was to be by herself.

✳✳✳

"I'm so wasted. I am such a big f'in' failure. To prove it, I just blew my full paycheck on booze, cocaine, and cards. There. You happy??? I'm broke and useless to you and David. Hope you had a fun night changing diapers." Luke rubbed his soiled hands over his irritated scalp.

She focused on his nearly shaven head, his nails full of grime, and his back broken by construction. Flagellated by his own mind, his torn and messy jeans, rumpled T-shirt, all of him collapsed under the weight of self-recrimination.

Nadia glued herself to the chair. She swung her long, black hair to cover her face. To hide from Luke, but also to give herself time, time to choose a different playbook. She stayed there, inside herself, just long enough to find the voice in her head trained by others, the

Self that had been forged by generations before her. She trampled her own pain and faked an answer.

"Luke."

He did not move, but lay absorbed in his inner conflict.

"Luke. You are home safely."

No reaction.

"Luke, you made it home safely. I love you. David loves you. We love you. I'm glad you are home." Nadia did not understand what she was saying. It didn't accord with her own distress.

Luke sat there. For a long time neither of them spoke. She turned to look at David in his crib. She focused on his chest heaving up and down, up and down. Once more their rhythm joined as it had during those lonely nights when they'd been left alone. Maybe she could love him once she rested up.

"Nadia."

She was afraid to hear what would come next. She had outrun her courage.

"Nadia. I need to go today. Like, I need to go to treatment again. I need to fix this because it's killing me."

In the simplicity and calm of his assertion, in the way he gazed at David, Nadia knew she would be alone again. She wondered whether he had hit a "bad bottom." It was all too quiet to be "rock bottom."

✸✸✸

On September 21, 2015, Luke walked into treatment at the Ottawa Royal Mental Health Center. He'd walked this path before, but he wanted to find the anguish that lurked inside. He wanted to throw it out in plain sight and confront it. He wanted to take its power away. He needed in a way he hadn't ever before to break its hold on him so he wouldn't strangle the life of his newborn son.

In the solitude of his room, beneath the burden of darkness, he heard an urgent sound well within:

The mirror is steamed with cloudy despair.
He's trying to find what once had stood there.
As the days turned to nights and the nights into weeks,
He's asking life questions but nobody speaks.

He's all by himself, no choice but grow fast,
And cover all pain that was brought from his past.
Years have gone by; the world still turns.
But stood still in his spot, the young boy's thoughts yearn.

Is it for answers he's been waiting to hear?
Or the curdling sounds of his thoughts and his fears.
No matter the noise, no matter the pain,
The flick of a light he feels in his brain.

Is it the response he's been wanting to get?
Could it all be gone, the hurt and regret?
The tangle and mess were dark, now it's bright.
Might these be something putting up a true fight?

The light starts to shine, the steam it recedes.
A man in plain sight, yet his young heart still bleeds.

October 16th, 2015, Luke walked out of Ottawa Royal Mental Health Centre after another 28-day treatment.

"Nadia, it will be different this time." Always the one who needed to talk. Nadia smiled, keeping her heart well-barricaded. Luke noticed that she was not holding David; she was clutching him. He walked towards her and she pushed David into his arms.

Luke knew his turn was up.

❉❉❉

Nadia told Luke she loved him and that she hated him all at once. She crept into a dark room and refused to come out.

In hushed tones, Luke had learned about postpartum depression from others. He ached as he watched Nadia reject their little angel's giggles. He yearned for Nadia to go to David's crib. He crayoned a happy family poster, but Nadia unpinned it.

Luke talked to her from the other side of the door. He told her stories of the life that awaited the three of them. They would go make snowmen in the winter snow and drink hot chocolate. They would splash in the lake and cool off with popsicles in the summer. They'd make huge piles of leaves and jump into them in the fall. Nadia could not hear him.

✳✳✳

Luke did not leave. Each day, he added another brick to the story, laying a new foundation. Day by day, the voice became a little louder. Then one day Nadia opened the door and walked out of the dark room. She wanted to bake a cake and make frosty icing. She wanted David to lick the spoon. She could possibly tolerate Luke standing on the other side of the kitchen counter and watching.

The ring on her finger could stay. Luke, the romantic, the man who asked her to marry him on an icy wintery day by the eternal flame of Parliament where they had first set eyes on each other. Luke, the man-boy who existed between the chirps and screeches of his metal detector headset and the excitement of the search for treasures in the park where everyone walked. Luke, the emerging father figure who chose to show up for little David's birth and stayed while Nadia duked it out with her rogue emotions. That Luke, well, he was a keeper.

Now she had to make herself a keeper. If she could get that baby fat off her body, she wouldn't resent David so much. It was not her son she resented; it was who she had failed to become that haunted her.

Luke left for his next construction gig. She was at the beginning of the beginning.

In the space of their physical separation, Nadia found herself breathing. She could watch over David sleeping while she recreated herself. She launched Fit and Fabulous Fresh Start—who she aspired to be, who she already was in one small but important part. She took on a new role as an Isagenix Independent Consultant. Her vision: "entrepreneur Momma whose mission is to inspire others to improve their health, well-being, and self-esteem and increase their pocketbooks." Now she would have to grow into all those aspirations.

The journey to Self would take her right back home. The only remaining question: would Luke be there? She knew David would be, and not with broken branches.

✳✳✳

"Daddy!" shouts David as Luke walks through the front door.

Nadia turns around to see Luke walk toward her. She hadn't expected him home this early.

"I took an earlier bus. We wrapped up the construction sooner."

Nadia looked at the jumble on the kitchen counter. David was covered in banana. Her lesson plan for next week was under a bowl of freshly cut avocado, and she was organizing Isagenix orders. Nadia was half-listening to something streaming on her phone with one earplug hidden behind her stack of black hair and the other dangling into her sports bra.

He followed the earphone cord as it swept down into her cleavage. He noticed the shake of her hips. He followed the contour of her body taking shape, no longer hidden in sweatpants. Leggings were so much sexier. His eyes shot up to look at her. They smiled at each other like shy kids. He swung around the counter and planted a kiss on her lips. David went wild clapping and putting his sticky hands on his mouth.

Weeks were long with each of them trying to catch up with life. Luke worked at a construction site that was an eight-hour bus ride away. The days were easier as he swung equipment around and followed the foreman's orders. The nights were the battleground. The boys, away from their family, told tales and played cards, chugging beer, casting him aside. He would lie in bed, ignoring the pain in his back, toying with sleep and staying clear of the drinking.

Nadia juggled caring for their son, teaching music for the family's benefit, and trying her hand at being an entrepreneur. She took on the supermom challenge and rebranded herself in the process. She amazed him with her energy.

❋❋❋

"Nadia, think you can put that phone away for a family dinner?" He smiled at her.

"I'm working. I'm not playing games, you know?" she shot back.

Her intensity sometimes frightened him. He worried that she was distracting herself too much from the pain he'd caused her. Often she seemed to be working too hard at being happy rather than enjoying their family. He wanted to talk about it but didn't know how to.

"Babe, I know. But sometimes you obsess. Nobody will die if you don't answer them right this minute." He knew his words were awkward, the word "obsess," a poor choice. "The company won't fail if you don't meet your sales target." He tried to relieve her from the self-imposed pressure of measuring her success.

"You're jealous," she snapped back.

"I'm not. We just said we wouldn't be the people who don't take time for their family."

"Hey, I give David all my time. What about you?" She headed for the door.

"Babe, stay. Let's talk," Luke said.

She kept walking. Talking was not her strong suit. He knew that. It puzzled him. He grew up thinking women were the ones who wanted to talk everything through. Then again, he never received guidance from a mother about these matters. Confusion and frustration jostled in his head. He couldn't figure out why she still didn't trust him. She was tiptoeing back toward the dark room.

"Hey, what's bothering you? Talk to me." He followed her up the stairs.

"Go spend time with your son. He doesn't understand that his daddy has to work out of town."

❈❈❈

The lights were dim in the park. He knew it was ridiculous to be out with his metal detector when he needed a tuque to cover his headset, and snowmobile mittens to keep warm. There wasn't much to listen for. Sure, the guys on the blogs could write about the hidden treasures fallen from people's pockets while playing with their kids in the snow. But, really, no one put an engagement ring in their pockets. The jewelry was all tucked away in layers of wool and fleece.

Imitation made him walk too fast and he couldn't steady the cadence of his swing. At this rate, he would damage the detector coil with the ice clumps. Where were all the sounds? Was something wrong with the control box? Had it frozen up? "Shit." He hit it once. Nothing was wrong.

It was Nadia. She'd managed to get into his head. He wasn't listening for the sounds. Then again, was he listening to her? What had she said during their last argument? She needed a little more fun, more people, more time playing instead of working, more time together on a date, more . . . She needed more than him.

He shook his head so abruptly that his headphones dislodged. He looked up. In the beam of light, he saw snowflakes. He drew his breath and watched it release into the mix of darkness and whiteness, distinct and dissolving into the brightness of the snowflakes and the obscurity of the night.

He could do this. He could be enough for Nadia, for David, and for himself. He could allow Nadia to be grumpy in the mornings. He could allow their son to be a wild screaming toddler and embrace his joy. He could allow his thoughts to wander just a little further into his past, bit by bit, and make his peace with it.

All he had to do was stay sober. And there's only one way to do sobriety. He was doing sober so he could keep on doing it. That's all.

✳✳✳

Luke walked into the bedroom. He'd opted to bring her coffee that morning instead of questions. Now it was late afternoon. If he didn't talk to her now, it would be supper time, bath time, and then mom entrepreneur time.

"You're pushing me away. We need to learn to talk to each other."

He noticed her turn towards the mirror. Was she looking at herself, at him, or at the past? She looked different to him, healthier and stronger. Did she see it? She was sexy, sexier than before. This sexiness attracted him, but it made him shy. It was more womanly, more assured, and more intimate. The vulnerability of their nakedness, he wanted that, but he needed more of his own self-assuredness. They needed to walk a little closer to each other's soul. Patience.

"Yes, let's talk," he said.

She failed to respond. She fidgeted with clothes in the closet.

"Nadia, I love you. Give it a chance. What's eating you up?" He tried again. It took more cajoling. Then with those big brown eyes, with the fire around the irises, she sat down on the bed. He came to her, took her hand and looked at her, not past her. He faced her and saw her.

"Rough week, Babe?"

"Yes."

"Tell me about it."

"What's there to say? Same old. Let's just have a good weekend while you're here."

"We will. But tell me, was it David? It's okay if it's hard sometimes. You are a mommy alone often."

Luke was unsure whether to just acknowledge this or apologize. His unknowing went to the core of his own ambivalence. The time apart gave him time to process their time together. The long bus rides, when the countryside turned into a string of repeating landscapes. He always looked but could never remember the order of things. Where was the garage with the funky mix of blue and orange signs? Did it come before or after that bus stop where there always seemed to be a passenger left over from a bad sitcom?

Silence.

Luke dipped his head down and looked up at her so close that his full view was of her. To make it a little easier, to honor the distance he knew she had to travel between her soul and her will to talk about herself, he closed his eyes and rested his forehead on her chin.

"Tell me," he said softly. To convince her it was safe, he stroked her forearm. Her skin, hot as a Sunday morning. This moment, together, theirs. David thankfully napping.

And she did. She talked first about work and the constant pressure of her little munchkin students twirling with inexhaustible energy. She described her week with David, one moment in love with his big blue eyes in his daddy-look-alike jeans, and then all her loose nerves when he spat out more food than he ate. She was exhausted.

"Luke, I need to do something that's for me. I want to take singing lessons."

There it was between them—a thread, a dialogue.

✳✳✳

Facebook postings became routine for Nadia. Focused on her "mompreneur" career, cheerleading her clients, mining for new ones, attending conferences. Her stage exceeded her childhood expectations. Her Isagenix followers, mentors, her friends and her family—her tribe—expanded steadily. Like the pebble in the pond analogy she favored, her circles of intimacy varied. Not everyone knew everything, but Luke knew most.

The shards of explosives from the past caught in her heart at times, but they no longer tore her down. Her tribe kept an eye on her, but she'd learned to ask them to close the circle around her when she needed support. They'd been there in August when she and Luke learned David would not have a little brother or sister.

With the briskness of September, she surrendered to gratefulness. She took to social media because of this message, she wanted to shout it.

> It's amazing what can happen when you let go and trust in God! My life has been blessed in numerous ways.

> Five years ago, I met up with a gorgeous man for coffee! Zero intentions but to make a new friend!

> In front of the Eternal Flame @ Parliament Hill he greeted me with a hug that let me know he'd hug me like that forever. Little did I know that he would be even more gorgeous on the inside!

> Luke, I trusted you with my fragile heart, and you have held it preciously ever since. What a beautiful journey we have been on so far.

> It's not only been unicorns and rainbows! We've been through some crazy stuff, but somehow what could have pulled us apart has only made us stronger!

> You make me laugh!

> You hold me when I cry!

You drive me nuts with your quirks (but I also find them adorable).

You are the amazing father I've dreamed of for my kids!

You are smoking hot (always a bonus).

You are my best friend, and I look forward to bitching and complaining at you on our front porch when we are old and grey! (Never said I was perfect.)

But most of all, I want to thank you for showing me that a past can be rewritten into beautiful new chapters!

I love you with all that I am! Your love, loyalty, and commitment is a precious gift I hold dear in my heart!

Happy anniversary my love! Looking forward to spending the rest of my life with you!

Luke noticed at random moments during the day that since becoming sober, time had slowed down—or was it that his heart and soul had entered his body? His mind was rightfully expelled to its proper place. His thoughts formulated, but without dictating. He observed her and the colors surrounding him. He saw the harmony and the discord through his feelings, not just through his brain.

He visualized Nadia walking to the kitchen from the living room and smiled. "Sappy," his brain scorned. Not really, his heart quietly murmured. The muscles in his face relaxed, and his pilot sunglasses rested better on his nose. He experienced his body differently, relaxed but charged with excitement. Sensuality, perhaps. Love, certainly.

Life on the sober side rounded the edges that had scratched all his surfaces. David already knew that, and Nadia was catching up quickly. They were taking different paths, but they intertwined often enough to know they were headed in the same direction.

✳✳✳

How do you celebrate a four-year-old?

"Pasta, cakes, and puddles!"

David wore his red raincoat, his blue and yellow rubber boots, and a little birthday hat. He jumped into the puddle of water and splashed all over while Luke took a slow-motion video complete with the exaggerated splash effects. They ate spaghetti, ravioli with lots of cheese, and then the cake.

The three of them sang "Happy birthday to you." David turned four on a Tuesday afternoon, September 25, 2018. All three of them were together in the little pasta joint, Mia Pasta, David's restaurant as he calls it, in the middle of the week.

This celebration contained so many more within it. It was a gala to honor their vision. Together they embarked on a quest for the life they yearned to create, not the life that was handed them through their genes. The time had come for them to stand up and walk out of the shadows.

Luke could not continue to work construction. He was pushing his back to the point that it would break. Nadia could not keep the lid on her entrepreneurial spirit. David could not grow up with his parents divided by distance.

Luke could stay at home, school their son in the mornings, and start his own eBay business. Nadia could reduce her teaching load, increase her Isagenix numbers and spend her afternoons homeschooling. David could spend his PJ time teaching his parents to laugh and take silly photos of the games he invented. They could redefine their family and include Luke's older sons and his daughter so that David could get to know his half-siblings.

And so they did.

Nadia spends more time on social media than Luke appreciates. Then again, she made him blush with tenderness when he read her October 16, 2018 Facebook posting:

Huge shout out to my love, Luke! Three years ago, today, you took back your life. Every step of your sobriety journey you have been strong, resilient and badass! To say I am proud would be vastly underrated. So grateful for this new path.

Life has hurled towards you blessings (and struggles) since, but you've kept on keeping on, one day at a time. My superman!

I respect you and your openness about addiction and the role model you are for the kids.

Happy 3rd! Here's to many more!

He has outgrown his hesitation to participate more buoyantly in the world. He responded:

Thanks, my love. It has been a rough rocky road at times, but you believed in me and stuck with me through the storms. I am forever grateful for you, and I love you forever and always.

❊❊❊

"My dad is an alcoholic still to this day. My dad's dad was an alcoholic who ended up finding sobriety. I'm pretty sure my dad's dad was a heavy drinker. Someday I'll have to tell David about this. I'm not going to tell him to do things one way or another. He'll be his own person. He'll have to make his own mistakes. But environment is really important. I want him to look at me and see me happy.

"Nadia and me, we have our moments. But we know the difference between moments and forever. I'd rather be with her forever. Those moments, I know they're just moments now. I can face them. We can face them."

✳✳✳

"Focus on yourself. You both need to be healthy. You want to help the other, but you can't really do anything, so you have to help yourself. The difference between my relationship with Luke and my former marriage is that I'm healthy now. I can deal with life differently now."

✳✳✳

David, with all his four and half years of wisdom and his old soul, looks up to Nadia and Luke from his bed as they tuck him in.

"Mommy and Daddy, we need to buy a magic wand so we can make everyone believe."

When Bedlam Becomes Quietude

[Tim & Chuck]

As a boy, Tim learned quickly that he and everyone around him were happiest when he cracked jokes. He grew into a clown because it accorded with his nature and allowed him to diffuse tension with a charming brashness. "Honeybunch, you look miffed as a bitch!" Or: "Don't be a tight-ass. It's not befitting a hunk like you." With his good looks, merry tongue, and soft touch, the anger directed at him never lasted very long. Tim learned to get his way with everything except the bottle. It had him by the throat.

Drinking had happened to Tim, not the other way around. He battled it from the time he was 12. Somewhere between the fairy tale of Florida and the frozen desert of Boston of his early thirties, he scared himself shitless. After a drinking binge that lasted long enough to exhaust him, he'd relieved himself in the Big Gulp on his night-stand and then blacked out. When he woke up, parched from the partying, he'd reached for the cup, having forgotten the night before. The fright was so total that he walked himself into an AA meeting, a room full of straight men.

Tim had picked the queen of hearts from the deck of cards. A gorgeous, 19-year-old deep-red-lipsticked lesbian swooped him up and dried him up with such flair, Tim forgot about drinking. United in their gayness and sobriety, they bonded. For months they told each other stories, shared dark secrets, and even managed to penetrate the AA fellowship without giving up their mutual solidarity.

There was only one power that could breach their deep bond: the bottle. The beautiful friendship crashed at her birthday party. They each returned to the hell from which they had emerged just long enough to experience their friendship. Tim burned every good thought of her and assumed she did the same. They'd ridden the wave of sobriety from Fantasy Island back to the shores of Jurassic hell.

Tim's family breached the crest of perdition along with him. His mother and father had blazed the trail countless times. No one was keeping track anymore. They trudged back up the same path equally unable to resist the call of the promised land. Each time, they tumbled down in a bundle of promises, amends, and make-believe hopes. Their innocent belief never ceased to amaze Tim. It was unclear to him who lacked the strength. Why should he care? He was eking out a life from this show.

Tim brilliantly hung on to this pattern for decades. His memory chest overfilled with bits and pieces of good times with family and friends. His mind did him the favor of erasing all the nightmares and barely remembering the well-being he might have felt in the rare moments of sobriety. In the end, the dry periods were like sprinkled chia seeds on gravy fries; they couldn't reverse the damage done by the alcohol binges.

Tim tried his luck at love in the early online dating game bolstered by a short period of sobriety when he was 34. It worked. Infatuated with Chuck, Tim panicked and headed for rehab. His intentions to give their love real oxygen were snuffed out three days later by the supposedly gay-friendly facility that strip-searched him before turning him over to the community of young, straight, super-bodied male drug addicts. Unable to withstand the taunting for being a Harry Potter lookalike and failing to connect with anyone, Tim left three days later.

The pattern recreated itself. Tim drank without limits until he was afraid to leave his bed except to relieve himself. He pulled the shades down and never turned off the TV. He pretended to watch shows that depicted a world as foreign to him as the deserts of Dubai. He talked gibberish to himself and baby talk to his pugs Hindie and Mod. Tim brought Chuck and his family to the very brink.

When everyone around him was about to explode, Tim sprang out of bed, showered, shaved, and emerged from the darkness. He appeared at breakfast looking green but filled his bowl with Fruit Loops and milk and brewed a strong cup of coconut tea. He dabbed his mouth and gushed enough tears to unfreeze Chuck's heart. He pleaded for leniency and promised to stop drinking. Chuck conceded.

Tim dried up alone in his room while Chuck handled the IT crisis line at work. Tim stared at the TV screen waiting for the hour to chime. The sound was the signal that Tim was allowed to swallow a smaller and smaller shot of vodka. This was the "tapering method" of detoxing at home. Tim, the self-perceived victim of this drying-out process, never cheated. He only drank what was measured out for him. He sweated with fear and anxiety knowing that eventually there would be no shot. He sweated in anticipation of the relief of not drinking. Gallons of Diet Coke, ginger ale, Fanta, and root beer flowed as Tim satisfied his cravings with sugary fizzy drinks.

Chuck and Tim sat on the leather couch separated by the pooches. Lyrics flowed from the Surround Sound speakers, filling the void in their dialogue when the TV was turned off.

Chuck watched movies and dramas but went to bed at 11:00 p.m. sharp without exception. He slept in the guest room. He moved his clothes into the closet, stuffed his underwear and socks in the dresser, and put away all his toiletries in the hallway bathroom. When *Intervention* came on, Chuck said, "I'm not watching this crap," and went to bed early. Tim took guilty pleasure in taping it and watching it after midnight. When the show's season ended, he watched the reruns until he ran out of soda pop.

After the first week, Tim suggested they walk the pugs. The shaking and noxiousness subsided as it always did after a few days of cold turkey terror. Tim pushed his body through the trauma by himself. The sweats, the puking, the endless wakeful hours were his alone. Even Hindie and Mod were not allowed in the jail that his bedroom became. Tim feared he might throw one of the old boys across the room. It was safer for him to be alone.

One week, then a second and a third passed. The three of them began to show promise of slimming up. The contours of their former musculature emerged behind the binging fat. They prepared healthier meals, watched more TV, and said quieter goodnights.

Darlene called Chuck at the office and inquired whether her son was still dry. When the answer was yes, she invited them for Sunday brunch. These visits home were the only time Tim and Chuck left the house together.

Inevitably, the good intentions bored Tim. His sheer will power collapsed.

"The hell with this!" Tim yelled and startled the pugs napping beside him. Hindie recognized the earthquake below the tone. Everything would be upset again. Hindie licked Tim's arm and headed for the kitchen dog bed where Mod, the wiser of the two, had already escaped. The pugs knew when to leave their master alone.

Tim believed he drank alone, but Chuck shadowed him. Wherever Chuck found a stash of vodka, he poured it out. Tim simply returned to the liquor store and replaced it on credit. Tim's artistic creativity inspired him to find more poetic hiding places. He liked to hide bottles in the porthole at the back of the living room speakers. The hidden vodka became the clichéd white elephant in the room.

Being left alone all day gave Tim a lot of time to fixate on his stashing strategy. It occurred to him that the hunting was contained to the inside of their house. He ramped up the cat and mouse game by pouring an entire liter of vodka down the garden hose and replacing the watering head: ingenious both in originality and convenience. Tim literally drank out of the water hose. Chuck never suspected.

✳✳✳

Chuck automated his life as meticulously as he debugged programs at work. Early to work, early home, and early to bed. Tim, the pugs, and TV satisfied his needs. Maturing, he contended with himself, meant that one increasingly enjoyed time at home. Fewer people in his life meant less drama and much less stress.

Tim could not be relied on to stay sober, which meant Chuck was always on call. Their lives had three, not four, seasons. A few months of dryness followed by a period of tension would crescendo in an explosion. Chuck synched his life to Tim's cycles. When Tim was happy, Chuck was happy, and their relationship thrived. When Tim crashed, Chuck followed.

Chuck's black hole was filled with self-recrimination either because he loved Tim insufficiently to keep him from relapsing or was too weak to leave him for a better life. Chuck faulted himself for choosing another broken relationship. He too had his own cycle that bottomed out with the same self-derision. He chided himself for his selfishness when his lover needed him. He tortured himself with endless questions: *If I leave him, what will he do? Where will he go? His parents will enable him. He will trip down the stairs like before, and who will call the ambulance?* Chuck waited for Tim. When it was time, he clambered out of the hole and joined Tim until the season turned cold again.

✳✳✳

Tim's parents counseled Chuck to leave Tim, yet they counted on him to monitor their son. "Here, Chuck. This will help you sort out your emotions. Maybe you can figure out how to deal with Tim in your life since you don't want to leave him." Darlene handed him a boldly masculine black leather diary.

"Thank you," replied Chuck. "I don't think so." Chuck wrote code: a system of communication appealing to him because the strings of letters and numbers had a consistent structure and definite meaning. He could rely on the same set of keystrokes to produce the same results each time. Plucking words from his soul, retrieving a mess of emotions and untangling the sensations coursing through him was out of the question. He could not predict what would tumble onto the page or what the results would be.

"I'm not a writer," he added to make clear there should be no expectations by either of them that he would undertake the task.

As for his friends, Chuck thought they were a fickle bunch. Paul and Barry, Tom and Brad, and all the others showed up for *espresso* martinis when martini bars were trending. When basil-infused cocktail bars and micro-crazy-horse breweries appeared on the scene, their friends began to choose bars that were longer drives from their home. Chuck let his friends drift away and absorbed Tim's friends as his own. Chuck told himself that he didn't have to follow the crowd. Tim's friends were now his friends. And Tim's friends stuck around.

The reality was otherwise. Exasperated by the volatile veering between rollicking drinking binges and sappy-eyed diet soda nights, Chuck's friends found other clubbers who could be counted on. They understood that they'd lost their buddy to Tim's charms. They no longer vied for Chuck's attention or his time. None of them guessed the trouble Chuck was in.

Not being a joiner or a follower, Chuck decided after two meetings that Al-Anon was not for him. He didn't need to attend six meetings before deciding, as "the program" recommended. He had no interest in sharing his experiences out loud and then listening to others essentially repeat the same stories in their own words. If he was going to venture into a circle of strangers and let down his guard, he needed a conversation. He needed opinions and, most of all, he needed answers. All that sobbing over what any decent programmer could see was a well-established pattern was crap. What he needed, what they all needed at these meetings, was a solution. What's the point of detecting the same bug over and over if you couldn't fix it?

That left Chuck with his parents as a possible sounding board; yet that was tricky. Chuck vaguely remembered his early childhood when his Dad was drinking heavily. But when he turned 12, Dad stopped cold turkey. No one talked about it. No one addressed the emotional fallout. There were other family members who had romanced the bottle, but Chuck was not sure who they were. In his world, no one went to rehab. They dealt with their drinking by stopping. They just got over it. At some point, there were more moments without drunkenness than with. The bad ones faded into the background and grew silent. Understandably, they advised their son, "If Tim can't stay sober, you'll have to leave him . . ."

End of conversation.

There were strangers as well: the veterinarian who spoke in innuendos too discreet for Chuck to understand.

"How is Tim? I could take care of Mod and Hindie when you're at work if he needs to take a month away."

"Tim, he's fine. No vacation plans for the moment," Chuck replied as he picked up the pugs. It never occurred to him that the vet was suggesting Tim go to rehab. Chuck thought the vet was referring to Tim's love of the Jersey Shore and resting from all his Crohn's complications.

❋❋❋

Tim was not fine. He was drinking again, from the heat of the summer and the unbearable fear of running out of booze. Tim drove to the liquor store trashed. The red lights flashed. The world conspired against Tim. He was charged with driving under the influence, the famous DUI dilemma. The terror of jail time had been so absolute—and intensified by the stories of what happens to gay men behind bars—that it transformed itself into a ghost-like hand that clutched the bottle out of Tim's reach.

For almost a full year he'd managed to stay sober. But the unrenewed terror eventually withered away. The ghost released its fingers long enough for Tim to snatch the bottle and run with it. And run he did, so far away from the fear that he forgot what he was afraid of in the first place. The bottle was his most loyal friend. Why had he walked out on his buddy? No reason, no reason at all.

The family crept to the edge once again. With the return of that sweet haziness, the world turned pink again. Tim professed his love for Chuck, his parents, nephews and nieces, aunts—anyone who had familial blood. Why was everyone so serious around him? He teased, joked, and found his quick tongue again. Newly romanced by the bottle, warmth and cuddles flowed from his soul after the parched days of sobriety. Everyone received his affection in the same way one embraces the last rays of fall before the frigidity of winter: with weariness.

❊❊❊

The intervention happened on a Wednesday. The day had been chosen for no reason other than the interventionist was available.

Tim prepared for his acupuncture appointment in Philadelphia. He slipped on his jeans, took a breath in so he could zip them up, then wiggled into his sneakers. He almost lost his balance as he tried to put on his pink T-shirt at the same time. He ran his hand through his messy sandy hair. He took a small swig from the flask and tossed it back into his underwear drawer.

The tangled sheets and blankets peaked on his side of the bed, the left side. A toppled Big Gulp cup, some medication bottles, a candy wrapper, used Kleenex, and a half inch of dust lay on his night table.

On the right-hand side, the night table was empty. Chuck had not used it for months, nor had he used his side of the bed.

People tiptoed into the living room downstairs, five to be exact: Chuck, Tim's sister Audrey, his mother and father plus a stranger. Their movements were anxious, as if they were attending a meeting with a doctor that would reveal a diagnosis no one wanted to hear but everyone had already guessed.

"Tim, you're going to be late," Chuck yelled with a nonchalance he did not feel. His words resonated up the stairs containing a high pitch to which Tim was oblivious. Chuck thought he would rather be at work. At least there, he could fix things. He knew how to handle the frantic calls on the IT help desk. He knew how to reboot computers, debug programs, and access information stranded behind forgotten passwords. Here he was helpless. He knew he needed to sit next to the empty chair.

Darlene sat on the other side of the empty chair. The short mother of Tim and Audrey possessed in energy what she lacked in height. No one ever underestimated her presence, least of all Tim. She silently willed Paul, the stranger in the circle, to succeed where she had failed. Both Darlene and Chuck looked up the stairwell, forgetting to breathe. Their eyes, trained to the same tension, moved from the stairs to the empty chair to the stranger.

He was the interventionist who knew no one in the room, yet he knew them all. "He'll come down when he's ready. Be patient." He stood in the middle of the circle. Dressed in a black turtleneck, black corduroys, and wafer-thin black wingtip shoes, he could have been a funeral assistant or a vampire enthusiast. The interventionist's somberness was too dark for Denny, Tim's father. Denny had stood by his son over the years, but at this very moment he wished he could erase himself from the situation. But the choice was not his. No father wanted to welcome his only son into such a circle.

Paul petted Hindie in his lap to comfort himself, not the dog. Hindie panted and looked from face to face. None of the faces smiled.

They followed Hindie's head and looked at one another wearing the same anxious memories and defeated desires for the impossible.

The stairs creaked. Hindie looked up and five other sets of eyes followed. Tim realized in a flash what was happening.

"Well, well, a little family pow-wow. And who might you be? Let me guess, you are "The Interventionist." Cool. Is there a hidden camera?" Tim smiled and waved at everyone in a regal fashion, from the wrist up. He slowed down to relish the moment. He already knew the outcome.

"Tim," started the interventionist.

"Butter Cups, I've seen the show many times. Let me make it easy for you. You'll be in and out of here in no time. I know the steps. Shall we start? My behavior is hurting you: blah-blah-blah. You love me and are concerned about me: blah-blah-blah. Who wants to go first?" Tim motioned to Hindie and Mod. "Come to poppa, my little darlings. It's storytelling time." He sat down in the place that was obviously his, the empty chair facing everyone.

Hindie abandoned Paul's lap, preferring Tim's, and gave its master a big lick on the chin. Mod, a little older, preferred to guard Tim by sitting at his feet. Tim pasted a fake smile on his face, planted his arm under his chin, lodging his head just above Hindie's and mimicked an eager child. "Who wants to read me their letter first?" He eyed his mother.

The interventionist, still stuck on the one syllable he had uttered, scrambled for the letters on the dining room table. He could feel Tim's stare on his back. He grew nervous as a debutant. He took the handwritten letter marked Darlene and walked over to her. He handed her the letter, placed his hand on her shoulder, and stood behind her. The strategy obvious to everyone: encourage the reader and impress upon the listener the strength of the circle.

Tim understood it differently. He interpreted Paul's stance less as support for his mother than a way to hide behind the group. With nothing more than his usual demeanor, Tim had stripped the interventionist of his authority in a few sentences.

Abandoned, the family unit recoiled onto itself, already projecting another botched effort. Everyone in the circle piled another layer of guilt onto their soul. Tim led the interventionist through the rest of the charade. It was unclear whether Tim played along out of some small measure of love for his family or whether to amuse himself. Tim focused intently on each reader. He tapped his fingers on his cheeks, attentive to their words, leaning into the space between him and them. They leaned away from Tim with each sentence. Their voices trembled while Tim's grew more assured.

"Thank you, Mom. I know this was not easy for you."

"Thank you, Dad."

"Oh, even you, my Sista."

And "Chuckie-pooh, you too."

When the last line was read, Tim stood up. He was shorter than the interventionist standing now behind Chuck, who was the tallest and the most shaken of them all.

"That was very touching, all of you. But, no, I am not going to rehab. Those tight ass folks don't know what to do with a fag like me. Besides, you know me. I can control this thing. So, nope, *nada*, not a fucking chance. Enjoy your little family party. I'm off to acupuncture." Tim reached for the car keys in his jean pockets and turned his back on them.

When they were just about to heave a sigh of relief that it was over, Tim turned around, walked back to his Mom, leaned over her, and planted a big, loud kiss on her forehead.

"Mumsie, you shouldn't waste your money on this chimpanzee. He is mute. Hope you have a money-back guarantee." Tim turned to face the interventionist still standing behind Chuck. Chuck busied himself folding the last letter, pressing the creases, and avoiding Tim's eye contact. "Are you an interventionist in training or what? You forgot to have each of them include an ultimatum in their letters. Really. You fucked up buddy. I'd look for another career if I were you."

Tim pranced towards the door as gay as an androgynous Tele-tubby. Halfway through the door, he turned around again. He beamed with confidence and arrogance as he addressed Paul.

"Hey asshole, make sure you give my Mom a refund and tell whichever rehab center you're from, no commission for you."

***

Emboldened by successfully thwarting the intervention and by the red wine, Tim walked into the kitchen carrying a monster plastic cup of boxed red wine.

"You are not going to drink this in front of me," said his mother.

"I'm sorry, Mom. I have to or else I'm going to be sick."

A wild woman trapped in his mother's body snagged the cup and threw it on the floor. The force of her gesture jack-hammered through Tim's impenetrable exterior. This woman, his mother, talked, raised her voice, and then screamed. *Poor Mumsie.* The exhausted shouting transformed her face into a contortion of flesh, wrinkles, and popping eyeballs. All this wasted effort. Deaf by practice, Tim stared hard at her until the vision of the woman he loved the most in the entire world blurred into a splash of distracting colors, relieving him from the obligation of seeing her.

"You are not fucking going to drink this in front of me," she yelled again. *"Fuck!"*

Mumsie had used the F-word. The shock of it broke his breath. She stared at the splattered wine, the mess of it, of all of this—their lives and their family. She continued to stare: too burgundy, it could be either his or her blood. Too easy to clean it up and pretend it hadn't happened, not even a broken glass. She'd lost control. She'd lost the fight. Again.

Except, she hadn't.

***

Tim had been so shaken by the terror of his mother's verbal lashing, he'd checked himself into a rehab. He, Tim, had done this to himself. He was going to try detox and stay with it again. He had asked his mom to drive him to prevent himself from changing his mind halfway there. Having resolved to do this, he gave himself permission to drink with abandon until it was time to go. He drank so much that by the time he hopped into the back seat of his mother's car, he forgot where they were going. Even the sight of Chuck loading his suitcase in the trunk meant nothing.

Sunrays penetrated the frost-covered ground along the rolling hills, a small gift of hope that February would eventually end. Tim sat in the back seat of his mother's car, flushed with heat from the Smirnoff he drained with a fat purple milkshake straw. He saw state liquor stores and fine wine outlets along the way oblivious to the distance growing between each one. He ignored the pubs in the same way he did the coffee shops and diners. He no longer remembered how it felt to drink in public. Aside from the rare Thanksgiving and Christmas family parties, he drank tucked under his duvet out of plastic cups. Less chance he would trip when in bed, less chance he would cut himself on shards of knocked-over glasses.

Darlene clutched the steering wheel and bargained with God. She offered to give up chocolate, trips to New York City, and even the Giants' football season. She reminded the Almighty that even a mother's heart could split open. She reminded Him of all that had passed. The misspent hopes, dashed after the first rehab treatment that became just one in a string of many, bringing her and Denny to the brink of financial disaster. The paroxysms of self-hate that drove Tim to drink more intensely after each relapse. She assured Him that Tim was a good boy, a kind boy, and that the burden of his Crohn's disease was sufficiently difficult that he should be relieved from the agony of his addiction.

Darlene had negotiated all these bargains with God before. If God released Tim from his drinking binges, she would volunteer at hospice until she was too old to stand up. Surely that was a fair trade: commute Tim's life sentence for a crime he did not commit in exchange for her commitment to care for the dying. She would replace their colostomy bags and hold their lonely hands as they died. God had to see that she could not lose her son, not this way. She didn't deserve to, no mother did.

Tim hummed to himself in the back seat, leaning against the cool window glass to temper the heat inside his head. A *beautiful equilibrium of temperatures*, he mused, fully consumed by his bodily state of well-being. Dialogues had long ago vanished from his repertoire. He spouted comic lines, yelled demands at Chuck, or slurred fibs of emotion to Hindie and Mod. He felt content with that corridor of communication.

Images of familiarity splashed around Tim's vodka-infused brain: the open field with the community baseball diamond, the rusted yellow teeter-totter next to swings with peeling paint, and the thin-crusted sand patch. His mind struggled to place these items in some context, but it was too much hard work. He closed his eyes and sucked the straw.

A memory came to disturb his back-seat slumber. He could not place it in time, but he did remember this same experience. This moment had happened before. Damn, he could be brilliant at times, remembering experiences from his past without much prodding. He amused himself by debating the extent of his mental prowess until the flashback could no longer be ignored.

Loneliness, sheer aloneness, waited for him at the end of this drive. He had been here once before. The sensation rather than the image from the time surfaced. Forlorn, abandoned in a room without his trusted friend, he lay for hours in a room at rehab where his brother-in-law had driven him. He had agreed to be there, but his resolve to make a life for him and Chuck had flip-flopped after just one night. The reality of life without his true buddy, the bottle, grew larger than the nightmare of his tormented relationship. No, he hadn't been ready for such a life. How would he deal with the pain of his disease? He wasn't facing his cursed Crohn's disease on his own. No one understood the excruciating pain in his stomach. A taxi ride had returned him to the safety of his bedroom at the small cost of $350 plus $10.99 at the local wine store.

Now, as the miles between him and his home mounted, he vaguely recognized the road. Someone else had driven him then. The silence, though. Yes, the silence was the running thread between both experiences. She drove without talking. She was too busy striking a bargain with God.

The memory of the landscape had burrowed itself in his memory attached to the shameful recollection that he had failed. He was headed to the same rehab. His mother had chosen the same place. How could she? This was the road to and from Hell. Tim sucked harder on the straw, grateful this time he had Smirnoff. With any luck, the stay would be over quickly. Just like the last time.

At least Tim would be able to ward off the repulsion he felt for himself when he thought of his mother's breakdown. He could tell himself he had tried. He had gone back to rehab. But it was not for him. Everyone would empathize, everyone would resume their roles, and life would go on. He would just feel less guilty about treating his Crohn's with alcohol. He promised, not God but his forever companions Hindie and Mod, that he would fully banish this trip from his recollection on his way home in a day or two. There was no point discussing this with his mother now. She was concentrating on the road. But they would talk when he came back. Maybe this time she would understand. What was clear in his mind was that he would not part ways with his blood brother, Smirnoff. They were not going separate ways.

❊❊❊

Chuck lived in a strange space between absolute relief with Tim's absence and the underlying tension that he would walk through the front door at any moment. Sudden freedom from the burden of caring for Tim created loneliness in one moment and an intense joy in another. Brave in his determination to reconnect with his friends, he picked up his cell phone but failed to dial. His courage was flooded by doubts of whether he would need to start dating again because a sober Tim might not love him anymore. Master of the house, no longer enslaved by Tim's moods and neediness, he reclaimed the kitchen and living room but could not bring himself to move back into the master bedroom again. The see-saw of emotions exhausted him.

As the hours turned into night and day again, Chuck slept as much to replenish his energy as to avoid the rawness of his feelings. He slept some more. Tension mounted as he waited for the phone to ring. Damn, Tim. Why was he not calling? Was he using his 15-minute telephone pass to talk with someone else?

Chuck marveled at the ease he enjoyed in their home without Tim there. Loneliness never crept in. His optimism quickly reappeared as he tossed all the empties and the stashes he found around the house. He cleaned out Tim's room. Hindie and Mod bounced and barked around like young kids scolded into submissive obedience. Chuck stacked the 'fridge shelves with cases of Coke, ginger ale, and 7-Up.

Chuck tackled his garage. He had abandoned his tools; he'd let Tim's boxes of jewelry making stuff infringe on his space. Projects lie unfinished: the patio herb planter Tim had broken when he'd fallen over drunk, the neighbor's neglected toaster oven he had promised to fix, and Darlene's floor lamp she'd now replaced. Chuck devoted himself to each project with undivided attention. His interest in rewiring grew again, so did his love of drilling, gluing, sanding, measuring, cutting, screwing, threading, nailing. He indulged himself in the joy of fixing things that could be fixed.

The call came. Tim's first call from rehab.

"Are you going to visit me this weekend?" Tim asked.

"When?" Chuck replied to give himself time.

"Sunday," Tim said.

In the silence that separated the question and the answer, thoughts terrorized each of them.

Tim's terror: *He's deciding whether he should come or let me wither away here. He's thinking about how early he needs to get up to make it on time. I know he is out bar hopping with his friends while I'm in here. There's no way Chuckie Pooh is staying at home by himself, especially not on a Saturday night. No one is fooling anybody here. I'm fucked. If he doesn't come, I won't make it.*

Chuck's terror: *I don't want to do this. He's locked up there. Can't he just stay? Can't we just leave him for a while longer? I promised Joe I'd fix his lawn mower over the weekend. I'm screwed. I must go. If he doesn't make it, I'll always blame myself. If I don't go, we don't stand a chance of making it.*

Chuck broke the silence. "Yeah. I'll go." They both hung up. What else was there to say?

On the first Sunday, they walked around campus and talked like tourists. Tim pointed and told Chuck stories about rehab. Chuck asked questions without caring about the answers. They discussed the family. Mostly they told stories about the pugs. Hindie and Mod were always a safe subject.

They talked 15 minutes every few days when Tim used up his telephone passes. Without the pressure of being together, they talked more openly and listened more intently. The following Sundays were easier. The conversation thawed, warming them at times but frigid on the edges when one of them tried to say too much too quickly. Bit by bit, the ice cracked: sometimes it melted, and sometimes it repositioned and froze over again. There were strange sounds caused by awkward pauses, nervous punch lines, and sentences left dangling in unfamiliar pitches. Energy surged but then flashbacks drained it. The visits were confusing, the time in between necessary.

Traveling between anxiety and hope, Tim stayed put at rehab. Chuck began to harbor thoughts that this time could be different. Darlene and Denny waited for their son. The pugs lifted their expectant heads in unison each time the front door opened.

By some unnamed Grace, time turned into 28 days.

***

Light emanated from the windows, bouncing strings of blues, greens, and reds on the mishmash of gems scattered all over the surfaces. Tim swirled around the third bedroom converted into his work-space. He paused to admire the earrings. He would describe them as "sparkly blue" when he posted these beauties crafted from Montana sapphire with clean diamond cut lines on eBay to sell them. "Incred-ible fireworks" in the form of a green gemstone quivered next to the sterling ring that awaited its centerpiece. Nestled among the jumble of colors rested the opal. A fossilized ammonite, rainbow colored, genuine Canadian stone that he would transform into an exquisite piece of jewelry to adorn a lovely female neck. This room energized his creative sensitivities.

Tim talked to his gems while he set them. He told them fairy tales, and they whispered stories about where they hailed from: Aus-tralia, Cambodia, Idaho, UK, the Caribbean. By the time they appeared on his eBay listings, they were old friends bonded by their time together. Everything was simple and safe here.

Each stone was polished by his touch. Each one bore witness to the days of sobriety that Tim accumulated. Each one heard him process his emotions since he left Caron two years ago. The sadness of the pain his Crohn's disease inflicted on Chuckie and his family, the isolation of his failure in the creative world after graduating from art school, the years of faking a career as a recruiter in corporate America, the dislocation of the bond between his sister and him, the shame and self-loathing covered by his dumbass behavior, all those sabotaging voices in his head shouting "bad, bad, bad boy," he left them bit by bit in the cracks of the gem. With each sale, his self-confidence grew.

Tim dragged himself to a few AA meetings but stopped. He did not belong there any more than a piece of amber fit into a bubble gum ring. He did stick to the outpatient sessions. The counselors helped him develop a more balanced view of himself, of his disease of addiction, and of his complicity with the painkillers to treat his post-surgery agonies. The counselors, like his former art professors, invariably forced him to look more deeply. His gems and his jewelry occupied his swirling brain, allowing Tim to become acquainted with the rough edges of his emotions.

Tim hated how his diseases robbed him of a chock-full better life. All the damn surgeries, the pain, the hospitals. He recognized that he'd turned himself into a clown. Sure, he loved his quick tongue and felt quite at home with his gay-boy, love-you-sweet-buns attitude that attracted the many fun seeking and affection deprived characters in his life. To use the cliché, he could get away with murder because everyone loved his attention. He flattered women with names of Baby Cake and men with Gorgeous Hunk. Behind the lightness hid a fear to test the authenticity of the friendships.

All his dependency on Chuck, not only to be his sexy chauffeur to medical appointments, but to clean up the messes from his Crohn's puking, to tend to his loneliness at the hospitals and calm his pre-surgery nerves. More than once, Chuck dissuaded Tim from strangling one of those wilted run-off-their-feet Miss Hot Lips Houlihan nurse look-alikes who insisted that Tim turn off the TV. Tim's hives were caused as much by his medical complications as his guilt about needing Chuck.

Chuckie Pooh didn't imagine when he fell in love with Tim that he would soon trade carrying shots to their loads of friends at a pub table to balancing trays of adult baby food, pills, and water from the kitchen up to their bedroom where Tim lay in a mound of bloated disaffection. Tim never intended to have to rely on Chuck's health insurance and finances. The subtext of all their interactions seemed to be that Tim always needs and Chuck gives. Tim resented his own constant needing. How could Tim know whether Chuck stayed with him because his armor, fashioned from caretaker steel since he was a kid, was stronger than his I-can-fix-anything self-image? That question was always an introduction to the more troublesome realization that Tim had no other options because their love and dependency were so tightly wound, neither knew how to release the other. Both were too afraid to see if they could stand free of one another without collapsing into each other.

With his shaky hands, his squirming belly, and blink-long attention span, Tim distracted himself with earrings, pendants, rings, and the odd cartoon sketch. These were certainties in his life. He knew how to measure and fit a diamond-cut sapphire into a dainty teardrop necklace or an overstated index finger ring. Jewelry making morphed Tim. It popped the top of his creativity that had been repressed for years. It made him less of a moocher. His eBay sales covered the soda cases and premium coconut tea that kept him sober. The chats with suppliers and buyers provided him a safe haven for narrow conversations with people unsuspecting of his fragile sober state and his previous inebriated dealings.

With time, Tim discovered other certainties in his life. Chuck did not resent him for his illness from Crohn's Disease, only for his addiction. Sobriety did not steal his glee for the New Jersey boardwalks, carnival pageantry, arcade shouts, and roller coaster rides by the beach. His friends did stick around when he was sober. He could cuddle with Chuck watching TV shows, sighing along with Hindie and Mod. Mumsie and Dad had aged but grew steadier in their love for one another. Love could endure.

❋❋❋

Rehab taught Chuck that Tim had to deal with his addiction, and he was along just for the ride. With Tim safe at home and without booze, Chuck unhitched from the joyride. The more time that separated them from Caron, the greater was the melancholy that drifted into Chuck's days. His emotions would percolate and dribble out of his corners. The living room couch trapped him. While Tim roared next to him, "Chuckie, this is outrageous. I love it!" and slurped his Diet Coke, Chuck choked on sadness.

"What the hell are you crying for?" Tim asked.

"I love your big brown eyes," Chuck said.

Tim teared up with joy, but Chuck teared up with heartache.

Handyman Chuck filled his time at home with fixing leaking taps, filling cracks in the bathroom floor, and straightening kitchen shelves. One by one he checked off the previously ignored home projects on the Honey-Do List. His activity staved off thoughts of Tim's inevitable relapse.

No one was there to fill Chuck's cracks. At first, he tried to tell Tim what the dark years had been like for him. "The time you were in bed for days so wasted and oblivious hanging on to Hindie, I was down here with old Mod trying to figure out what to do. Do you have any idea what it feels like to see the man you love try to drink himself to death and not be able to do anything to help him? I was dazed at work, sleep deprived and so alone."

"You want to talk about alone? Try being in rehab with 29 straight men who think your being gay is a bigger problem than drinking. Try being away from your family and friends for 28 days. Try figuring out how you to manage pain in your stomach so excruciating you want to die," Tim replied.

Chuck clammed up. There was no point. They could see each other but they could not understand each other. Chuck knew what being on the outside felt like. As the poorest kid in his class, he'd learned to tuck his wants away. No point wishing for what you cannot have.

Without the pressure to constantly search for booze stashes to clean out, Chuck found time to reacquaint himself with his emotions. At first, Chuck had to separate his feelings from what Tim told him he was feeling. The similarities between his work and his internal condition were obvious. The alcohol played the same role in their relationship as a Trojan virus infecting a computer. Disguised as a legitimate way of socially interacting, drinking is like malware to someone with a substance use disorder; it destroys everything by hacking into your system. Addiction gains malicious access, infects your thoughts and emotions, remotely controlling you to act in a self-destructive way. Rebooting a computer is just as ineffective as leaving the drinker.

Chuck was a program with a bug. All those years of Tim's drinking had recoded Chuck into focusing only on Tim: his Crohn's, his physical pain, his social needs, his this and that. Chuck needed to find his source code and reprogram it to bypass Tim.

Solitude and time helped Chuck focus on his process. As he cleaned the living room he mulled over all those resentments from Tim's drunken slurs and his own nasty retaliatory responses. He cringed when he remembered Tim yelling "You're with me because you're so boring no one else wants you" and his shameful response: "Spoken like a real drunk who can't see how disgusting he's become." One by one, he took as many painful memories as he could endure and placed them in the context of the disease. He considered them until the sting he felt was gone. He rewired his brain to examine his own emotions and actions. He became aware of his self-defeating behavior and his way of abdicating responsibility for his own life by being Tim's five-star caregiver.

Chuck practiced forgiving Tim and then forgiving himself. He weeded the little patch of green in the backyard and pulled out the roots of his anger anchored deep within by accepting that life was not fair. Grudgingly, Chuck admitted to himself that Tim had a point. He was a little boy wanting to save his best friend so he could feel himself a superman.

❋❋❋

"Tim, tell me you're not watching that show again?" Chuck asked with more than an obvious hint of disapproval as he carried some chips and Diet Coke into the living room.

"I am, Chuckie Pooh. You know I never miss an episode." Tim replied.

"It's bad for you. It gives you ideas on how to drink, places to hide your bottles, and how to get away with it." Chuck's shoulders tightened under his baggy T-shirt. "It makes me wonder if you're thinking about it, you know, romancing the idea of drinking." His voice pitched uncontrollably. The acrid taste crawled up his throat.

"It's okay, Honey. Relax. *Intervention* is my AA. It makes me sad to see how destroyed these people are. This was me four years ago," Tim said, glued to the screen.

Silence.

"Come on, Babes. It reminds me of why I'm a cheap date now. Why Coke is my drink of choice. It grounds me," Tim said, placing his hand on Chuck's restless leg. "It's my obligation to watch it. You know I don't miss an episode. Ever."

Tim knew the show's format and the emotional ping it looked to trigger in its audience. He hadn't seen this episode before, but it was always the same. The show chronicled people like Tim grinding their lives into bits and pieces until they crashed. It documented the emotional horrors inflicted by this disease on everyone around them, slowly depriving everybody of oxygen, to see if anyone would be left standing. Tim knew his brain would slowly atrophy the memories of his own destructive path. He watched the show to remember. He was not giving that "f'n" disease a chance to get near him again.

Chuck fiddled with the potato chip bag, unsure to do.

Tim softened his grin. He turned his full attention to Chuck and playfully blinked his brown eyes. He looked directly at Chuck, the man he loved, and recognized fear. Chuck returned Tim's gaze. Chuck saw in it Tim's acknowledgment of his need not to forget.

Chuck held the gaze of this precious soul, the man he loved and would continue to love. In that moment, between Hindie's heavy breathing and a soap commercial, they'd managed to be vulnerable to each other.

"Sweetie, if it's okay with you, I'll skip this episode," Chuck said.

"That's fine, Babe."

"I'll finish up the dishes," Chuck said.

"Sounds good. I'll call you when it's over. We can watch whatever you like next." He plunked a kiss on Chuck's cheek and returned his attention to the show.

As Chuck returned to the kitchen, he threw a look back at Tim as he took his place next to Hindie. He let out a soft "hum" and shook his head with a big silly grin. He hummed as he cleared the sink. *Just like that. We can talk. I can walk away and he can stay, and we can come together again.* Chuck's mind drifted to last night and how warm and easy their lovemaking had been. *Each being their own person sure was a turn-on.*

***

"Honey, I'm going to pass out. Do not call the ambulance," Tim said with surprising force and promptly passed out.

Chuck called Darlene. She was on speed dial.

"Call the ambulance, Chuck. I don't care what he said. We can't play with his life." Darlene said, taking charge.

Three days later, Tim woke to a white coat, Chuck, and his mom and something stuck to his side. The prognosis was worse than the previous ones: perforated colon, 10 percent chance of survival. And that thing stuck to his side was a shit-bag which everyone preferred to call by its proper medical term: a colostomy bag.

Tim knew with the greatest certainty of his life that he was done with alcohol. He wanted to live more than he wanted to die. No way would he tempt fate now that he couldn't even hold his shit inside. At least he hadn't lost his sense of humor.

The gratitude Tim experienced in that hospital room felt freaky. He realized that sobriety was his lifesaver. Without it, he would have woken up in a casket.

Six months later, he woke up alone with a blasting hangover in his bedroom. He consoled himself that the headache was far less painful than that cleaver tearing up his stomach. He reached for his Big Gulp cup. Empty. Damn, did he finish all that vodka last night?

"Chuck, where's my fucking vodka? You steal it again, you sandbag?" Tim yelled from under the blankets.

"I'll bring you up some Coke," Chuck replied from downstairs.

"I don't want bloody pop; I want vodka. I can't deal with this hell. My stomach is killing me."

"The vodka is killing you. Stick with a natural death."

"Fuck you, Chuck. I'll get it myself." Tim got to his feet. When he made it to the door only a few feet away, he realized Chuck had barricaded him. The idiot had moved the dresser so Tim could not get out. "What the hell are you doing? Holding me hostage again!"

"Preventing you from injuring yourself, asshole. Remember last time you were this drunk, you went down the stairs head-first. No, you can't remember. You were so drunk, you passed out."

"Stop being an ass. I want a drink, so I'll drink. You can't stop me."

Appearing from nowhere, Chuck suddenly was face-to-face with Tim. He tossed Tim on the bed.

"Lie down, you jerk. You aren't going anywhere. I'll get you whatever you want except booze."

"That's the only thing I want. Get out of my goddamn way. Get off me." Tim balled up his fist and punched Chuck in the gut with all his anger. It was the first punch he'd thrown in his life.

Chuck reacted by throwing Tim back on the bed, sitting on top of him and slapping him across the face. Stunned by his own physical aggression, he got up and ran downstairs.

"Darlene, it's Chuck. I just hit Tim. I can't do this again. He has been drinking for three days. You or Denny need to get over here. We're out of control," Chuck said.

"Chuck, call the cops." Darlene said.

"But I hit him," Chuck protested.

"Call the cops. He hit you first. He needs to go to jail and sober up. He can't drink in his condition. Nothing will stop him now that he's started. Call the cops. I'm on my way," Darlene said and hung up.

The relapse had lasted four days. Tim had never punched anyone before. Chuck had never lost control like this. The beast had awoken with such ferocity, neither one of them knew how to exist. The cops gave Tim a choice: ER or jail. Tim chose ER. ER led to a bed at Princeton House which led to out-patient treatment.

Worse than the humiliation of returning to rehab was resetting the clock. Tim had blown over 1,800 days of sobriety. He had to learn to face that he was now only hours sober. His self-image was shot to pieces.

✳✳✳

The pink cloud reappeared. This time Chuck knew how to recognize the hues, and although it was pretty, he was less mesmerized by it. He knew that although he wanted to support Tim, Tim was the only one who could stay sober. His addictive condition was permanent. If Tim needed to bask in the beauty of the pink cloud to get back on track, he could give him that space.

Chuck knew that Tim counted on his health insurance and his salary. He relied on Chuck when he was sick, too. It was so easy for Chuck to pull out his superman cap. This time around he resisted the urge. He stuffed his hands in his jean pocket and headed for his garage. There was a ceiling fan to fix and a baseboard to repaint. The neighbor had asked Chuck for help to repair his leaking bathtub faucet. Chuck realized his sanity lay in performing those small tasks. He could be Mr. Fix-It in his garage shop but not in Tim's head.

✳✳✳

"Honey, I'm going back to painting," Tim announced as he walked into the bedroom.

"Back to painting?" Chuck asked.

"Well, you know, I did graduate from Art school, mister," Tim winked. "I talked to Mumsie and we're going to do paint night with a twist at her place."

"We? With a twist?" Chuck asked sitting down on the bed after stripping down to his boxer shorts.

"It's up to you if you want to join. It'll be a blast with the girls. They need to blow off some steam," Tim said. "It's extra cash," he added.

"Sounds good. I'll come once in a while, but I don't promise to stick around every time."

"Deal."

They snuggled under the covers. Chuck liked that they chatted now before falling asleep. In the dimness of the bedroom and the warmth of their embrace, they often broached the stickier issues. Chuck felt safe when they talked this way. Even if sometimes the subjects were a bit out of his comfort zone, there was something special about it. The two of them chatted to the sound of Hindie and not so young Mod snoring like hogs.

"Sweetie, you think it's safe to do paint night with a twist?" Chuck asked, treading lightly.

"Honey bunch, you know I haven't touched the stuff for three years now," Tim said, managing to keep the reproach from his tone.

"I know. It's just that painting and booze—that was another part of your life," Chuck said. "Before me," he added.

"Babes, we need to keep moving forward. I'm not in the past anymore. I'm a social animal, you know that. I feel good about it. The relapse, I think I needed it to happen. I needed to see just how this disease could whip my ass so quickly."

"It's a nice ass," Chuck interrupted.

"Thanks, Babes. It's hard for me to think about sometimes. All it took was three days of drinking, and I smacked you. You, Chuckie Pooh, the guy who is always there for me. No matter what. I'm not going to do it again. I guess I just needed that one reminder," Tim said.

Chuck stroked the back of his neck and said, "You know this thing is always going to be around us? It will never be a completed project."

"I know, Babes, like my Crohn's and my crummy health. But you in my life, that's complete," Tim said. "Ah, who's getting all lovey dovey now?" Chuck teased.

"Who's getting all funny duddy?" Tim replied.

They fell asleep. Neither of them dreaming fairy tales, neither of them immune to the risks of their life together, but with a quiet certitude that they could and would grow old together just like their parents.

You're the One

[Bill & Chantal]

Chantal stared at the phone, willing her fingers to dial the number. Bill had given it to her yesterday, in this same room, their home office. *"Call Rick for me tomorrow, after I am gone. I just can't do it."* He was Bill's best friend, and she hardly knew him. Why had she taken on this responsibility? It was one of many questions she needed to answer for herself in the next month.

"Rick, it's Chantal."

"Hi." Rick said. There was an uncomfortable silence at the other end of the line. Chantal had never called him before.

"Rick, Bill asked me to call you. He won't be able to talk to you for the next 31 days. He's in rehab."

"Rehab? Has he been in an accident?"

"Alcohol rehab, detox rehab, treatment rehab," she said.

"What the hell? He's not an alcoholic. Bill enjoys his drinks, but he's the most together man I've ever met. What's happening? What have you done to him?" Rick's tone grew accusatory.

"Rick, listen, it's the right thing. Bill can't control his alcohol anymore."

"Give the guy a break. He's in the middle of an ugly divorce, his kids are upset, and his mother just died. Anyone would be drinking their way through that. He does not have a problem—he's just in a tough place. He's been to hell and back since he left his job. Where is he? I'll call him." Rick was shouting.

"Rick, he is where he needs to be." She hesitated. Where was the line between convincing Rick and shaming Bill? "He can't control it anymore. He has vodka in his juice at six a.m., Kahlua in his coffee at nine, wine starting at lunch, and Scotch for dessert," Chantal said.

"He isn't an alcoholic. You have to get him out of there. He doesn't need this right now. He needs his friends."

"He's where he needs to be. If he doesn't belong, the rehab will release him. They told me they assess people in the first 24 hours. Rick, I am his friend, and I love him more than anything. He needs this, trust me."

"No. I want to talk to him. Where is he?" Rick pressed.

"Rick, I'll keep you updated. He can't talk to anyone right now. He'll call you when he can. He wanted me to let you know. I have to go now. Bye, Rick." She hung up.

Chantal collapsed back into the wingback chair. She glanced up at the diplomas on the wall: undergraduate, law school, MBA, Ontario Law Society, and New York State Bar. She felt bewildered at how she'd ended up on this call.

Less than one year ago, Chantal and Bill had moved to Philadelphia. She had bought a brownstone house in the Art Museum area where they could both have a fresh start. They craved roots. They yearned for a home. Neither of them had any local history of jobs, family, or friends. They could finally explore the depth of their feelings for each other. They could recharge after years of high-powered executive careers on expat assignments and invent a common future. That had been the dream. Reality, however, had turned out differently.

The moving boxes were still unpacked when Bill received a call that his mother was gravely ill. Chantal knew how to deal with family crisis, and in less than twelve hours, the Jeep was packed, the house secured, and the drive to London, Canada, began. She had that take charge, put-everything-on-hold gene embedded in her soul. No conscious choice or deliberation was needed.

The months of illness were grueling. Chantal stood by Bill at his mother's bedside. She did not shy away when the woman she barely knew asked her to swab her mouth or brush her hair as if Chantal had been her daughter-in-law. Chantal had conceded her place when Bill's estranged wife, legally separated but emotionally entangled, claimed her right to see her mother-in-law. The humiliation Chantal was subjected to by this woman at the funeral reception had burned a deep scar on Chantal's heart—right next to those left by her own father.

The struggle between Bill and his ex-wife—as decreed by the courts a month later—engulfed the new couple's lives, darkening their every step in Philadelphia. Buried below all the dirt of divorce, his resentful adult children, the grieving for his mother, their move across the country, and early retirement, was another truth yet to be unearthed: Bill was a high-functioning alcoholic.

✳✳✳

Chantal sat on the couch in the darkness of a late January afternoon. She chased away the images that tormented her—scenes littered with a broken mirror, unending nights of slammed doors, and hurtful words as each held onto the other, each damaging the other. Caught in a cataclysm neither could understand or control, they questioned everything, from their relationship to the essence of their individual lives.

Chantal eased and teased her mood by listening to the Köln Concert, empathizing with the pain Jarrett felt when he improvised the masterpiece. Grasping for bits of comfort in books, she wistfully hoped that she too could claim some moment of lucidity in her distress. She hardly noticed that her cup of Rooibos tea was cold. The book she held irritated her just as the out-of-tune piano had nearly provoked Jarrett into cancelling the performance that had become her beacon in troubled times. If only she had the option to call off her appearance in this drama. Or, did she? She resented the book she was trying to read: *Of Course You're Angry: A Guide to Dealing with the Emotions of Substance Abuse.* She snapped it closed and tossed it on the stack of equally offensive titles on the coffee table: *The Recovery Book, Co-Dependent No More, Games Alcoholics Play, One Day at A Time,* and *Courage to Change.* Great new reading list.

The internal opera began:

> ***The overture:*** *Chantal, learn all you can. You are up to the challenge. You have the strength of two. You must take control of this mess.*
>
> ***First aria:*** *Why does he get off the hook?*
>
> ***Chorus:*** *He's not responsible for his drinking because he has an illness.*
>
> ***Second aria:*** *Isn't that convenient for him?*
>
> ***Chorus:*** *You are responsible for your life. You are a certified Co-dependent. Go fix that.*

She threw the remote at the stereo. She wanted to pounce on something, anything. But there was no prey, only this inner voice she could not silence. She curled up once more on the sofa.

Damn this Hell that Bill had caused in her life! This was her home. She did not have a drinking problem. She wanted to enjoy a glass of wine in front of her fireplace, like normal people do. She had paid her way in life. Now she longed to sip on her wine while listening to Ravel and reading Isabel Allende while cuddled up with her lover. Why did Bill have to spoil this long-awaited time? Why did guilt have to strangle her wish for something so ordinary?

Chantal found herself in a strange place. She loved a man who was in rehab. Everyone around him, except his sister, was in denial. Chantal had not kicked him out of her house even though he'd corrupted the peace within it. They were not married. They had no children. In fact, she had absolutely no commitment from him. It would have been much easier to leave him, but she was making the harder choice to stay.

Why?

> Letter from Bill, January 25, 2009,
> from Caron Treatment Center
>
> Dear Chantal,
>
> I thought we had a really great first date today. I hope you didn't mind my 25 rehab chaperones that were with us. Actually, it felt very much like a first date and sort of like seeing you at Penn's Landing a year ago after so long. I was nervous at first, but once I connected with those blue eyes, then everything felt warm and peaceful. And I felt so much love for you. I really do think of it as my first date of sobriety and what an amazing, sexy woman to have that first date with. I'm very lucky.
>
> I'm feeling really good tonight. I have you, the love of my life, and I'm taking care of the one thing that would have come between us. So, the future looks really great from here. So much ahead to look forward to! This week I'll be working on my treatment plan and goals for the year which we can share next Sunday on our second date. I'm making a big assumption that you like me, and that we'll have a second date.
>
> Have a great week! Take care.
>
> Love You Big Time (LYBT)
>
> Bill (xoxo)

Chantal settled into her favorite tea shop and watched people walking by. Some were dressed for winter while others pretended it hadn't arrived, coddling their morning coffee cups for warmth. She preferred looking out the window to focusing on the task at hand. It was unfair that she had to write the "Cost Letter." It was part of the process. "Loved ones"—she hated that term—were asked to write a letter to the alcoholic explaining exactly what the disease had personally cost them.

Bill had been gone for ten days now, and she was stuck with this homework assignment. She was confident she had sufficiently self-flagellated for being blind to his crash. She now understood Bill had a disease. She had dutifully attended regular Al-Anon meetings, as well as the Sunday talk at Caron before the first weekly visit, and had committed to participating in the Family Education Program in two weeks.

She wrestled with the anger stirred by the requirement that she write this letter. She knew that counselors and others would read it. It felt like an intrusion into her personal life. Her resentment was growing. The burden seemed unjustified given their brief history. Then she thought of Rick. Who else could write this letter but her?

Chantal knew herself well enough to understand that her anger was a simple cover-up for her fear. She was trapped. She was being called upon to be honest. The truth would hurt Bill and shame her. Bill's Achilles heel had always been guilt. Sober, he would have to obey this compulsion. She would be the necessary casualty of his deep-seated need to fix his family. She knew she might mean a lot to him, but she was not his family.

Chantal's own Achilles heel dovetailed his disease handsomely. She was the poster child for the dutiful daughter. She had consciously abdicated her right to walk away. She would stand by his side while he tried to right his life. She was trading on the hope that with a clear mind, he would choose her and their life together. She was gambling with her future after all the effort she had invested in creating it. Was she crazy?

The thought that Bill's love for her might have been a substance-induced illusion gnawed at her incessantly. In the space left by his absence, she now questioned every tender moment, every soulful confidence, every magic moment they had savored together. If alcohol had controlled him, who was he?

The letter. She owed him the letter. How he reacted to it would be the early warning signal of whether he planned to stay. She wrote.

February 2, 2009

Philadelphia

Dear Bill,

First and foremost, I love you. You are the love of my life. I will always feel deeply about the bond that we share. Since I met you and during the years that followed, as our relationship developed from friendship to soulmates to love, I saw in you a man I respected who had strong values, who could be genuine and spontaneous, a man who cared about people (not things and titles and how much). I saw a man who was so affectionate, who cared for his physical well-being, and who reflected on life and searched for his own spirituality; a man who could be strong yet loving, who could lead yet be a friend; a man who could travel the world and stay at the Ritz and yet sit quietly on a deck and appreciate the moon and the stars. That man was and is YOU, Bill, my Green Eyes.

Yes, the alcohol and the drinking changed you. It's been such a long, tortuous, and painful road, which makes it difficult for me to express the emotional cost.

The first and foremost cost of your drinking is loss of TRUST. You have lied to me in so many ways and so often.

The second cost has been my self-confidence and self-esteem as a woman.

The third cost of your drinking is that I became sick, too. I began acting in ways I could not control, trying to stop you from drinking.

She filled in all the gaps of what she needed him to know. She realized that her own healing depended on telling her truth and with both taking responsibility for themselves. Long after the lunch rush came and went at the tea shop, the task was complete. No one had disturbed her.

✵✵✵

They were like two kids looking at brochures for summer camp with glossy photos of the endless wild activities that promised— no, that guaranteed—fun times ahead. Squeezed in together, they compressed the space that separated them on the couch. They flipped through catalogues and brochures from the heaping pile of Eden experiences. The Omega Institute calendar highlighted a half dozen courses, from Borofsky's course in couples' communication to Pema Chödrön's "Smiling at Fear." The registration forms for cycling goaded them to improve their time on 100-mile rides now that it was possible to set such goals. Their favorite was the Backroads cata- logue, offering five-star luxury cycling anywhere from Burma to Peru, which Chantal had intentionally left slightly out of reach. The ques- tion loomed large in her mind whether Bill was ready for vacationing with other couples who would want to share stories over drinks.

"Everything has to be counterintuitive from now on," Bill said.

Chantal winked back at him, unsure what that meant. She figured a nonverbal response was safest. Since Bill's return two days ago from rehab, she'd learned that this phrase was his new mantra. It sounded like rehab insider jargon to her, but she was willing to go along with whatever Caron prescribed. They had sobered him up, and now she had to keep him that way. She knew that was not correct Al-Anon self-talk, but Bill was not going to relapse because she missed a beat.

"From now on, I want to plan everything. Vacations, workouts, AA meetings, meditation time. It's time to be full on. No more procrastinating," Bill said.

"Fine with me. You're preaching to the converted," she replied, hoping the cliché would sound convincing.

Three hours later, their calendars fully penciled in from March until the end of December 2009, the former CEO and General Counsel were back on track.

✳✳✳

Bill looked at the calendar. Today was May 19, 2009. He had nailed it. He smirked. He was in charge of his life. He had completed the famous 90 meetings in 90 days dictated by AA, but he had done it his way. He had skipped two days and then attended two meetings a day. One time, he even attended three meetings in one day. He was a former CEO. He knew that the final number and deadline counted; everything in between was just fluff. Leaders found their own ways to the bottom line.

Bill knew it irritated Chantal. He knew she wanted him to follow "The Program." He was sober for now, and that was enough. He was still considering whether this was a lifetime commitment. He would determine whether he had a glass of wine, not the almighty Higher Power.

Bill was downright smug about his life. He was not craving alcohol the way all those my-name-is-so-and-so-I'm-an-alcoholics did at the AA meetings. Bill played the part, shared when it was his turn, read the Big Book, and even journaled—anything to keep his therapist happy. His sponsor could hardly utter a sentence in front of 20 mostly lost men who struggled to read out loud. He had given speeches to Wall Street investors. Soon, very soon, he would leave all this navel-gazing behind, jump on his motorcycle and enjoy his hard-earned retirement on his own terms.

At least he did not have to worry about "people, places, and things." Philly was new to him. What things could possibly trigger someone to drink? That was nonsense. People? He knew no one in town except Chantal, and she was his biggest cheerleader. He was lucky to have her in his corner. She could have his heart, but his head and soul were off limits to her. Between his alcoholic mother he escaped from as soon as he could and his alcoholic ex-wife he had stayed with far too long, he had enough experience with alcoholic women to keep all women at arm's length.

The guys at AA backed him on that: "You get to have your privacy. You're sober now so you can have all the space you want. It's called boundaries." Bill liked that. Compartmentalizing his life was his specialty. Sober, he would now excel at it, and he had AA jargon to defend it.

He took all those thoughts with him to Rittenhouse Square. He lit up his big fat Ashton cigar, took out his Mont Blanc pen, and cracked the spine on his leather diary, courtesy of Chantal. How did he feel? Fantastic. He began to write about the juice he'd made for breakfast, the weight he had lost, and all the amazing facts of his sober life, avoiding any reflections on his emotional state.

✳✳✳

Chantal welcomed the opportunity to visit the Kimmel Center when Bill bought tickets for an evening of Indian fusion music. She longed for an elegant evening out after all their meetings at coffee shops. The Kimmel would be safe; they could stay in their seats at intermission and taxi home, avoiding the lure of any bars. After his five months of sobriety, Bill confused her. She had lost her ability to read him. He carried a patch of fog around him that made it impossible to gauge his emotions. Their desires were often trumped by missed cues on his part and overthinking by her.

Tonight was no exception. Was he nervous about going out all dressed up like old times and triggering a craving? Was he excited because he had formally asked her out on a date? At times like this, she caught glimpses of the Bill she had fallen in love with: romantic, spontaneous, and thirsty for communion. These brief appearances of his former self allayed some of her doubts about his commitment to their relationship.

"Blue Eyes, let's get out of here," he said before the concert had finished. "It's a gorgeous night for a walk. It's been so long since we've just been impulsive." He took her hand and led her out.

When he held her hand a few blocks later to help her into a horse-drawn carriage—clearly pre-arranged—she laughed and forgot about the past. When they approached Penn's Landing, overcrowded by partygoers, and she read the disappointment on Bill's face while he redirected the driver, she stopped breathing.

Bill nervously chatted about all the highlights of their relationship, anxious to fill the silence while they settled into an outdoor table at Twenty Manning where they had been dropped off. Once the Perrier was served and the waiter walked away, Bill dropped to one knee.

"Will you marry me?"

"Yes."

In that moment, neither cared about the advice of "The Program" about not making important decisions in the first year of sobriety. Five months was close enough.

✳✳✳

Bill diligently attended AA meetings, met with his sponsor and engaged in regular therapy. Chantal embraced her own private therapy to understand the family disease she had welcomed into her home and vowed to defeat. Chantal and Bill attended Omega Institute courses for growth, laid down their executive hats and performed rituals, participated in communication workshops, scoured their souls to understand their childhood scars, and learned to meditate. They were aligned in their desire for recovery. Bill scheduled their "For me, for you time" sessions, a practice they had learned at Omega. The point was to create intimacy through physical closeness without resorting to sexuality to distract from the fear of being emotionally vulnerable.

"I've put together a playlist," Bill said, sounding awkward and excited. He loved Chantal's body and her open sensuality. When words failed him, making love to her seemed the only way he could express his love for her. It frustrated him that tension from all of the recovery efforts, especially the therapy, often crept into their sexual interaction. The sensation of her skin, the weight of her head on his chest, and the intimate caressing provoked within him a sense of belonging he had not experienced before. His peace was often shattered by looking into her eyes and seeing sadness encircled by fatigue. Guilt would shoot through him instantly. His body would either respond mechanically, draining the connection he desperately sought, or refuse to perform, shaming his already bruised male ego.

"Great sound," Chantal said.

She approached him naked in the candlelight with a tinge of nervousness given away by that certain laughter he knew so well. He had to restrain himself from engaging her in foreplay. The strict rule of the practice of standing close to each other required that there was to be no kissing, foreplay, or lovemaking during or immediately afterwards. At this moment, it took all of Bill's self-discipline not to rebel and do it his way. He knew Chantal would be disappointed, and he thirsted for the emotional connection that was promised if they regularly allowed each other to stand so close and unguarded to one another.

Bill stepped forward, standing within such proximity that he could feel her breath but not touch her. To the rhythm of the music they breathed together. They inhaled and exhaled slowly and intently, following the tempo of the music, then began to breathe faster and faster until the music reached its crescendo.

The next step was the trickiest. Excited and in sync, they would sit with intertwined legs, supported by pillows, in such a way as to face each other at eye level. Without saying a word, listening to the ambient music, they would hold each other's gaze for five minutes without speaking. They could hold hands for balance but not to caress.

Over the years, they had come to affectionately call each other "Blue Eyes" and "Green Eyes." Within this safe space, free from the complication of words, intonations, and insinuations, they could look at one another and see each other. Bill loved this time. He would peer into her Blue Eyes with assurance. If he saw sadness, he offered her a smile through a gaze straight from his soul. On the days when his Green Eyes were clouded with doubt and self-contempt, he saw her Blue Eyes affirm her respect for him.

When the bell chimed, the hardest part was not to jump all over her and descend into sexual bliss. The connection was so profound after such closeness, that it begged to be demonstrated after their desire for each other had grown so raw and palpable. To follow the instructions, Bill would reach over and tickle her and they would play-fight like lions.

"Raarrhh," Bill said. "Let's call this 'Jungle Time.'"

Chantal roared back. She laughed with great abandon. This was a ripple in time. All the work he was doing in therapy, in AA, in recovery, was aimed at achieving this closeness with his Blue Eyes expanding to infinity.

✳✳✳

"Bill, tell me about your relationship with your mother," the therapist asked.

"She resented her kids. She had a love affair with rum and Coke. She taught me to keep secrets from my father. I went away to do my MBA as far as I possibly could. I hate that I abandoned my little kid sister to her. But I had loving grandparents who took me in during summer breaks and showered me with love." Bill knew the routine by now.

"What do you want to talk about? Clearly this subject doesn't interest you."

"I've been to enough retreats, men's groups, seen a few shrinks and so forth. I get it. My mother did not teach me to love. I married the image of my mother. My family is a mess. I have to take antidepressants; my life is so pathetic. Chantal says I show no affection and that she feels alone. I am taking the Twelve Steps to resolve this. Did I miss anything?" Bill said slowly to emphasize his ineptitude.

"What do you want to talk about?"

"I want to talk about this Zoloft and how it's messing up my sex drive. I hate it. I don't want to be on an antidepressant. Never have been. Why do I need it now? I'm fine without it," Bill said.

"Are you?"

"I'm in a fog now and can't be a real man with my wife. So, no, I don't need it," Bill said.

"It takes time, Bill. Give it time."

Bill decided that Therapist Number Four had outlasted his usefulness. He would need to hire another.

✽✽✽

It had been Chantal's idea to host a New Year's Eve party with a ritual. First, the guests would go to the rooftop deck and burn a piece of paper on which they had written all their pain and suffering for 2010. After the main course, they would return to the rooftop and set off helium balloons carrying their lists of intentions for

2011. After dessert, to welcome in the New Year with generosity, they would place a stamp on an envelope that contained a check to their favorite charity.

Chantal now stared at twelve flipchart-sized papers each representing a month of 2010. The tally overwhelmed her. In January, Bill had postponed their wedding indefinitely. He felt no joy for their impending nuptials. In February, they had returned home early from a trip to Thailand because one of his children had crashed, ending up in medical rehab for 17 days. March to April was filled with the rollercoaster of their relationship's downward spiral into the greatest darkness of her life as Bill struggled with his medication and inner demons. In August, Chantal lost her grandmother, a woman she adored, who had long inspired her to "live life to the fullest."

Fall had wreaked one devastation after another upon her, beginning with surgery in September for an ovarian cyst. Chantal had never been sick in her life. More worrisome to her was the risk that Bill would relapse, triggered by memories of visiting his mother in the hospital. In October, the biopsy revealed that Chantal had ovarian cancer, both aggressive and life-threatening. With no time to lose, a few days later she had robotic surgery. When she came to, she awoke to thirteen angry phone messages. Her father had unexpectedly died of a heart attack. Her brother and her father's wife were at war. November brought chemo treatment. By December, she had little resilience left to absorb the news that her mentor was sick and unlikely to celebrate the New Year.

Chantal had insisted on hosting this 12-person sit-down dinner party at home only one day after her fourth chemo treatment to convince herself and Bill that life was normal and on an upswing. Neither were convinced that any part of their story would have a happy ending. Chantal's cortisol level was still bouncing off the charts and concerned her doctors.

"Sweetie," Bill said as he observed her list of painful memories sprawled across the living room floor. "You are the love of my life.

I know it is hard to believe right now, but we will make it through this." He never looked her in the eye. He brushed her one remaining strand of hair, careful not to touch the beret that covered her bald head, then left the room. He failed to give her the hug she craved to support his words.

She immediately resented his pretended closeness. It felt so mechanical. He did all the right things: massaging her feet aching from the steroids, bringing her ginger drops for the nausea, and handling all the anxious calls from family and friends. But he would not shed a tear, he would not shout his anger, he would not crawl over the wall he had built around his soul. He called her soulmate, but they both knew it had become a make-believe statement.

Chantal reigned in her surging anger to focus on her intentions for 2011. At least she had a purpose. It might not be practicing law anymore, but she intended to become an author. If she could defog her chemo-fried brain and begin to write again, she would be all right.

In March, one year after Bill's rehab, she needed to find a calling of her own until they figured out their lives. The universe had obliged. When Bill took Chantal to Thailand, he introduced her to Dr. Amporn Watthanavongs, the founder of a Thai charity that educates street children. For years Bill had sponsored kids who attended FORDEC (Foundation for Rehabilitation & Development of Children and Family) schools and programs. When Dr. Amporn found out Chantal was an attorney, he assumed she was a good writer. He spontaneously asked her to write his life story. She instantly accepted, believing that working on a book about Dr. Amporn's life would give meaning to hers. An impoverished child, orphaned at 5 and a boy soldier at 14, Dr. Amporn became a well-educated man best known as a foster father of 50,000 street children of Thailand. He remained an active philanthropist in his late 70s. She was inspired to focus on this endeavor.

Soon she would be strong enough to return to her writing studio—a room of her own, as Virginia Woolf called it. It was also her sanctuary away from the turmoil of recovery that ruled their home. It was her sanity and her safe place. Bill did not have a key.

✳✳✳

Retirement challenged Bill. He adored the concept of freedom; exercising it proved more difficult. Addiction had robbed him of his peer relationships. He longed to discuss business with his friends Henry and Mirko and to reminisce with former colleagues about the Western Union days when his career was at its apex. Addiction had plunged him into a dark, lonely, idle hole.

Bill felt ready to emerge from obscurity. He wanted to travel again. At heart, he was an adventurer and explorer and always would be. All the expat assignments in Bangkok, Buenos Aires, and Paris had nourished his boyhood need to discover the world. Hopping planes, making decisions, and shaking up the world—that was his core. Time was up on this social isolation. He could handle being around drinkers now. He was convinced of that. He was not going to keep them in quarantine for the rest of their lives.

Bill and Chantal had negotiated their way through the first year of an alcohol-free home. Bill knew he had pushed Chantal into serving wine to over 50 guests at their parties before she felt comfortable with it. He noticed when she sent the last guests home with corked wine bottles. He cornered her. "You don't trust me?" He could be hard on her.

He wanted Chantal to understand that he was ready to resume a full life. Alcohol free, yes, but he wanted to build on all the relationships she had been forging for them in Philly. What better way to prove his resolve then a trip to the heartland of wine: Italy? If he could handle that, he could handle anything.

Chantal rose to the occasion. She organized a series of home exchanges to avoid the temptation of the lobby bar for him. The first two weeks were spent in a townhouse in Montecatini Terme. Immediately upon arriving they stocked groceries, thus avoiding the need to linger in cafes, which was one of Bill's favorite pastimes when he lived in Paris before he retired. Cognizant of Chantal's unease with the trip, Bill intentionally placed the Big Book and Twelve Traditions on the night table. He also made a point of penciling in an AA meeting in Florence. He was more curious and intent on collecting bragging rights back home by attending than believing he would need the support of the fellowship.

By the time they reached Venice and ten days into their trip, Bill had grown accustomed to the constant sight of outdoor cafes brimming with patrons enjoying wine. His Coke and ginger ale were always more expensive than the local reds. Piazza San Marco greeted them as they disembarked from the ferry. Eager to please Chantal's mother who had joined them for part of the trip to celebrate her birthday, Bill insisted they sit at the Piazza to listen to the live orchestra while they admired the grandeur of the Basilica.

Bill's romantic fervor surfaced. Charmed by the moment and his love for his fiancé who sported an attractive, silvered baby-length hairdo, a testament to her courage to face her cancer and not hide in shame, he felt the urge to toast their upcoming wedding next year with a glass of champagne. He broke his charming ways by immediately ordering a sparkling water and cappuccino ahead of the ladies' choice.

The waiter looked at him for an uncomfortable minute.

"Nothing else?" he asked.

"That's all," Bill said.

"No wine?" He asked under what Bill felt was a demanding glare.

"No. *Grazie,*" Bill replied.

The next day Bill found himself irritated by the lightheartedness of all the tourists on the gondolas and especially angered by the café patrons enjoying their afternoon wine. He made a fuss everywhere they stopped. He even refused to pay for the espresso he'd ordered before they were shown to their table because there were no seats available on the patio. The waiter threatened to call the police. Bill walked out. The discomfort, not to mention the embarrassment he'd caused Chantal and her mother, did not shame him. He felt justified. Bill marched ahead and left his fiancé to deal with the mess and make amends on his behalf.

Bill could not help the anger that swelled within him. Why could everyone, even people who appeared to be teenagers, sip wine all afternoon and he could not. Life was a fraud. Had he not earned the right to enjoy himself? He felt as if he had the word "alcoholic" tattooed on his forehead. The waiters were taunting him. He felt no compassion for the untenable position in which he'd placed Chantal. He almost always ordered her wine for her. He bullied her into drinking as proof of her trust in him. Then he resented her for drinking.

Bill desperately wanted to order a glass of chilled red Chianti, not a stupid cappuccino. That was it. He was experiencing his first craving a full 21 months into sobriety, but when he called his sponsor that evening, he heard himself glaze over the truth.

"I'm not craving a drink. I'm just angry I can't enjoy the experience of being in Venice with my fiancé. It's messed up," he said.

"Bill, that's craving. Find a meeting," his sponsor said.

Bill followed his advice. Instead of meandering the cobblestone-flowered alleys of Venice in hand with his fiancé and teasing her sensuality, he attended an AA meeting at the Instituto Canossiano Fondamenta de Le Romite. Unlike at home in Philadelphia, Bill needed to share. He raged at the local culture until he was spent, and everyone listened to him attentively. For the first time he felt the power of the meeting.

A retired lawyer, Jim, cleverly shared a well-kept secret among locals on how to deal with aggressive waiters.

"I've lived in Venice during four years of my recovery. There is an unspoken code in Italy that if you don't drink alcohol, you order a

Gingerino. It's like a Campari and soda, same ruby color and slightly bitter taste but without the alcohol. Once you order this drink, you will not be presented with a wine list or have the Chianti pushed on you." Jim said.

This excellent practical advice had alleviated the frustration of ordering in restaurants and returned his enjoyment for European café life. However, the trip continued to push Bill's tolerance of life without the sophistication of ordering fine wines. He kept his weekly appointments with Suzanne, his new recovery therapist, via Skype. Suzanne had an innate sense of his internal stirrings. She probed him about the lack of enthusiasm in his description of the trip. Bill reluctantly admitted that the hiking and sitting in Italian parks had given him time to reflect. He did not want to take antidepressants anymore. He was grateful that Suzanne had switched him to Bupropion which did not affect his daily lovemaking as Zoloft had. That said, he did not need it.

Suzanne drove a hard bargain with Bill to stay on it. She convinced him that his body had just begun to adjust to the new medication; and with his wedding just a few months away, this would not be a wise time to confuse his body. "Think of your honeymoon," she said as finishing touch to her argument.

✳✳✳

On May 19, 2012, in the presence of 110 guests, Bill and Chantal exchanged their vows at the Top of the Tower in Philadelphia. This was a great celebration. Tables were identified with country names where their guests had traveled from: Russia, Serbia, Sweden, Mexico, Canada, to name a few. Dr. Amporn, the central character in Chantal's book, had traveled from Thailand. Among the guests were 55 friends that Chantal and Bill had cultivated in their brief four years in Philadelphia. These people had dressed up for murder mystery nights, showed up for book signings, cycled with them, shared cigars and played tennis with them, and raised funds for worthy causes. Most of them knew about Bill and Chantal's recovery, but some did not.

Family members from Canada were present; others attended in spirit by way of a memorial table for the people they had lost since being together: his mother, her stepfather, her grandmother, her father, and her mentor.

Chantal and Bill had found an equilibrium called life in recovery. Although they still teetered, sometimes quite abruptly, they knew how to recalibrate. Confident they could overcome all that life sent their way, they finally joined hands and walked down the aisle.

Chantal opened her heart to Bill before all those gathered and offered Bill her vows:

> *Upon the currents of life, you flowed into mine,*
> *halfway around the world,*
> *a familiar soul in an exotic land;*
> *Life rarely trumpets the arrival of a treasure.*
>
> *I found in you a worthy explorer of life,*
> *curious about the human spirit,*
> *a lover of food, nature and the globe.*
> *Courageous to face any challenge:*
> *a 100-mile bike ride,*
> *a journey deep into your soul,*
> *a small kitchen or*
> *a long trail into the woods.*
>
> *The Fates challenged our union,*
> *through the valleys of death, addiction and cancer,*
> *the peaks of France, Canadian Lakes, Mexico and Philly,*
> *we learned that love is like the tidal movement,*

sometimes to recede or to return,
sometimes gently or passionately,
always with the knowledge of our freedom to grow
and our responsibility to honor our commitment to each other.

To you, My Lion,
with your kind heart, always giving,
To you, My Soulmate,
who desires to live fully,
To you, My Sweetie,
for your cookies, ice cream and French toast,
To you my Renaissance man,
plays, mud, ascots, speedo, incense,
jazz, woods or Rialto bridge,
To you, My Biker and Cyclist,
for being the best travel companion,
To you, William David Thomas,
the man I am proud of and admire and love deeply.

I, Chantal Christine Jauvin, promise
to border and salute your journey,
to assume as broadly as I can our existence together,
to never know you fully so you can always grow,
to challenge you to be the great person that you are,
to sit with you in the silence of pain or the unknown,
to protect your sobriety always,
to travel, eat, dance, meditate, cook, roam and read
here or everywhere,
to co-create the adventure of our life together,
wherever it leads,
wherever we take it.
I promise to be there with you until the end.

And Bill offered Chantal his vows before everyone:

I will open myself to compassion for you
I give myself to our relationship
I commit myself to our marriage
There will be a you, a me and an us,
we will grow as a couple and as individuals,
I vow to take responsibility for our relationship
I vow to take your life in my hands
Our marriage will be our dual destiny together:
our oyster, our adventure and our spiritual journey.

I am honored to participate in your life with grace.
I vow that in our relationship, intimate and enduring,
together we will practice wellness, grow spiritually and
build healthy relationships.
With you, Chantal, I have experienced loving joy for the
first time in my life, and then I knew bliss.

You have faithfully guarded my sobriety,
and without that I would not be here.
I vow to protect you and our relationship.
I vow to share my truths with you.
I vow to encourage your passions.
I vow to nurture your gentle, caring heart.
Together we will grow our roots in Philly
while we continue to roam the world on our own terms.
You are my Lioness, my lover, my rock.
You are my soulmate in thought, leather and lingerie.

We met under the stars of Africa
but it was under the winter stars of Muskoka
that I knew you were "the one."

Marital bliss filled Bill with overconfidence. Without the guidance of his doctor or the knowledge of Chantal, he stopped taking his antidepressant. After one and a half years of marriage and five years into sobriety, life became complicated again. They both lost control.

"Can you try to keep this relationship talk to two hours?" Bill asked, setting the stage.

"Sweetie, can we try to keep it neutral? These relationship talks have helped us in the past. Let's give it a try. We can't go on like this," Chantal said.

"Ok. I'll go first. Three compliments: You look beautiful. You cooked a great dinner last night. You keep in touch with your friends," Bill said.

"Thank you. Your three compliments: You were patient on the tennis court with me today. You looked into my eyes when you talked to me yesterday. You reached out to John to make new friends."

"Next. I honor your discipline to keep writing," Bill said.

"I honor your perseverance in attending therapy, going to AA meetings, and seeing your sponsor," Chantal said.

Bill rolled his eyes. Chantal ignored it and waited for the next part of the relationship talk. She was anxious to get through the first part, knowing that the aim was to create a connection before they addressed weekly issues in the second part of the talk. This week, the connection was broken, and the compliments felt like a charade. Dutifully, they would go through it until they put up their shields for what would be a repeat of the last couple of weeks: an argument. These relationship talks were held in public places to help keep them orderly.

"This week, I give you a bottle of inspiration to uncork when you get writer's block. My second gift is a bubble of silence because you keep saying you talk too much."

Bill had zinged her. That was not a gift, it was a veiled attempt at controlling her so she would not raise all the issues they'd faced during the week. Chantal dug her fingers into her chair and ignored the bait.

"Thank you for the gifts. This week, I give you sunshine to brighten your mood. I also give you an opportunity magnifying glass to help you find what you want to do next." The last gift had sounded like a good idea when she'd written it down in preparation for their talk. Given the tension between them right now, she thought it might backfire.

"It's your week to go first. What do you want to talk about?" Bill asked without thanking her for the gifts, as the process required him to. She ignored that as well.

"I feel like you are being so passive-aggressive towards me. What am I doing that angers you so much?" Chantal asked.

"Here we go with the therapy talk. I'm so goddamn tired of all this. I don't need it. I don't need an antidepressant. I'm fine," Bill said, standing up.

"I don't need you," he shouted.

Stunned, Chantal shrunk under the glares of morning coffee drinkers enjoying their morning paper on the terrace. She fumbled for words.

"Sweetie, sit down. Let's try to figure this out," she said.

"I don't want to figure anything out anymore. You don't like the way I talk to you. 'I don't look in your eyes anymore.' 'I don't have any affect.' 'I'm not building any relationships.' 'I don't phone my kids often enough.' All you do is criticize me. You want emotions, here's some emotions: I don't give a damn!" He kept on shouting as he walked away.

❄❄❄

Distraught and in free fall, Chantal didn't know if she could keep her relationship together. She didn't even know if she wanted to anymore. She hardly knew if her body would hold up. The internal trembling, the sleeplessness and stress, were her enemies. Her cancer was not yet in remission and her cortisol levels were still off the chart every time she had blood work.

"Chantal, I told you it would take a long time," Kathleen said.

"Kathleen, you have been with me through all of this. You prepped me to meet Bill's therapist, Dr. Frank, when I didn't want to, just months after my chemo. You've helped me deal with the childhood wounds left by my father. You've seen me jubilant when Bill proposed and we got married. All along you told me it would take time," Chantal said.

Chantal continued, "He has been sober five years now. FIVE years. How much longer?"

"Longer, much longer, Chantal. When you asked to come to my office together last week, I was reluctant," Kathleen said.

"It's unbearable. He stopped seeing his therapist, number seven I think. I've lost count. He was seeing him twice a week. AA meetings, sponsor, men's group . . . He won't take medication, and he is clearly depressed. I don't see much hope. Do you?" Chantal said. She wanted a definitive answer.

"Chantal, Bill is a deeply wounded man. He needs more time to heal. He is doing all of this to show you he is doing it, but it's a form of rebellion. When you were both in my office, I could see that he's not emotionally available," she said.

"Kathleen, I've worked hard with you, and I've recovered my self-confidence. I've created boundaries. Sometimes they get fuzzy, but usually I realize it and I have tools and support to deal with it. My friends Anne and Janet are the best support network. I feel that the time has come to stop therapy. My marriage is in shambles, but I have found my footing again. I have your number. I'll call you if I need you," Chantal said.

"I agree, Chantal. Stay close to your soul. I am confident you will make the right choices for yourself."

With those words, her five and a half years of therapy with Kathleen ended.

✳✳✳

As Bill's world collapsed around him he watched it with detachment, puffing endless cigars and playing at therapy. His raft was drifting out of reach. No, he was swimming away from her out of disgust for himself. He hated who he had become. He found his existence pathetic, looking at life through the looking glass.

On the outside, he was in his prime, the most physically fit of his adult life, with a chic home near the Art Museum and the best travel companion, his wife. They were experiencing the world together: sky diving in New Zealand, then best man and maid of honor for Mirko and Jelena in Jamaica, attending opera at La Scala in Milan, cycling and hiking in Peru. Chantal had such thirst and energy for life. He loved her, and then he pushed her away. He marveled at the fact that she'd held on so long.

On the inside he was a lost sheep wandering a dark, deep forest. Five years of sobriety without relapse and yet no joy. This was his lowest point—lower than rehab, his divorce, and even rejection by his own grown children. What was the point of being sober?

Faced with his dejection, he saw his wife making her own way. She completed the manuscript for her book despite all the turmoil in their life. She had created a haven for herself at her writing studio. Chantal was the strongest woman he knew. He admired the way she'd faced her cancer, written her first book, and created a diverse network of friends and acquaintances in Philly. All the while, he floundered. More than once he found himself taking it out on her.

Then she did it again: she showed up. She suggested a full-out couples' therapy retreat in their own home with Paul and Connie, who had previously led them through a personal weekend of relationship building in Connecticut. Bill knew that Chantal trusted Paul in a way he found threatening. Paul embodied the image of an emotionally available husband and a man who'd broken the cycle of addiction in his own family. That was a tall order for Bill.

The retreat was intense but did not ward off the storm. Bill could not bring himself to stop rebelling inwardly and outwardly.

A month later, Bill reflected on his conversations with Paul. One of the few pleasures left in his life was having a cigar in their backyard, which he and Chantal had affectionately named the Bamboo Café. They had transplanted two clusters of bamboo that were part of the décor when they had exchanged their wedding vows. Such a romantic idea, Bill snickered to himself.

"Sweetie," Chantal said as she came into the Bamboo Café.

"My Lion, I love you deeply, but I can no longer live like this. I know we are meant to be together. Perhaps in another lifetime. I have started to look for a divorce attorney," she calmly added. She turned around and quietly went back into the house.

Everything stopped for Bill. Then everything swirled out of control. He was panicked by moments and relieved by others. The woman he loved and knew was his soulmate, his Blue Eyes, his Lioness was leaving him. He pleaded with her for more time. He guilted her back to Thailand as one last attempt to save their marriage.

Before they left, he made two important decisions. First, he hit the pause button on therapy, men's groups, sponsor, everything except one AA meeting a week. Second, he would go back on his antidepressants.

❋❋❋

Chantal stared at the computer screen. "Sweetie! Maverick wants to publish my book."

Bill showed up. Together they talked through the contract that arrived while they were cycling together along the Gulf of Thailand. "Unsupervised," Bill loved to say, when they cycled without a group. They celebrated the signing of her first book deal with a candlelight dinner, feet touching the sand to the sound of the ocean. He ordered her a glass of champagne and himself a ginger ale.

"To the love of my life: I am so proud of you. I don't know anyone who gives so much of herself. Congratulations, My Lioness, you deserve this." Bill toasted her.

Knowing that the summer and fall would be consumed by the publication and marketing of *The Boy with a Bamboo Heart*, they took their first European cycling trip on the French coast. They started in Brussels, saw Chantal's family, and then cycled down the Normandy and Brittany coasts. The two of them, alone, on an adventure. They celebrated again, somewhere in a small French village, when Maverick Publishers sent the proofs of the book cover. The fresh air, cycling all day, and the oysters worked their magic.

On November 6, 2015, Chantal sat across from her husband on the 52nd floor of a swanky restaurant overlooking the Bangkok skyline, celebrating the successful launch of her book at the Foreign Correspondents Club in Bangkok the night before. The buzz she felt was not from her fear of heights but from the energy that encircled them. There he was: Bill, charming, handsome, full of ideas, switched on, and looking straight into her eyes. He had made peace with taking an antidepressant; he'd decided his path to recovery was to engage fully in life. Rotarian, mentor, investor, board member, cyclist, sponsor—he was even trying his hand at sketching and baking.

***

It seemed they always found themselves in a foreign land when it was time to celebrate. Marking ten years in recovery was no exception. They sat by the river under the stars of Myanmar in a restaurant Chantal selected after several recommendations. The quiet evening was perfect for the occasion. Even the restaurant's name "Seeds" was appropriate. It was a few days before their guided cycling trip began in Bagan, the ancient city of thousands of pagodas, where they would experience their first hot-air balloon trip together. Another first.

Bill looked at Chantal. He saw her fully. He could sense her anticipation, feel her jubilation, and experience her elation. Times had changed for him. He'd become attuned to her.

"My Lion, for the gift of time you have given us, congratulations on your 10th anniversary. Not only have you maintained your sobriety, you've reclaimed your life and made our relationship possible. I am here for you and with you. I love you," she said.

She handed him a gift. His smile betrayed his boyish eagerness to open it.

Chantal had given him the gift of time back. The Montblanc Heritage watch symbolized their recovery. It was engraved with "Love you My Lion—10 years." Chantal had given him time to face his disease. She'd given him time to heal. And now she was giving him time to live their vows together.

"My Lioness. You're the one," Bill said.

The First Date

[Sherri & Larry]

On their first date, the three harbingers of Larry's future manifested themselves, but it was too early—or perhaps already too late—for him to understand. A self-assured, desirable bachelor, evident by all the phone numbers pushed into his hand by well-intentioned match-makers, Larry knew his wit and good looks were in demand. His status as a medical resident didn't hurt either.

Sherri burst into Larry's life. A majorette with national titles, she combined smarts with physical prowess as head baton twirler for the University of Miami. Highly focused and daring, she twirled fire.

Sherri wasted no time informing Larry during their first telephone conversation that she'd recently appeared in the hot new film, *Porky's*. Larry immediately went to Blockbuster's and rented the movie. He did not regret that he'd asked her out on a blind date.

"Happy birthday," Sherri said as she unapologetically handed Larry a big, red balloon with birthday wishes scrawled in metallic ink. "How about that? My balloon for you matches your little red convertible." She roared with laughter. This was the first of many surprises that Larry did not expect from Sherri.

"Thank you. Ready for dinner?" Larry asked, pulling out of her parents' driveway. He may not have been blushing, but he did find the gesture adorable. The perfect gift for a blind date with a 33-year-old male bachelor, he snickered to himself.

"Yes, as soon as you stop and pull up that car top. I spent a lot of time fixing my hair and don't want to look like I just came in from the Wild West," Sherri said. Larry obliged. He shook his head as he regretfully pulled the top up on his Mazda—the first of many times that Sherri would get what Sherri wanted.

Dinner flowed smoothly as they took turns sharing stories about their college experiences. There was an ease to their exchange. Before dessert arrived, Sherri excused herself. Larry only found out much later that she had secretly called her father from the pay phone during the meal to tell him she'd met the man she would marry.

Sherri's big personality coincided with Larry's own love for life's effervescence. In college he'd acted on stage and performed in musical comedies. The funny messages Sherri left on his answering machine contrasted with the seriousness of the operating room and the sick children who populated his days at the hospital. Never one to falter, on December 1st, less than three months after their first date, Larry proposed. Sherri said, "Yes."

❊❊❊

Movement was a constant in Sherri's life. As a good little girl, she did well in school under the constant gaze of her mother. At times, her mother's control felt palpable, like a shadow that extended its reach to straighten Sherri's shoulders and prevent her from moving either left or right. When Sherri discovered baton twirling at the age of 11, she tasted freedom. She could spin, swirl and pivot to her heart's content. Her happy place shrank to the space between her hand and her baton. She commanded the baton and her mother watched. Sherri released the straightjacket of her adolescence by twirling. Each trophy she earned as a majorette allowed her to travel further away from home.

Although Sherri told everyone that her college choice was predi-cated on her twirling opportunities, it was a subtext for how far she could go to escape her mother's reach. The University of Miami seemed far enough from New Jersey. This silent act of rebellion against her mother sacrificed the closeness she enjoyed with her father. She had to make the bargain worth the trade.

The University of Miami may have been known as the "Public Ivy," but to Sherri it was the land of the free. Her eyes were wide open to everything from disco biscuits to pot-to-vodka and the intoxicating mix of it all on campus. She tried it all. The harder she marched and twirled, the harder she inhaled and drank. Although she maintained her cues with the baton, the effects of partying were beginning to manifest. Miami in the late 1970s was laying the groundwork for the rise of Miami Vice. Sherri-the-heavy-partier was laying the ground-work for Sherri-the-functional-addict.

Salvation came with *Porky's*. It gave Sherri a reason to take a semester off school. It also allowed her to camouflage her extracur-ricular activities. One person it did not fool was her father. When the shooting on the movie was complete, Sherri's father guided her back to a university closer to home. It was Rutgers University that awarded Sherri a Bachelor of Science in Psychology and Special Education.

Graduation meant work, which required some way of controlling drinking and drugging. Perhaps more problematic was the fact that Sherri was living under her parents' roof. Skipping out on work was not an option under the hawkish eye of her mother. Sherri trans-ferred her baton twirling skills into balancing her life. The hinge was the drugs and alcohol. On the one hand, there was the advertising job in New York and the responsible accountant fiancé she'd dated, possibly to find a way out of her mother's reach. On the other, there were the martinis and joints consumed with unrestrained abandon. She ditched the boring accountant fiancé and hung onto the booze and pot.

Larry was the tipping point. Accomplished, charming, and with a boyish sense of humor, he could handle her scary mother. This man, she could trust. At 25 years of age, less than one year after their first blind date, Sherri stepped into her new role as the wife of a Doctor.

Life came quickly at the newlyweds. First came the devastation: Sherri's father passed away only seven weeks after he'd walked her down the aisle. The pillar of her family life crumbled. Sherri retreated into vodka. Morning, day, and night, it numbed her pain.

Life tripped Sherri up. After years of flips, cartwheels, and five-hour days of twirling, Sherri slipped on a dislodged brick in the driveway of her home while walking with Larry. The worst of it was that she couldn't even blame the alcohol. It happened in a rare sober moment. Embarrassed but in pain, she consulted a doctor. This man, a doctor who was not her husband, offered her a second love affair: Valium.

As with all totally consuming love affairs, the force of the attraction weakens the mind and enhances the senses. In Sherri's case, her courtship with narcotics quickly became an obsession which numbed the pains of life.

❊❊❊

Larry understood the herniated disc, the first miscarriage, and the complicated pregnancy. He understood surgery, prescription medications, and psychological trauma. What he did not understand was the depth of his wife's battle.

Larry had his own juggling act to attend to. He was a physician, a surgeon, and head of a urology clinic. He took his duties as father and husband seriously but with necessary detachment from domestic details. Given Sherri's back issues and the two bundles of joy running around the house, he hired Mia and Brigitte for their Caribbean joie de vivre and love of hard work. They rotated housekeeping shifts and kept the household functioning during Sherri's growing absences. In the end Larry had to turn to a live-in housekeeper.

"You've been drinking today," Larry raged one night as he walked in the door and found Sherri at the kitchen counter pretending to finish up washing dishes for the meal Larry knew full well she hadn't prepared or helped with the cleanup.

"Well, good evening to you, Mister I'm-So-Important-Surgeon-I-can-breeze-in-at-10:00pm-and-criticize-my-wife-first-thing-through-the-door. How was your day, Larry?" Sherri said.

"I don't like your tone or your lying," Larry said.

"Just like you. Telling me what's going on instead of asking? Your patients must love that. I'm in pain, Larry—you know, physical pain, post-surgery pain, complicated-pregnancy pain," she said, her tone louder with each enumeration.

Larry looked at her, too tired to move or to resist the pull of the argument. He knew this loop and the energy it would drain out of him. Yet, he knew he would engage. It would anger him later that he had succumbed to the temptation, but these duels and the sarcasm had become their only way to relate.

"Oh wait, you forgot that when you visited me in the hospital you weren't a physician on his rounds. You were my husband. You remember the tubes, the IV—all that stuff you're so damned knowledgeable about? That was me, your wife, not some nameless patient. That was me in pain, suffering and alone."

"I know what pain is, Sherri. I deal with it every day."

"Do you? Do you really know what it feels like when your body hurts so bad you want to die? No, not you, Mister Perfect. You superman." She knocked over the empty glass tumbler as she mocked the super-hero figure.

"Your motor skills, Sherri. They tell the truth. It's obvious you've been drinking," Larry said as he turned his back to leave the kitchen.

"Oh, don't you dare! Don't you dare diagnose me! And don't you dare leave the kitchen. I haven't had a drink in days. We need to talk about those babies upstairs—you know, your daughter and your son," Sherri shrieked, pointing at the ceiling.

"No. We're not going to talk about anything. You're drunk, and I have surgery in the morning. Whatever it is, it can't be that important because I would have heard about it from the housekeeper," Larry said.

"You insensitive bastard!" she yelled at his back.

Larry spun around to face her. He saw the dark-circled eyes covered by layers of makeup. He saw the half-peeled nail polish from her last attempt to make herself attractive. He saw a broken woman: a survivor of four miscarriages, back surgery, spinal leaks and spinal fusions. He cared for Sherri, but she was buried somewhere inside this other woman. This other woman was ugly with her lies, her drinking, her constant misery, blaming him and her mother for her pain. His patients suffered too, but they were not as destructive as this.

The image of his patients came crashing through the moment, the image that always saved him from his personal misery. Doctor Larry breathed in deeply. A protective cloak fell over his heart, and his brain clicked into crisis mode. He needed to quickly evaluate the best approach: a quick, aggressive intervention or a gentle, therapeutic treatment.

Sherri stormed by him, grabbed her jacket and keys hanging in the foyer, stopping just long enough to engage his gaze. She threw her head backwards with all the soap-opera flair of a starlet.

"I did not have a drink today, but now I'm going out for a drink. See you around, Dr. Zhivago," Sherri said calmly with complete control. She slammed the door behind her.

One of the babies started crying. Before Larry could calm himself enough to go upstairs, the other had joined in. He wanted to go to them, but knew the nanny would pacify them before he could cool his blood. He waited until the wailing was replaced with a sweet Caribbean melody. When he heard the footsteps retreat from the babies' room, he went to them. Larry caressed his daughter and kissed her on the forehead and repeated the gesture with his baby boy. He refused to let his thoughts wander to their mother. The children had loving nannies who cared for them as their own.

Relieved to be alone in his bedroom, Larry rehearsed his nighttime mantra. The children are still babies and well cared for. Sherri will come around soon enough to mother them. She was receiving the best medical care. He was doing the right thing, concentrating on building his practice to care for all of them. Eventually they would be a happy family. He then reviewed all the reports and instructions for the next day's surgery. All the mental boxes checked, he allowed himself to fall into a brief, fitful sleep.

Two days later, when Larry came home early enough to tuck the children in, he saw Sherri's car in the driveway. It took him longer than usual to turn the ignition off in the car. He stepped out and inspected her car, looking for dents. There were none. He felt a small amount of relief until he spotted the Caesar's Casino parking ticket. He wondered how much Sherri's little temper tantrum had cost him this time.

He walked around the car twice to calm himself down. He knew too well that once he stepped into the house it would not be a quiet evening. He would face the usual barrage of recriminations for his failings as a father and husband, not to mention as a physician. Guilt in Sherri triggered her big bully personality. This in turn triggered Larry's best improv skill: sarcasm.

He walked through the door and said, "Well, well, well. Miss Wonder Woman graces us with her presence. How was Atlantic City?" There was no point delaying the inevitable.

✳✳✳

Months morphed into years and time became a jumble of dramas. Sherri saw her husband, children, and housekeepers buzz around her as she shrank. Her life was absurd. The medical explanation given to the children by their doctor father was that Mom suffered from a chemical imbalance. Mom was unwell. No one questioned the diagnosis, nor did they ever let the words alcoholic or addict slip into the family conversation.

✳✳✳

"Sherri, take that book away. I don't want to see it in the living room. You think our kids can't read." Larry glared at the cover: *The Verbally Abusive Relationship: How to Recognize It and How to Respond.*

"You self-centered, arrogant, selfish man. You think I don't understand what you're doing?"

"You mean taking care of the kids? Taking care of you? Look at you! Have you looked in the mirror lately? I've had it up to here with your pains. I empathize. But get yourself together, Sherri. If not for me or you, for the kids. You're not bipolar. You are using again. I don't know where you get it, but you're not yourself."

"I get it from Canada, and I need it. I can't stand the pain. You say you care, but you don't. You like it when I'm weak because it makes you look and feel strong. You like pointing out all my failures. My mother sees it. She sees the way you treat me."

"Let's not talk about her now." Larry cut her off. His rib cage tightened and his mind raced to take charge before his rage did. Entangled in this internal duel, he failed to notice the presence of two little pairs of eyes.

"Yes, let's talk about her. You don't get to dictate everything. You're a bully and verbally abusive. I won't take it anymore." Sherri grabbed the flower vase and threw it on the floor. "I am strong. See that. I am strong." She charged at him. In her fury, she was strong. He could not contain her brute physical strength fueled by a lousy self-help book.

He disentangled from her and caught sight of his children.

"Go to your rooms," Larry shouted. He did not want them to see their mother like this.

The children ran up the stairs. Sherri charged at his chest with her arms as if to tackle him. He protected himself while she kept charging at him. Terrified by her rage, he did the unimaginable. He made the call.

They came within minutes. They brought the white jacket. The screaming stopped. They took Sherri away. The children didn't come down to ask what had happened to their mother. They stayed in their room.

This was the first of Sherri's periodic absences when life would return to normal.

✳✳✳

Everyone in the household assumed a role and held onto it as best they could. Sherri's role was the good girl doing her best to be a good mother, yet ravaged by cravings and failings. She collected rehab experiences as others collect frequent flyer miles. She calmly returned from each 28-day program determined to get it right this time. But whether it was a return from sunny Florida or cold Minnesota, whether from the Mayo Clinic or The Meadows, the demons were more devious.

At the beginning the children would welcome her back with cards, balloons, and flowers, full of stories to share from her absence. They craved a "normal" mom and quickly forgave. As the peace eroded and the fun-crazy mom transformed into the unpredictable, unreliable crazy mom, they began to wait— even pray—for her departures.

Sherri does not recall which rehab it was, but she recalls marking her birthday there. She remembers because her youngest daughter made a video clip wishing her happy birthday. Her older sister pouted in the background. She eventually mumbled a wish, but what struck Sherri was her daughter's eyes. She recognized pain. She understood that she was running out of time to be the parent she wanted to be.

Larry playacted his roles with ever-increasing ease. His public appearances involved personifying the talented surgeon he was and the happy family man which he definitely was not. Behind the scenes he was the logistics director extraordinaire as he performed his many hidden roles. He coordinated the housekeepers, took care of all home repairs and expenses, attended to Sherri's intake and discharge from rehabs, participated dutifully in Family Education

Programs and couples' therapy. He financed the kids' private lessons, his wife's endless treatment, and paid the many counseling bills. He also battled his mother-in-law, who portrayed him as the cause of all of Sherri's problems.

The one role that was not playacted was that of the loner. Exhausted by the pretending and the attending, he found himself letting his phone go to voicemail when a friend's number appeared. He took to running to avoid social contact at the gym that might lead to invitations he would have to turn down. He spent more time listening to sad R&B songs in the dark. Those vibes were the only intimacy he knew. He would not walk away from his responsibilities no matter how hard it was. Period.

Much in the same way that tasks at work denote the hierarchy of power, the levels of accountability in a family dictate the hierarchy of trust. The more menial the work, the less authority is involved. Sherri couldn't be counted on to have dinner ready for the kids, attend basketball games, or even replenish Larry's shaving cream. Her name was stripped from the bank accounts, and she couldn't make any appointments or plans for the family. Her only ally was her mother, who could be relied upon to villainize Larry.

Time was bullying Sherri into a person she didn't want to be, into moments she would regret and never regain. Time was hurling her into a future where she could no longer face herself or her husband, much less care for her children. Robbed of time and memories, she populated the wasteland in her heart with Percocet and Vicodin washed down with vodka.

＊＊＊

"It's baloney, Sherri, and you know it! I'm not attending another family education program. I know more about substance use disorder at this point than about new urological advances. The answer is "no." And I refuse to have the kids participate as well. They have their hands full with their own private counseling. They have enough to deal with than to go another round with you. Have fun at rehab. See you in 28 days," Larry said.

The sadness and the resentment took turns gnawing through the last of Larry's resistance. He could barely contain his jealousy when he saw the family holiday beach photos on his colleagues' desk. He searched the happy moments of others to find some sign of distress. Why did he have to be so blind on that blind date? Why did he have to carry not only the physical frailness of his wife but her substance abuse as well? Why couldn't he have a happy family life? Hadn't he worked hard enough to earn it?

❋❋❋

On the twelfth try, Sherri decided she would try harder to do things the right way. This time Sherri didn't get the housekeeper to smuggle in Vicodin to get her through rehab. She didn't lie to her counselors. She decided she'd take to heart the AA slogan "Fake it until you make it." She was ready to fake the rest of her life to make it because what she wanted most was to have her family back. Her youngest was 13 years old, so vulnerable. Sherri did not know her two other children, and they certainly did not know her. All of them had been interacting with their mother through the prism of addiction since they were born.

Yes, addiction. Sherri had to bear the burden of the word. Larry was not verbally abusive. It was her disease, her substance use disorder, that was emotionally abusive of her. The psychiatrist, the counselors, and the sponsors had all told her that although she couldn't be cured, she could put this disease into remission forever. Why hadn't she heard them before? Now she did, and she wanted full-time and long-term remission. There was a treatment: it was called sobriety and recovery.

The treatment was simple but hard. It started with a routine: up at 7:00 a.m. to make breakfast for the kids, coffee for Larry, and give a peck on the cheek to whoever was willing to receive it. At the beginning there were not many takers. To the gym at 9:00 a.m. Then pick up groceries and attend an AA meeting. Spend a few hours on the internet building a small retail business. Avoid all Canadian pharmacy websites. If tempted to drink, call her AA sponsor to talk through the craving. Prepare dinner and serve it at 5:30 p.m. sharp, with or without Larry.

This was called consistency, although to Sherri it was Groundhog Day. Not easy for the woman who loved spontaneous decisions and impromptu outings. The thing about this recovery plan was that it called upon her to put caring for her family ahead of her own whims. If she died of boredom, at least she would not die alone. "Slow and steady" became her mantra.

She paced herself. At first it was buying Larry a new razor. Then it was the pressed shirt on a hanger for the social gathering with residents after work. She reignited her joy for cooking and made Larry's favorite dishes on the weekend. She offered help with the children's school activities. She accepted their hesitancy but jumped if they said "yes." Sometimes, she would try her hand at a spontaneous act, but one she'd premeditated and discussed with her sponsor. Would it be okay to take a detour from after-school practice to stop for ice cream with her son if it meant arriving home 30 minutes late? Yes, as long as she texted the housekeeper to let her know. Sometimes, she would prep tomorrow's dinner ahead of time so she could stop at a little boutique on the way home from her AA meeting and keep her schedule on track. The small acts of impulsiveness within a strict schedule helped her reconnect with herself.

She waited—days, weeks and a month—until he was ready. Then the invitation came to join Larry at a professional social function. Sherri was elated. She dressed up, put on her makeup, and looped her own necklace. It was worth it. When Larry came to pick her up, she saw it. She saw that slight moment of recognition. It passed quickly, overshadowed by his habit of telling her what to do. She was ready; she'd rehearsed the evening with her sponsor at least five times.

Sherri did not expect Larry to pay her much attention. His job was to mingle with his colleagues; her job was to be present and pleasant.

"Good evening, Sherri. It's lovely to meet you. Larry, where have you been hiding your beautiful wife? Can we offer you a glass of champagne?" the host charmingly offered.

"No, thank you. I'll have sparkling water. I'd rather waste my calories on dessert," Sherri said firmly with a slight theatrical flair.

Everyone laughed. Larry relaxed.

It was a beginning.

❊❊❊

The irony did not escape Larry. He'd been role-playing for 27 years when their marriage counselor asked him whether he'd be willing to role-play with Sherri.

"Isn't that what we've been doing since we got married?" Larry shot back at the therapist.

"Let's try to tone down the sarcasm, okay? A simple 'yes' or 'no' will do."

"Okay," Larry said.

"I want you to reverse roles. Sherri, you'll enter the room as Larry after work, the way you would like him to be. Larry, you'll welcome Sherri home the way you'd like to be treated. Go ahead, Sherri," the counselor directed her.

"Hello, Sherri. I'm home," Sherri said and then walked over and placed a tentative kiss on Larry's cheek.

Larry, pretending to be Sherri, accepted the kiss and froze.

"How was your day? Make any internet sales?" Sherri said to keep the role-play going. She sat down next to Larry.

"Yes, I did. I also found a new recipe to make your sweet tooth happy over the weekend," Larry responded tentatively. He put his hand on Sherri's knee, mechanically uncomfortable with being under the watchful eye of the therapist.

"I look forward to it. Shall we plan a date night on Friday?" Sherri asked. She felt a little manipulative since she'd wanted to ask Larry for some time, and the therapist's office felt safe.

"Okay," Larry responded.

Sherri looked at the therapist for help. He said nothing.

"I'll take you out for a movie and ice cream," Sherri offered.

"I would love that," Larry answered.

And so it happened that date night became a Sherri and Larry tradition. A time just for the two of them. The same way Monday night became cuddle-on-the-couch-and-watch-the-TV-series-*24*. The more they saw Jack Bauer fight the bad guys one at a time, the more relaxed they became in living their marriage one day at a time. Larry's sarcasm turned into fun, dry humor. Sherri's unpredictability turned into fun surprises.

The next round of counseling focused on telling each other their truths. The counselor asked each of them to sit across from one another. She wanted them to first affirm their love and then tell the other a truth about their hurtful behavior. The other was to listen and say nothing until the counselor directed them to.

"I don't like it when you drink. I know you have a disease. It still hurts me, and I can't trust you," Larry said quietly looking directly at Sherri.

The therapist motioned for them to just breathe and look at each other. The therapist let the silence continue until the charge of electricity in the air dissipated. He then nodded at Sherri.

"I don't like it when you yell at me. I know you're angry. I feel small and vulnerable in those moments," Sherri said.

They held each other's gaze and stayed silent. Then Sherri took the initiative.

"I'm sorry I've hurt you. Will you forgive me?"

"Yes," Larry said without pause.

Sherri motioned towards Larry. The therapist stopped her. He let them both sit with the moment. Sherri fidgeted. The silence ticked away.

"Yes, I forgive you Sherri," Larry repeated.

The therapist nodded approvingly to Larry but said nothing. Larry took a deep breath and refocused his gaze on Sherri.

"I'm sorry, too, Funny Girl," Larry said.

Sherri could not remember the last time Larry had apologized to her. She felt that she was always trying to catch up for the past. His words settled between her guilt and shame gremlins, elbowing them to make just a small amount of place for themselves.

And so, this too was a new beginning. Each of them learned to apologize. These brief intermissions in the blame game allowed them to peer beyond their masks to consider the possibilities of altering the script of their relationship. The rehearsals in the therapist's office crept into their conversations in the car, in the kitchen, and in bed when they kissed goodnight.

❊❊❊

Sherri and her sponsor formulated a strategy that effectively applied to every situation: "Do the right next thing or the great next thing." To Sherri that meant during Hanukkah she would not only prepare potato latkes with more ardor but also decorate with attention to detail.

To the tunes of Cat Stevens, Sherri cut and arranged snow white lilies and blue delphiniums in the crystal vase. She tucked at the table runner to make sure it sat just right, no wrinkles. She set a little gift next to the plates of the two youngest children. They sparkled in silver ribbons. She could not wait to see their eyes when they opened them. She might have gone overboard a little, but she thought Larry would not mind too much. He loved these traditional family moments. For him, she had handwritten the prayers he would say as he lit the candle.

In the background, she heard Cat sing *Hard Headed Woman*. That particular tune often called her attention. She hummed along. Over time, the meaning of the lyrics had changed for her. She'd found that hard-headed woman within herself. She knew that hard-headed meant determined and willing to stay sober. No, like Cat Stevens, she didn't need any "fancy dancers" anymore. Gail, her sponsor, was helping Sherri take herself for who she was, not her disease.

This, tonight, the evening with her family, was possible because Sherri had found her sobriety and stuck to it. It was a victory she could humbly celebrate privately. She rewarded herself by making her home festive and welcoming. She anticipated the moment when each of her children would walk in, and their faces would light up.

Sherri tucked her AA coins somewhere in the table setting as a reminder that each family gathering resulted from holding steadfast to "One Day at a Time." First, it was one coin, then two, and now she had three coins for her three years of sobriety. At times she giggled to herself. She was creating a whole new take on the story she'd read as a little girl: "The Gold Coins That Went a Long Way."

Larry also made it possible for her and the two of them to celebrate. She noticed how he manipulated his schedule to be at home more often and how he found a way to get there a little earlier on special occasions.

"Like the hot pink helium balloon?" she'd ask him when she managed to surprise him.

"Perfect gift for a blind date," he would reply.

✳✳✳

People, places, and things: Sherri had learned that well. Know your triggers and avoid them at all cost. She never romanced the pharmacy. She raised her level of alertness any time she came near those little cylindrical, childproof, amber-brown pill bottles. There was only one label for those: DANGER. She steered clear.

The one thing she forgot to be wary of was her own body. The pain that exploded in her left ear raised her pain threshold beyond what she remembered experiencing during her various surgeries. The ENT doctor who attended quickly diagnosed an outbreak of shingles in her left ear canal. Empathetic to the severe pain caused by this viral infection, the doctor prescribed Vicodin. Sherri stayed silent and reached for the script.

The internal reptile voice laid to rest three years ago whispered ever so slightly into her brain:

"You've got this. You've been sober three years. You are strong-headed. You are fierce. You are determined. One pill every four to six hours. No need to say anything to him, you can handle this."

Sherri did not have this. Her disease had her. Within a few days, the torment was no longer the shingle in her ear, it was her addiction. Desperation took over her resolve, her recovery, and gave her back her shame.

She reverted to her devious behavior, fueled by narcotics that commanded her brain to find and consume more and more. On the internet, she discovered some Canadian pharmacies that would FedEx her some pills. She found herself in her fluffy purple housecoat and matching slippers chasing the delivery truck that she'd missed. Oblivious to neighbors, the postman, or anyone walking their dog, she jumped in her car in her pajamas and followed the truck until the driver stopped and handed over the pills. For good measure, more than once she picked up a 40-ounce bottle of vodka by way of a detour back to the house.

Outwardly, she performed the charade. She cooked dinner but with less effort. She continued to talk to "her girls" about their recovery. She skipped her own AA meetings and calls to her sponsor. She picked up her old habits with the ease of an expert.

✻✻✻

"Larry, it's Sherri. You have to take me to Caron, and you have to do it now," she screamed into her phone.

"Relax Sherri, you've done this talk so many times. You—," Larry responded impatiently, looking at his watch.

"You don't understand. I'm using again! I need to go back to rehab. For me, Larry, for me! I don't want to die! I don't want to lose the children. I don't want to end up killing myself."

In the few minutes it took Larry to absorb the news, the trauma of all the past years intruded into the moment, flooding him with flashbacks: Sherri screaming at the kitchen counter, his holding the two babies and pacing the bedroom alone, the 911 calls, and the utter desolation he'd experienced. The drawbridges went up. He went numb. If he'd needed to fill in a chart with his own diagnostics, he would have written PTSD—post-traumatic stress disorder.

"Pack your bags. I'll drive you." He hung up.

Larry called his older brother from the car. They—his mother and his brothers—had always stood by him. As he drove home he triaged the details of the children's and the household needs he would have to take charge of again. "Damn it, Sherri." He slammed the steering wheel hard. The car veered slightly, before he regained control.

Ice formed around the edges of his nerves. Everything inside went numb. He couldn't allow himself to dwell on the past, or even on the immediate future. He knew the drill. He'd have to sit the children down and tell them, again.

✻✻✻

On April 21, 2008, Sherri reset her sobriety counter to day one. Sherri knew that she was also resetting the trust-o-meter with Larry and the kids. It took all the techniques and the many hours with her psychiatrist and Gail, her sponsor, to remember that this was the disease. This is what substance use disorder did to you. It took over. You became someone else.

"Larry, I'm so sorry for this relapse. I have a disease. I'm responsible for my sobriety. I accept that," Sherri said, looking at her husband but not moving too close. They were in the kitchen, and she was the one who was out of place. She desperately wanted to go back to those years of sobriety when she'd been queen of the kitchen. She wanted Larry to want to come home to the family and to her happy and relaxed, not anticipating the worse. "I have to battle the shame. I relapsed. I also went back to treatment voluntarily and quickly. That's progress, isn't it?" she asked.

"It is. I'll do my best to be home for dinner tomorrow night, but I can't promise." He moved toward her, hesitated, stepped aside, and left the kitchen.

"Progress, not perfection," Sherri whispered to herself. He hadn't kissed her, but they also hadn't fought.

***

"Hello, this is Sherri," she said as she picked up the phone in the kitchen. She was in her happy place, making Larry's favorite carrot soufflé.

"Hello," a tentative voice said on the other end of the phone.

The voice was familiar; but distracted, Sherri could not quite place it.

"It's me, Sarah. I know, it's been ten years. I thought maybe it was time to call," the female voice said.

"Ah, . . . Sarah." How long had it been? Eight, maybe ten years since they'd spoken.

"Thank you for calling," Sherri said, not knowing where to begin. Afraid Sarah might hang up, Sherri ventured the truth. "Sarah, it's been so long. I'm so happy to hear your voice. I'm eight months sober. Well, I would have been almost four years sober . . . Anyway, it doesn't matter now. I just want you to know, we can talk now." And talk they did.

Sarah and Lenore had slowly drifted away from Sherri. Caught up in the storm of addiction, Sherri had done nothing to resume the friendships. She'd told herself the usual story: her girlfriends' children, husbands, and lives came first and they did not have time to be involved in her problems. Under the surface of this self-lie, Sherri knew that not even her best friends could battle the monster that dictated her life. Besides, at the time she'd lost interest in them.

Two weeks later, Lenore, the third member of their inseparable trio called Sherri. Sarah and Lenore had had not told each other they would reach out to Sherri. Sherri's joy was magnified by the gift of both long-lost friends reaching out because they missed her. The three of them talked for hours. Before long they were sharing their lives planning new adventures as in the good old days. The happy beneficiaries would be their families. Sherri had not lost her touch for creating lighthearted and fun gatherings. Together, the three women were a powerhouse. Sherri began to trust the gifts of recovery.

❋❋❋

Progress creates forward momentum. Although Larry needed time and a lot of signs to believe that this recovery period would last for long, he had to admit that it felt different this time. The transition from treatment to home life transpired without the same anxiety. He began to forget about the relapse and see the Sherri he'd fallen in love with. She counted one, two, and three years of post-relapse sobriety. His count was different.

Larry added the many times that Sherri had called the insurance company to deal with that claim for the fallen tree damage, showed up with a freshly pressed shirt, gathered their friends to celebrate his birthday, drove the kids to their friends, or planted some flowers in the garden.

Larry admired the slow and steady way Sherri rebuilt her relationship with the girls and his son. She took interest in their lives. At times, he did think she could overcompensate for her past absences with a bit too much generosity. He understood. He just needed to keep her in check.

Yes, he just needed to keep her in check. That thought was foul on so many levels, he admonished himself. First, it implied the game his psychiatrist warned him against. Larry might be the responsible one, keeping the family together, but he was also the "enabler." He contributed to the family disease. That was a tall order for Larry to accept. For a long time, maybe even a few years, Larry had transferred the anger he felt towards Sherri onto the professionals whose help he sought. Of course, he tried to control his wife. He could not let her run wild with three young children in the house. Not to mention all the debt from rehab, therapists, and psychiatrists for the entire family. It was a miracle the dogs did not need therapy.

Stop, he commanded himself. Control the silent introverted "awfulizing"—such a genius medical term—that is what Larry needed to do. Control himself, not Sherri. He'd accepted the expenses, written the checks, hired the housekeepers. He'd perhaps even played the martyr in the name of keeping the family together. Stop, he dictated to himself.

Larry redirected his thoughts. He visualized the last time they'd gone to New York City, walking hand in hand after watching *Tootsie* on Broadway. Sherri's spontaneous demand for an old-fashioned soft-serve cone. She had such a big personality and such exuberance. His lips formed a silly smile. He looked forward to the getaway weekends to New York City, their Friday night, and the family trips she planned. Sober, Sherri brought laughter into their lives. Her love flowed beyond their immediate family. He needed to acknowledge her more. Not as the bigger person in the relationship, but as the humbler person recognizing that Sherri had worked the hardest. She battled a disease to keep him.

"Thank you, Larry. I saw your public post on Facebook for our anniversary. So simple, so profound, so you. I've reread it a few times: 'Happy 23rd—we are blessed—love you—Larry.' I appreciate it," Sherri said.

"Oh, if you're happy with that, I guess you don't want this little box." Larry dangled the purple-wrapped ring-sized box with a big silver bow.

"Larry, you shouldn't have!" Sherri could not hide her delight. She loved glitter, though she no longer yearned for it.

"Remember, appearances can be deceiving. I was blind on my blind date," he teased. He could do that now. They talked about the past, both seriously and sometimes, like now, even lightly.

Unable to control her excitement, she tore the paper off. Stunned, she pulled out a key chain from the box.

"You didn't?"

"I did."

"Without me?"

"You saw it. You know the one in Margate."

"Oh my! Oh my!" Sherri feigned a faint scene.

Recovery was full of surprises. Good ones. This was the beach house in Margate, the one off the bridge. She knew exactly which one. If you turned left, you ended up at Caesar's Casino. If you turned right, you ended up at their new beach house. Larry trusted her to make the right turn.

❋❋❋

Sherri understood that trust needed to be earned incrementally. She had consistently made the right turn to Margate, she attended her AA meetings five times a week, and she never missed an opportunity to build up the family. Her psychiatrist agreed it was time for her to raise the ante with Larry. She decided a date night at that little Italian restaurant would provide a more relaxed scenario, and Larry wouldn't be able to rush off to work.

"Larry, I'd like to talk about something that has been on my mind. And it's not a trip to Paris," Sherri said. She wasn't so good at dry humor. It had sounded better when she'd practiced with her sponsor.

Larry took a sip from his cocktail, looking relaxed, and even in the romantic lighting, Sherri could see he was more amused than alarmed.

"Do you trust me now?" Sherri asked making sure she modulated her tone to make the question as neutral as possible, carefully deciding to use the word "now."

"Yes." He replied simply. No tension rising, although he did momentarily glance at the menu he already knew by heart.

"I think it's time. I want my name back on the checking account," Sherri said.

"It took you long enough to ask. I'm surprised it took you this long. You know: What Sherri wants, Sherri gets." He winked at her. "I'm starving. I'm in the mood for that fettuccini."

Two weeks later the freshly printed checkbooks arrived with both their names. Sherri smiled. Nothing changes if nothing changes, went the slogan. She had changed. There was proof in black and white. As the slogan promised, so something had changed; she could make household financial decisions.

✱✱✱

"Larry, I have an email from the director of alumni affairs at Caron," Sherri informed her husband.

Sherri's internal voice no longer pushed her towards the pill bottles, but it still held power. The power to shame her, to make her feel small and incompetent. The email triggered Sherri's insecurity. Had she failed as an AA-sponsor? Had she forgotten to follow-up with someone just out of treatment? She recoiled at what misstep caused a formal email to be sent to her.

"Sherri, relax. You give them your soul. You're wearing out the roads between our place and Wernersville with all your volunteer work. I'm sure it's nothing serious. Let's finish unpacking. There's an ocean waiting for you out there. Did you bring a red bikini to go with that red helium balloon of yours?" Larry teased.

The email was followed by a call. There with her feet in the sand, her husband with an umbrella drink as she fingered her diamond AA pendant, she held her breath.

"Sherri, we would like to present you with the 2011 Community Service Award at the next gala," an official sounding voice said.

"I accept." This was better than winning an Oscar. Well, almost. Sherri started to mimic an acceptance speech after she hung up.

Larry indulged Sherri's theatrics and clapped. Sherri saw a little water formation in the corner of his eyes that could be mistaken for tears of joy.

❄❄❄

Larry selected his words with caution but did not mince them.

"Sherri, you have to cut the puppet strings your mother holds you with. She's in a good place with a lot of care. I understand she had an accident, but you couldn't have prevented it. You don't need to be at her constant beck and call."

"Larry, she's my mother. I may not always have been close to her, but she's in her eighties and she never picked up a drink. She did something right."

"Sherri, this has nothing to do with your mother's teetotaling. She fell, she had an accident, but she has turned that into new leverage over you. You can't go running every time she calls."

"Larry, she has only me."

"WE also have only you. And it's our turn. Full stop."

"Are you telling me what to do?"

"I'm telling you it's time you draw the line."

"Oh yeah? According to who? Is that a threat?" Sherri moved towards him.

"According to me, your husband. No, it's not a threat. It's an observation of facts. She comes between us." Larry decided to end there before this argument turned too heated.

Sherri stepped back and sat down.

He noticed her taking a deep breath. He remembered the technique: Wait and look at her. Say nothing. Time felt heavy. He preferred pushing it along. His instinct was to race time—a skill well-honed in the operating room, from the sense of urgency when faced with a situation he couldn't fully control. He forced himself to wait a little longer. He had nothing left to say, but he could easily keep going. He was good at improvisation; in fact he liked it. It was stopping that was difficult. This was also crucial when he felt he held the high hand.

"You're right. I'm sorry. I need to work on my boundaries with my mother. I don't need to run daily errands for her. Once a week is more than enough," Sherri said, meeting his gaze.

Satisfied the matter was resolved, Larry nodded and walked out of the kitchen. As he passed her, he intentionally brushed her bare arm. Touch to reconnect, a small gesture he remembered from his high-priced therapist.

✳✳✳

It's June 2, 2019, at the Steps to Cure Sarcoma Walk. Larry, Sherri, and their daughters wear the green T-shirts. They are a team. They are raising money and awareness for people who must combat this vicious cancer that attacks their connective tissues. They're also cre-ating meaning for what a family in recovery stands for. Sherri and Larry hold hands as they begin the walk. When they cross the fin-ish line, Larry takes out his phone and points to it. Right on cue, his daughters shout:

"We miss you, little brother—see you at the beach house. In how many days, Mom?"

Larry points the phone at Sherri.

"In too many days—that's how many days." She blows a stage-worthy kiss at her son.

Before they see him in August, Sherri and Larry will celebrate 32 years of marriage. Because Sherri gets what Sherri wants, Larry will put up the top on his grey Mercedes convertible with the two golden doodles and Noah the cat in the back seat as they drive down to the beach house in Margate for a private celebration in their happy place.

Acknowledgments

The work of the eye is done.
Go now and do the heart-work on the images imprisoned within you.

—Rainer Maria Rilke
Letters to a Young Poet

A heartfelt "thank you" first and foremost to my husband, William Thomas. You have taken so many risks since we began our life adventure together: motorcycling in Colorado, cycling in Myanmar, trekking in Patagonia, even skydiving in New Zealand. Yet your most courageous undertaking has been putting in the "heart-work" required to live life not only as a sober person but as someone in recovery. The chaos of addiction was more frightening for me than jumping out of that plane over Queenstown. Without the upheaval brought into our lives by this family disease, I may never have faced my own fears; nor would I have dealt with my inner landscape as profoundly as I have. Thank you for choosing to stay in our relationship through the long years it took for us to find our healthy selves and bring them together in our relationship. This book would not exist without you; nor would I know that such an intimate love is possible.

I want to express deep gratitude to all the people who first walked with us, both knowing and unknowing, during our early chaos, and who said "this way," who said "a little longer," and who sometimes did nothing but hold us. To those who said "enough" and those who challenged our blindness to what needed seeing; to those who showed patience and listened to us as we worked on the images imprisoned within; to all of you, I say, "Thank you." Anne, Janet, Ileana, Leonard and Muriel,

Mary, John, Robert, Rick, William, Peter, Micki, our therapists, our sponsors, our fellowship cohorts, our families, our friends—far too many to individually name—you were, and are, all instrumental parts of our recovery and this book. To my mother, *un merci du fond de mon coeur* (thank you from the bottom of my heart). I owe a special thank you for teaching me love, waiting for me while I attended to my relationship with Bill, and always encouraging me to be me.

I extend my deepest appreciation to the couples who participated in this book and especially the couples who agreed to share their journey: David and Leslie, Nadia and Luke, Tim and Chuck, and Sherri and Larry. I am honored and humbled that you entrusted me with the telling of your recovery stories. Thank you for your generosity of heart, your time, and your trust. I have the greatest respect and admiration for your willingness to give voices and faces to couples in recovery. I also want to thank Douglas and Pat, Rick and Susan, and many other couples, wives, husbands, and partners whose stories are not specifically told in this book but are included in the story of Tom and Carole.

To Jeremy, I owe a special "Thank you." When Bill and I approached you, you said "YES" with great enthusiasm. Not knowing where the path would lead, you joined in with your knowledge, expertise, and questions and challenges—always willing to do a little more and a little more and even a little more. I'm very grateful for the ease of our collaboration. The ASCENT Approach is the result of our joint work. I also wish to thank Dina H. Harth, a Philadelphia-based licensed psychologist, for her important feedback and generous gift of time to discuss the early iteration of The ASCENT Approach with Jeremy and me. Your insights were invaluable.

I wish to acknowledge the support of Caron Treatment Center in Wernersville, PA, and their staff. Their care and support were essential both to Bill's sobriety and to our recovery. I wish to extend my deep gratitude to Doug Tieman for his tremendous support of this book from the very beginning, the help of the Caron counseling team who shepherded my early thoughts on the book's structure, as well as David

Rotenberg, Cheryl Knepper, Christopher O'Reilly, Karen Pasternack, Kristin Campbell-Salamone, Margaret Schroeder, Hayley McMullen, Amy Durham, Jills Simmons, Pam Smith, and many others who are part of the Caron family. Thank you also to Pat Feeley who supported the project with such enthusiasm; I wish you well in your new endeavors.

A big and heartfelt "thank you" to my team. I extend a special thank-you to Ann Corcoran in Philadelphia, who is the glue that keeps my life and Bill's together. She wears far too many hats to be able to list here, each task mastered as competently as the other. Marchalita Mapili in the Philippines, who typed out all the interviews, grew the awareness of our project in social media, and completed dozens of other tasks with enthusiasm. Lin Wai Phyo (Kevin) in Myanmar, my research assistant, diligently hunted down materials, summarized papers, and always willingly looked up one more thing for me. Wendy Leonard in Florida patiently corrected and formatted the manuscript. Paris Alexander Walker in California diligently edited early versions and provided thoughtful feedback on my writing. Umar Javed in Pakistan redesigned my website and brought new life to my online presence. Their talents are as wide and their dedication as diverse as the regions of the globe they come from.

I had the tremendous good fortune to be introduced to Lisa Smith, author of the acclaimed memoir *Girl Walks Out of a Bar*. Lisa's dedicated passion to destigmatize substance use disorder has put her at the forefront of the movement to advance well-being in the legal profession. She graciously presented my manuscript to SelectBooks and introduced me to its CEO, Kenzi Sugihara.

I owe an immense debt of gratitude to Kenzi for believing in *Love Without Martinis* and moving forward with its publication while we face a global pandemic. A special thank you to Nancy Sugihara who read every word until each sentence was understandable to those familiar with recovery and those new to recovery. Without her endless patience, this book would not read as smoothly and as clearly. Also, I wish to thank Kenichi for shepherding my book through the various stages of production and distribution so that it may find its way into your hands.

I have deep gratitude for my publicist Gretchen Crary of February Media. Because of her considerable efforts, tireless enthusiasm, and wealth of experience, my book is reaching far more readers and supporting many more couples.

I also wish to thank all the people who touched us by the strength of their relationships, whether in recovery or not; and the bond of love of others such as my great-aunt Liliane and my great-uncle Terry, who inspired us to engage in a lifetime of heart-work.

Recommended Readings

A complete list of the books and articles which informed this book are found in the bibliography. However, in creating The ASCENT Approach, Dr. Jeremy Frank and I relied on specific works we felt would be beneficial to specifically set out here. In developing the six practices, our thought process was largely informed by the following works:

Brown, Stephanie, and Virginia Lewis. *The Alcoholic Family in Recovery: A Developmental Model.* New York: The Guilford Press, 2002.

Larsen, Earnie. *Stage II Relationships: Love Beyond Addiction.* New York: Harper One, 1987.

Nakken, Craig. *Reclaim Your Family from Addiction: How Couples and Families Recover Love and Meaning.* Minnesota: Hazelden Publishing, 2010.

Vaillant, George E. "Alcoholics Anonymous: Cult or Cure?" *Australian and New Zealand Journal of Psychiatry*; 39: 431-436.
https://doi.org/10.1080/j.1440-1614.2005.01600.x

In addition to the works listed above, the following book discusses the need for connection to be fully realized as human beings:

Hendrix, Harville. *Getting the Love You Want: A Guide for Couples.* New York: St Martin's Press, 2008.

For the definition of addiction:

https://www.asam.org/resources/definition-of-addiction

For the concept of codependency:

Hendrickson, Ellen. "Is Your Relationship Codependent? And What Exactly Does That Mean?" *Scientific American* online (January 7, 2017).
https://www.scientificamerican.com/article/is-your-relationship
-codependent-and-what-exactly-does-that-mean/

For the concept of the continuum of readiness to change based on the Transtheoretical Model of Change:

Prochaska, J.O., DiClemente, C.C., & Norcross, J.C. "In Search of How People Change: Applications to the Addictive Behaviors." *American Psychologist,* 47 (1992): 1102–1114. PMID: 1329589.

For the concept of different pathways to recovery:

https://www.samhsa.gov/sites/default/files/recovery_pathways_report.pdf

Bibliography

Books

Al-Anon Family Group Head Inc. *The Dilemma of the Alcoholic Marriage*. Virginia: Al-Anon Family Group Headquarters Inc., 2007.

Barnett, Robin. *Addict in the House: A No-Nonsense Family Guide Through Addiction and Recovery*. California: New Harbinger Publications, 2016.

Beattie, Melody. *Codependent No More: How to Stop Controlling Others and Start Caring for Yourself*. Minnesota: Hazelden Publishing, 2016.

Beattie, Melody. *The Language of Letting Go: Daily Meditations on Codependency*. Minnesota: Hazelden Publishing, 2009.

Berg, Beverly. *Loving Someone in Recovery: The Answers You Need When Your Partner Is Recovering from Addiction*. California: New Harbinger Publications Inc., 2014. Kindle.

Benton, Sarah Allen, *Understanding the High Functioning Alcoholic*. Westport: Praeger Publishers, 2009.

Brown, Brené. *The Gifts of Imperfection: Let Go of Who You Think You're Supposed to Be and Embrace Who You Are*. Minnesota: Hazelden Publishing, 2010.

Brown, Stephanie, and Virginia Lewis. *The Alcoholic Family in Recovery: A Developmental Model*. New York: The Guilford Press, 2002.

Cameron, Julia. *Floor Sample: A Creative Memoir*. New York: Tarcher Perigee, 2007.

Chapman, Gary. *The 5 Love Languages: The Secrets to Love That Lasts*. Chicago: Northfield Publishing, 2015.

Chödrön, Pema. *When Things Fall Apart: Heart Advice for Difficult Times*. Boston: Shambhala, 2016.

Dan F. *Sober but Stuck: Obstacles Most Often Encountered That Keep Us From Growing in Recovery*. New York: Hazelden Publishing, 2010.

De Marneffe, Daphne. *The Rough Patch: Marriage and the Art of Living Together*. New York: Scribner, 2018.

Diane and Glenn A. *Step Up to Love: A Twelve-Step Guide for Couple Recovery*. Virginia: World Service Organization, 2009.

Dold, Catherine, Howard Eisenberg and Al J. Mooney. *The Recovery Book: Answers to All Your Questions About Addiction and Alcoholism and Finding Health and Happiness in Sobriety.* New York: Workman Publishing Company, 2014.

Dunion, Paul. *Shadow Marriage: A Descent into Intimacy.* New York: iUniverse, Inc., 2006.

Fletcher, Anne M. *Sober for Good: New Solutions for Drinking Problems—Advice from Those Who Have Succeeded.* Boston: Rux Martin/Houghton Mifflin Harcourt, 2001.

Frederiksen, Lisa. *If You Loved Me, You'd Stop! What You Really Need to Know When Your Loved One Drinks Too Much.* California: KLJ Publishing, 2008.

Freud, S. *A General Introduction to Psychoanalysis.* New York: Boni and Liveright, 1922.

Griffin, Dan. *A Man's Way Through Relationships: Learning to Love and Be Loved.* Nevada: Central Recovery Press, 2014.

Griffin, Kevin. *One Breath at a Time: Buddhism and the Twelve Steps.* New York: Rodale Books, 2004.

Gottman, John and Julie Schwartz. *Eight Dates: Essential Conversations for a Lifetime of Love.* New York: Workman Publishing, 2018.

Hendrix, Harville. *Getting the Love You Want: A Guide for Couples.* New York: St Martin's Press, 2008.

Johnson, Sue. *Hold Me Tight: Seven Conversations for a Lifetime of Love.* New York: Little, Brown & Co., 2008. Print.

Johnson, Susan M. *Attachment Theory in Practice: Emotionally Focused Therapy (EFT) with Individuals, Couples, and Families.* New York: The Guilford Press. 2019

Katherine, Anne. *Boundaries: Where You End and I Begin.* New York: Simon & Schuster, 2000.

Kennedy, Patrick J. and Stephen Fried. *A Common Struggle: A Personal Journey Through the Past and Future of Mental Illness and Addiction.* New York: Penguin Random House LLC, 2015.

Larsen, Earnie. *Stage II Relationships: Love Beyond Addiction.* New York: Harper One, 1987.

Lawford, Christopher Kennedy, and Beverly Engel. *When Your Partner Has an Addiction: How Compassion Can Transform Your Relationship (and Heal You Both in the Process).* Texas: BenBella Books, 2016.

Lerner, Harriet. *The Dance of Anger: A Woman's Guide to Changing the Patterns of Intimate Relationships.* New York: Harper Collins Publisher, 2014.

Levoy, Gregg. *Callings: Finding and Following an Authentic Life.* New York: Three Rivers Press, 1997.

Ling, Walter. *Mastering the Addicted Brain: Building a Sane and Meaningful Life to Stay Clean*. California: New World Library, 2017.

McGee, Michael. *The Joy Recovery: The New 12-Step Guide to Recovery from Addiction*. New York: Union Square Publishing, 2018.

Meadows, Martin. *Daily Self-Discipline: Everyday Habits and Exercises to Build Self-Discipline and Achieve Your Goals*. New York: Meadows Publishing, 2015.

Nakken, Craig. *Reclaim Your Family from Addiction: How Couples and Families Recover Love and Meaning*. Minnesota: Hazelden Publishing, 2010.

Neill, Neill. *Living with a Functioning Alcoholic—A Woman's Survival Guide*. Qualicum Beach, B.C.: Neill Press, 2011.

Pruett, Sue. *Our Marriage: Surviving Addiction and Thriving in Sobriety*. Indiana: AuthorHouse, 2010.

Sinor, Barbara. *Tales of Addiction and Inspiration for Recovery: Twenty True Stories from the Soul*. Michigan: Modern History Press, 2010.

Steinberg, Neil. *Out of the Wreck I Rise: A Literary Companion to Recovery*. Chicago, London: University of Chicago Press, 2016.

Treadway, David C. *Before It's Too Late: Working with Substance Abuse in the Family*. New York: W. W. Norton & Company, 1989.

Journal Articles

Dethier, Marie, Christelle Counerotte, Sylvie Blairy. "Marital Satisfaction in Couples with an Alcoholic Husband," *Journal of Family Violence* 26, no. 2 (February 2011): 151–162. https://doi.org/10.1007/s10896-010-9355-z.

Fals-Stewart, William, Timothy J. O'Farrell, and Wendy K.K. Lam. "Behavioral Couple Therapy for Gay and Lesbian Couples with Alcohol Use Disorders," *Journal of Substance Abuse Treatment* 37, no. 4 (December 2009): 379–387. https://doi.org/10.1016/j.jsat.2009.05.001.

Graff, Fiona S., Thomas J. Morgan, Elizabeth E. Epstein, Barbara S. McCrady, Sharon M. Cook, Noelle K. Jensen, and Shalonda Kelly. "Engagement and Retention in Outpatient Alcoholism Treatment for Women," *The American Journal on Addictions* 18, no. 4 (February 2010): 277–288. https://doi.org/10.1080/10550490902925540.

Hansen, Mary, Barbara Ganley, and Chris Carlucci. "Journeys from Addiction to Recovery," *Research and Theory for Nursing Practice: An International Journal* 22, no. 4 (September 2008): 257–275. https://doi.org/10.1891/0889-7182.22.4.257.

Hendrickson, Ellen. "Is Your Relationship Codependent? And What Exactly Does That Mean?" *Scientific American* online (January 7, 2017). https://www.scientificamerican.com/article/is-your-relationship -codependent-and-what-exactly-does-that-mean/

McCrady, Barbara S., Adam Wilson, Rosa Muñoz, Brandi Fink, Kathryn Fokas, and Adrienne Borders. "Alcohol-Focused Behavioral Couple Therapy," *Family Process* 55, no. 3 (September 2016): 443–459. https://doi.org/10.1111/famp.12231.

McCrady, Barbara S., Elizabeth E. Epstein, Sharon Cook, Noelle Jensen, and Thomas Hildebrandt. "A Randomized Trial of Individual and Couple Behavioral Alcohol Treatment for Women," *Journal of Consulting and Clinical Psychology* 77, no. 2 (April 2009): 243–256. https://doi.org/10.1037/a0014686.

McCrady, Barbara S., Elizabeth E. Epstein, Kevin A. Hallgren, Sharon Cook, and Noelle K. Jensen. "Women with Alcohol Dependence: A Randomized Trial of Couple Versus Individual Plus Couple Therapy," *Psychology of Addictive Behaviors* 30, no. 3 (May 2016): 287–299. https://doi.org/10.1037/adb0000158.

O'Farrell, Timothy J. "Review of Outcome Research on Marital and Family Therapy in Treatment of Alcoholism," *Journal of Marital and Family Therapy* 38, no. 1 (January 2012): 122–144. https://doi.org/10.1111/j.1752-0606.2011.00242.x.

O'Farrell, Timothy J. and Abigail Z. Schein. "Behavioral Couples Therapy for Alcoholism and Drug Abuse," *Journal of Substance Abuse Treatment* 18, no. 1 (January 2000): 51–54. https://doi.org/10.1016/S0740-5472(99)00026-4.

O'Farrell, Timothy J., Keith A. Choquette, Henry S.G. Cutter, Elizabeth D. Brown, and William F. McCourt. "Behavioral Marital Therapy With and Without Additional Couples Relapse Prevention Sessions for Alcoholics and their Wives," *Journal of Studies on Alcohol* 54, no. 6 (January 2015): 652–666. https://doi.org/10.15288/jsa.1993.54.652.

Owens, Mandy D., Barbara S. McCrady, Adrienne Z. Borders, Julie M. Brovko, and Matthew R. Pearson. "Psychometric Properties of the System for Coding Couples' Interactions in Therapy—Alcohol," *Psychology of Addictive Behaviors* 28, no. 4 (December 2014): 1077–1088. http://dx.doi.org/10.1037/a0038332.

Prochaska, J.O., DiClemente, C.C., & Norcross, J.C. "In Search of How People Change: Applications to the Addictive Behaviors." *American Psychologist*, 47 (1992): 1102–1114. PMID: 1329589.

Rychtarik, Robert G. and Neil B. McGillicuddy. "Coping Skills Training and 12-Step Facilitation for Women Whose Partner Has Alcoholism: Effects on Depression, the Partner's Drinking, and Partner Physical Violence." *Journal of Consulting and Clinical Psychology* 73, no. 2 (April 2005): 249–261. https://doi.org/10.1037/0022-006X.73.2.249.

Rychtarik, Robert G., Neil B. McGillicuddy, and Christopher Barrick. "Web-based Coping Skills Training for Women Whose Partner Has a Drinking Problem," *Psychology of Addictive Behaviors* 29, no. 1 (March 2015): 26–33. https://doi.org/10.1037/adb0000032.

Schumm, Jeremiah A., Timothy J. O'Farrell, Christopher M. Murphy, and William Fals-Stewart. "Partner Violence Before and After Couples-based Alcoholism Treatment for Female Alcoholic Patients," *Journal of Consulting and Clinical Psychology* 77, no. 6 (December 2009): 1136–1146. https://doi.org/10.1037/a0017389.

Thomas, Cheryl L. "The Influence of Addiction Recovery on Couple Relationships: A Qualitative Examination Through a Bowenian Lens," Electronic Thesis or Dissertation. University of Akron, 2012. http://rave.ohiolink.edu/etdc/view?acc_num=akron1334715161.

Vaillant, George E. "Alcoholics Anonymous: Cult or Cure?" *Australian and New Zealand Journal of Psychiatry*; 39: 431–436. https://doi.org/10.1080/j.1440-1614.2005.01600.x

Walitzer, Kimberly S. and Dermen H. Kurt. "Alcohol-focused Spouse Involvement and Behavioral Couples Therapy: Evaluation of Enhancements to Drinking Reduction Treatment for Male Problem Drinkers," *Journal of Consulting and Clinical Psychology* 72, no. 6 (December 2004): 944–955. http://dx.doi.org/10.1037/0022-006X.72.6.944.

About the Author

Photo by Mark C. Morris

CHANTAL JAUVIN is an attorney, writer, and adventurer. Born in Canada, she is a citizen of the world. While working for a top tier Canadian law firm and later as general counsel of a Fortune 500 company, she has lived in Japan, Mexico, Cambodia, Russia, the United States, and Austria. She has addressed central banks from Spain to South Africa, worked with companies from Ghana to Uzbekistan, and mentored attorneys from Dubai to Mumbai.

When she is not involved with her community, she loves to travel the world on two wheels. She and her husband have pedaled over 10,000 km in faraway places.

Her first book, *The Boy with a Bamboo Heart,* has been translated into French and Serbian. All author proceeds for the book are donated to a children's charity in Thailand.

To learn more about her work and to schedule a book group chat with her, please visit her website www.chantaljauvin.com.